Lecture Notes in Computer Scien

Commenced Publication in 1973
Founding and Former Series Editors:
Gerhard Goos, Juris Hartmanis, and Jan van Leeuwen

Andrew Butterfield   Clemens Grelck
Frank Huch (Eds.)

Implementation and Application of Functional Languages

17th International Workshop, IFL 2005
Dublin, Ireland, September 19-21, 2005
Revised Selected Papers

 Springer

Volume Editors

Andrew Butterfield
University of Dublin
Department of Computer Science
O'Reilly Institute, Trinity College, Dublin 2, Ireland
E-mail: Andrew.Butterfield@cs.tcd.ie

Clemens Grelck
University of Lübeck
Institute of Software Technology and Programming Languages
Ratzeburger Allee 160, 24538 Lübeck, Germany
E-mail: grelck@isp.uni-luebeck.de

Frank Huch
University of Kiel
Institute of Computer Science
Olshausenstr. 40, 24098 Kiel, Germany
E-mail: fhu@informatik.uni-kiel.de

Library of Congress Control Number: 2006938912

CR Subject Classification (1998): D.3, D.1.1, D.1, F.3

LNCS Sublibrary: SL 1 – Theoretical Computer Science and General Issues

ISSN	0302-9743
ISBN-10	3-540-69174-X Springer Berlin Heidelberg New York
ISBN-13	978-3-540-69174-7 Springer Berlin Heidelberg New York

Typesetting: Camera-ready by author, data conversion by Scientific Publishing Services, Chennai, India
Printed on acid-free paper   SPIN: 11964681   06/3142   5 4 3 2 1 0

Preface

The 17th International Workshop on Implementation and Application of Functional Languages (IFL 2005) was held in Dublin, Ireland, September 19–21, 2005. It was organized by the Department of Computer Science at Trinity College, University of Dublin.

IFL 2005 was the 17th event in the annual series of IFL workshops. The aim of the workshop series is to bring together researchers actively engaged in the implementation and application of functional and function-based programming languages. It provides an open forum for researchers who wish to present and discuss new ideas and concepts, work in progress, preliminary results, etc., related primarily, but not exclusively, to the implementation and application of functional languages. Topics of interest cover a wide range from theoretical aspects over language design and implementation towards applications and tool support.

Previous IFL workshops were held in Germany (Lübeck, Aachen and Bonn), the UK (Southampton, Norwich, London, St. Andrews, and Edinburgh), in The Netherlands (Nijmegen and Lochem), in Sweden (Båstad and Stockholm), and in Spain (Madrid). In 2006, the 18th International Workshop on Implementation and Application of Functional Languages was held in Budapest, Hungary.

We have continued the innovation introduced for IFL 2004, in which the term "application" was added to the workshop name. Our aim was to reflect the broader scope IFL has gained over recent years and to make IFL even more attractive for researchers in the future. The number of researchers attending IFL 2005 and the subject range of submissions demonstrated the appropriateness of this modification. Continuity with previous workshops was maintained by keeping the well-known and familiar acronym IFL.

Continuity and consistency with previous workshops are ensured by the presence of the IFL Steering Committee (`http://www.ifl-symposia.org/`) formed of experienced former Programme Chairs and other researchers with a strong historical connection to IFL. Papers are selected using a rigourous refereeing process involving at least three external referees, with higher standards pertaining to papers that are co-authored by Programme Committee members. Each paper is discussed anonymously and on camera before being ranked for inclusion in the final proceedings. Decisions are adjudicated by the Programme Chair, who is precluded from submitting any paper. The Programme Chair also directs discussion and voting on the award of the Peter Landin Prize, using a secret ballot.

IFL 2005 attracted 53 researchers from 14 different countries. Most participants came from Europe: 12 from the UK, 5 each from Germany and The Netherlands, 3 from Hungary, and 1 each from Belgium, Denmark, Greece, Portugal, and 19 from Ireland. We also welcomed two participants from the USA, and one each from Canada, Brazil and Mongolia. During the three days of the workshop 32 presentations were given, organized into 10 individual sessions. The draft proceedings distributed during the workshop contained 37 contributions. They were published as Technical Report TCD-CS-2005-60 of the Department of Computer Science, Trinity College, University of Dublin. This volume follows the IFL tradition since 1996 in publishing a high-quality subset of contributions presented at the workshop in the Springer *Lecture Notes in Computer Science* series. All participants who gave a presentation at the workshop were invited to resubmit revised versions of their contributions after the workshop. We received 22 papers, each of which was reviewed by at least three members of the international Programme Committee according to normal conference standards. Following an intensive discussion the Programme Committee selected 13 papers to be included in this volume.

Since 2002 the Peter Landin Prize has been awarded annually to the author or the authors of the best workshop paper. The Programme Committee was pleased to give this prestigious award to Clemens Grelck, Karsten Hinckfuß, and Sven-Bodo Scholz, for their contribution on "With-Loop Fusion for Data Locality and Parallelism." Previous Peter Landin Prize winners were Olivier Danvy, Arjen van Weelden, Rinus Plasmeijer, and Pedro Vasconcelos. IFL 2005 was generously sponsored by the Department of Computer Science at Trinity College Dublin. We are grateful to them for their financial and organizational support. We wish to thank all participants of IFL 2005 who made this workshop the successful event it was. Last but not least, we are indebted to the members of the Programme Committee who completed their reviews in a very short time frame.

August 2006   Andrew Butterfield, Clemens Grelck, Frank Huch

Organization

Programme Committee

Matthias Blume	Toyota Technological Institute at Chicago, USA
Andrew Butterfield (Chair)	Trinity College Dublin, Ireland
Clemens Grelck	University of Lübeck, Germany
Zoltán Horváth	Eotvos Lorand University, Hungary
Frank Huch	University of Kiel, Germany
Joe Kiniry	National University of Ireland Dublin, Ireland
Hans-Wolfgang Loidl	Ludwig-Maximilians University Munich, Germany
Frédéric Loulergue	University of Paris XII, Val de Marne, France
Simon Marlow	Microsoft Research, Cambridge, UK
Marco T. Morazán	Seton Hall University, NJ, USA
Joseph Morris	Dublin City University, Ireland
Barak Pearlmutter	National University of Ireland Maynooth, Ireland
Rinus Plasmeijer	Radboud Universiteit Nijmegen, Netherlands
Peter Thiemann	University of Freiburg, Germany
Phil Trinder	Herriot-Watt University, Edinburgh, UK
Germán Vidal	Technical University of Valencia, Spain

Additional Reviewers

Peter Achten	Radu Grigore	Annette Stümpel
Bernd Brassel	Michael Hanus	Malcolm Tyrrell
Peter Divianszky	Mikolas Janota	Abdallah Al Zain
Robin Green	Sven-Bodo Scholz	

Sponsoring Institutions

Department of Computer Science, Trinity College, University of Dublin.

Table of Contents

Contributions

A Framework for Point-Free Program Transformation[*]

Alcino Cunha, Jorge Sousa Pinto, and José Proença

CCTC / Departamento de Informática, Universidade do Minho
4710-057 Braga, Portugal
{alcino,jsp,jproenca}@di.uminho.pt

Abstract. The subject of this paper is functional program transformation in the so-called *point-free* style. By this we mean first translating programs to a form consisting only of categorically-inspired combinators, algebraic data types defined as fixed points of functors, and implicit recursion through the use of type-parameterized recursion patterns. This form is appropriate for reasoning about programs equationally, but difficult to actually use in practice for programming. In this paper we present a collection of libraries and tools developed at Minho with the aim of supporting the automatic conversion of programs to *point-free* (embedded in Haskell), their manipulation and rule-driven simplification, and the (limited) automatic application of *fusion* for program transformation.

1 Introduction

Functional Programming has always been known to be appropriate for activities involving manipulation of programs, such as program transformation. This is due to the strong theoretical basis that underlies the programming languages: the semantics of functional programs are easier to formalize.

As with any programming paradigm, different functional programmers use different styles of programming; it is however true that most advanced programmers resort to some concise form where functions are written as combinations of other functions, rather than programming by explicit manipulation of the arguments and explicit recursion. For instance a function that sums the squares of the elements in a list can be written in Haskell as

```
sum_squares = (foldr (+) 0) . (map sq)  where sq x = x*x
```

A radical style of programming is the so-called *point-free* style, which totally dispenses with variables. For instance the function `sq` above can be written as `sq = mult . (id /\ id)`, where the infix operator /\ corresponds to the *split* combinator that applies two functions to an argument, producing a pair, and `mult` is the uncurried product.

The origins of the point-free style can be traced back to the ACM Turing Award Lecture given by John Backus in 1977 [1]. Instead of explicitly referring

---

[*] This work was partially supported by FCT project PURe (POSI/CHS/44304/2002).

A. Butterfield, C. Grelck, and F. Huch (Eds.): IFL 2005, LNCS 4015, pp. 1–18, 2006.

arguments, Backus recommended the use of *functional forms* (combinators) to build functions by combining simpler ones. The particular choice of combinators should be driven by the associated algebraic laws.

In the modern incarnation of these ideas, the combinators correspond to morphisms in a category (where the denotational semantics of the language are constructed) and the desired laws follow directly from universal properties of this category. What is more, this approach extends smoothly to the treatment of recursion in what is known as the *data type-generic* approach to programming [8,14]. This allows one to reason equationally about functions obtained by applying standard *recursion patterns*, thus replacing the use of fixpoint induction.

The generic aspect of this approach comes from the fact that all the constructions are parameterized by the recursive data types involved in the computations. It is widely accepted that this style is a good choice for reasoning about programs equationally and generically. It has also proved to be fruitful in the field of *program transformation* [4], where well-known concepts like folding or fusion over lists were first introduced by Bird to derive accumulator-based implementations from inefficient specifications [2].

As a simple example of the kind of transformation we mean, in the function `sum_squares` given above, the fold can be equationally fused with the map to give the following one-pass function, where `plus` is uncurried sum.

```
sum_squares' = foldr aux 0  where aux = curry (plus . (sq . fst /\ snd))
```

The drawback of using this radical point-free style is that, as the examples in this paper show, programs written without variables are not always easy to write or understand. In fact, it is virtually impossible to program without using variables here and there. Pointwise vs. point-free is a lively discussion subject in Haskell forums; the goal of the present paper is to present a set of libraries and tools that support point-free program transformation, but this includes the automatic translation of code to point-free form, so that programmers may apply point-free techniques to their code with variables.

Specifically, we present here the following components, which are all freely available as part of the **UMinho Haskell Software** distribution.

Pointless: A library for point-free programming, allowing programmers to type-check and execute point-free code with recursion patterns, parameterized by data types. With the help of extensions to the Haskell type system, we have implemented an implicit coercion mechanism that provides a limited form of structural equivalence between types. This has allowed us to embed in Haskell a syntax almost identical to the one used at the theoretical level.

DrHylo: A tool that allows programmers to automatically convert Haskell code to point-free form with recursion patterns. In particular, we employ the well-known equivalence between simply typed λ-calculi and cartesian closed categories suggested by Lambek [12]. This serves as the basis for the translation of a core functional language to categorical combinators, extended by the first author [3] to cover sum types. A second component here is the application

$$\frac{}{\Gamma \vdash \star : 1} \qquad \frac{\Gamma(x) = A}{\Gamma \vdash x : A} \qquad \frac{\Gamma[x \mapsto A] \vdash M : B}{\Gamma \vdash \lambda x.\ M : A \to B} \qquad \frac{\Gamma \vdash M : A \to B \quad \Gamma \vdash N : A}{\Gamma \vdash M\ N : B}$$

$$\frac{\Gamma \vdash M : A \quad \Gamma \vdash N : B}{\Gamma \vdash \langle M, N \rangle : A \times B} \qquad \frac{\Gamma \vdash L : A + B \quad \Gamma \vdash M : A \to C \quad \Gamma \vdash N : B \to C}{\Gamma \vdash \mathsf{case}\ L\ M\ N : C}$$

$$\frac{\Gamma \vdash M : A \times B}{\Gamma \vdash \mathsf{fst}\ M : A} \qquad \frac{\Gamma \vdash M : A \times B}{\Gamma \vdash \mathsf{snd}\ M : B} \qquad \frac{\Gamma \vdash M : A}{\Gamma \vdash \mathsf{inl}\ M : A + B} \qquad \frac{\Gamma \vdash M : B}{\Gamma \vdash \mathsf{inr}\ M : A + B}$$

$$\frac{\Gamma \vdash M : F\ (\mu F)}{\Gamma \vdash \mathsf{in}_{\mu F}\ M : \mu F} \qquad \frac{\Gamma \vdash M : \mu F}{\Gamma \vdash \mathsf{out}_{\mu F}\ M : F\ (\mu F)} \qquad \frac{\Gamma \vdash M : A \to A}{\Gamma \vdash \mathsf{fix}\ M : A}$$

Fig. 1. Typing rules

of a standard algorithm that converts recursive functions to *hylomorphisms* of adequate regular data-types, thus removing explicit recursion.

SimpliFree: A tool for manipulating point-free code. Its use will be exemplified here: (i) for the simplification of the very verbose terms produced by DrHylo; and (ii) for program transformation by applying fold fusion.

Organization of the Paper. Section 2 introduces the languages used in the paper, and Sect. 3 reviews notions of point-free equational reasoning, with the help of an example. Pointless, DrHylo, and SimpliFree are described in Sects. 4, 5 and 6. Finally Sect. 7 concludes the paper.

2 The Pointwise and Point-Free Styles of Programming

In both styles, types are defined according to the following syntax.

$$A, B ::= 1 \mid A \to B \mid A \times B \mid A + B \mid \mu F$$
$$F, G ::= \mathsf{Id} \mid \underline{A} \mid F \otimes G \mid F \oplus G \mid F \odot G$$

We assume a standard domain-theoretic semantics, where types are pointed complete partial orders, with least element $\bot$. 1 is the single element type, $A \to B$ is the type of continuous functions from A to B, $A \times B$ is the cartesian product, $A + B$ is the separated sum (with distinguished least element), and μF is a recursive (regular) type defined as the fixed point of functor F.

Id denotes the identity functor, $\underline{A}$ the constant functor that always returns A, $\otimes$ and $\oplus$ the lifted product and sum bifunctors, and $\odot$ composition of functors. For example, booleans can be defined as $\mathsf{Bool} = 1 + 1$, natural numbers as $\mathsf{Nat} = \mu(\underline{1} \oplus \mathsf{Id})$, and lists with elements of type A as $\mathsf{List}\ A = \mu(\underline{1} \oplus \underline{A} \otimes \mathsf{Id})$.

Pointwise Language. Terms with variables are generated by the grammar

$$L, M, N ::= \star \mid x \mid M\ N \mid \lambda x.\ M \mid \langle M, N \rangle \mid \mathsf{fst}\ M \mid \mathsf{snd}\ M \mid$$
$$\mathsf{case}\ L\ M\ N \mid \mathsf{inl}\ M \mid \mathsf{inr}\ M \mid \mathsf{in}_{\mu F}\ M \mid \mathsf{out}_{\mu F}\ M \mid \mathsf{fix}\ M$$

Apart from variable, abstraction, and application, we find $\star$, which is the unique inhabitant of the terminal type (as such, it equals $\bot_1$); fst and snd are projections from a product type and inl and inr are injections into a sum type; $\langle \cdot, \cdot \rangle$ is a pairing construct, and case performs case-analysis on sums. Associated with each recursive type μF are two unique strict functions $in_{\mu F}$ and $out_{\mu F}$, that are each other's inverse. These provide the means to construct and inspect values of the given type. Whenever clear from context, the subscripts will be omitted.

The typing rules are presented in Fig. 1. We now show examples of terms in this language.

$$
\begin{aligned}
&\text{zero} : \text{Nat} && \text{nil} : \text{List } A \\
&\text{zero} = \text{in (inl } \star) && \text{nil} = \text{in (inl } \star) \\
&\text{succ} : \text{Nat} \to \text{Nat} && \text{cons} : A \to \text{List } A \to \text{List } A \\
&\text{succ} = \lambda x.\ \text{in (inr } x) && \text{cons} = \lambda ht.\ \text{in (inr } \langle h, t\rangle) \\
&\text{swap} : A \times B \to B \times A && \text{null} : \text{List } A \to \text{Bool} \\
&\text{swap} = \lambda x.\ \langle \text{snd } x, \text{fst } x\rangle && \text{null} = \lambda l.\text{case (out } l)\ (\lambda x.\text{true})\ (\lambda x.\text{false}) \\
&\text{distr} : A \times (B + C) \to (A \times B) + (A \times C) \\
&\text{distr} = \lambda x.\ \text{case (snd } x)\ (\lambda y.\ \text{inl } \langle \text{fst } x, y\rangle)\ (\lambda y.\ \text{inr } \langle \text{fst } x, y\rangle)
\end{aligned}
$$

Recursive functions are defined explicitly using fix. For example, assuming that mult : Nat $\times$ Nat $\to$ Nat, the factorial and length functions can be defined as

$$
\begin{aligned}
&\text{fact} : \text{Nat} \to \text{Nat} \\
&\text{fact} = \text{fix } (\lambda f.\ \lambda x.\ \text{case (out } x)\ (\lambda y.\ \text{succ zero})\ (\lambda y.\ \text{mult } \langle \text{succ } y, f\ y\rangle)) \\
&\text{length} : \text{List } A \to \text{Nat} \\
&\text{length} = \text{fix } (\lambda f.\ \lambda l.\ \text{case (out } l)\ (\lambda x.\ \text{zero})\ (\lambda x.\ \text{succ } (f\ (\text{snd } y))))
\end{aligned}
$$

Point-free Language. The set of combinators that is of interest to us comes from universal constructions in *almost bicartesian closed categories*, that is, categories with products, non-empty sums, exponentials, and terminal object. See for instance [13] for a thorough treatment of the subject.

The point-free language contains the constants fst, snd, inl, inr, in, and out, with the obvious types, and also the set of combinators given below. To convey the meaning of each combinator, we give its definition in the pointwise language.

$$
\begin{aligned}
&(\cdot \circ \cdot) : (B \to C) \to (A \to B) \to A \to C && \text{id} : A \to A \\
&(\cdot \circ \cdot) = \lambda fgx.\ f\ (g\ x) && \text{id} = \lambda x.\ x \\
&(\cdot \vartriangle \cdot) : (A \to B) \to (A \to C) \to A \to (B \times C) && \text{bang} : A \to 1 \\
&(\cdot \vartriangle \cdot) = \lambda fgx.\ \langle f\ x, g\ x\rangle && \text{bang} = \lambda x.\ \star \\
&(\cdot \triangledown \cdot) : (A \to C) \to (B \to C) \to (A + B) \to C && \text{ap} : (A \to B) \times A \to B \\
&(\cdot \triangledown \cdot) = \lambda fgx.\ \text{case } x\ (\lambda y.\ f\ y)\ (\lambda y.\ g\ y) && \text{ap} = \lambda x.\ (\text{fst } x)\ (\text{snd } x) \\
&\overline{} : (A \times B \to C) \to A \to B \to C \\
&\overline{} = \lambda fxy.\ f\ \langle x, y\rangle
\end{aligned}
$$

It is convenient to have derived combinators corresponding to the operation of the product, sum, and exponentiation functors. These can be defined, respectively, as $f \times g = f \circ \text{fst} \vartriangle g \circ \text{snd}$, $f + g = \text{inl} \circ f \triangledown \text{inr} \circ g$, and $f^{\bullet} = \overline{f \circ \text{ap}}$.

The point-free language contains only values of functional type. As such, elements of a non-functional type A are denoted by functions of the isomorphic type $1 \to A$. The previous examples can be written in the point-free language:

zero : $1 \to$ Nat

zero = in $\circ$ inl

succ : Nat $\to$ Nat

succ = in $\circ$ inr

swap : $A \times B \to B \times A$

swap = snd $\triangle$ fst

distr : $A \times (B + C) \to (A \times B) + (A \times C)$

distr = (swap + swap) $\circ$ ap $\circ$ ((\overline{inl} \triangledown \overline{inr}) \times id) $\circ$ swap

nil : $1 \to$ List A

nil = in $\circ$ inl

cons : $A \to$ List $A \to$ List A

cons = $\overline{\text{in} \circ \text{inr}}$

null : List $A \to$ Bool

null = (true $\triangledown$ false $\circ$ bang) $\circ$ out

The language also contains a recursion operator: the *hylomorphism* recursion pattern. This was introduced with the first study of recursion patterns in a domain-theoretic setting [13], and was later proved to be powerful enough to allow for the definition of any fixpoint [14]. It is defined as follows.

$$\text{hylo}_{\mu F} : (F\,B \to B) \to (A \to F\,A) \to A \to B$$
$$\text{hylo}_{\mu F} = \lambda g.\ \lambda h.\ \text{fix}(\lambda f.\ g \circ F f \circ h)$$

Function h computes the values passed to the recursive calls, and g combines the results of the recursive calls to compute the final result. The recursion tree of a function defined as a hylomorphism is modeled by μF. The factorial and length functions can then be defined in the point-free language as follows.

$$\text{fact} : \text{Nat} \to \text{Nat}$$
$$\text{fact} = \text{hylo}_{\text{List Nat}}\ (\text{zero} \triangledown \text{mult})\ ((\text{id} + \text{succ} \triangle \text{id}) \circ \text{out}_{\text{Nat}})$$
$$\text{length} : \text{List } A \to \text{Nat}$$
$$\text{length} = \text{hylo}_{\text{Nat}}\ \text{in}_{\text{Nat}}\ ((\text{id} + \text{snd}) \circ \text{out}_{\text{List } A})$$

Naturally, other derived operators can be defined using hylomorphism. The following correspond to the well-known *fold* and *unfold* recursion patterns:

$$\text{fold}_{\mu F} : (F\,A \to A) \to \mu F \to A \qquad \text{unfold}_{\mu F} : (A \to F\,A) \to A \to \mu F$$
$$\text{fold}_{\mu F} = \lambda g.\ \text{hylo}_{\mu F}\ g\ \text{out}_{\mu F} \qquad \text{unfold}_{\mu F} = \lambda g.\ \text{hylo}_{\mu F}\ \text{in}_{\mu F}\ g$$

3 Point-Free Program Transformation

The basic laws of the non-recursive calculus are given in the appendix. We will exemplify their use in the context of a non-trivial program transformation taken from [4]. We resort to the following fold-fusion law to treat recursion:

$$f \circ (\!| g |\!)_F = (\!| h |\!)_F \quad \Leftarrow \quad f \text{ strict } \wedge\ f \circ g = h \circ Ff \qquad \text{cata-FUSION}$$

where we use the compact notation $(\!| g |\!)_F$ for $\text{fold}_{\mu F}\ g$ (strictness conditions are discussed in detail in [4]). Consider the function isums::[Int]->[Int] that computes the initial sums of a list.

```
isums []     = []
isums (x:xs) = map (x+) (0 : isums xs)
```

This can be optimized by introducing an accumulating parameter to store at each point the sum of all previous elements in the list. We first define an operator $\oplus :$ List Int $\times$ Int $\rightarrow$ List Int as $\oplus (l, x) = \mathsf{map}_{\mathsf{List}}$ $(\overline{\mathsf{plus}}\ x)\ l$. The function isums can then be written as the fold isums $= (\!|\underline{\mathsf{nil}} \triangledown \oplus \circ \mathsf{swap} \circ (\mathsf{id} \times \mathsf{cons} \circ \underline{\mathsf{zero}} \triangle \mathsf{id})|\!)$.

The optimized function isums_t can be calculated from the equation $\mathsf{isums}_t = \overline{\oplus} \circ \mathsf{isums}$, or $\mathsf{isums}_t\ l\ y = \mathsf{map}_{\mathsf{List}}\ (\overline{\mathsf{plus}}\ y)$ (isums l) pointwise, which plays the role of specification to the transformation. It can be checked that one obtains by fusion, with F the base functor of lists,

$$\mathsf{isums}_t = (\!|\underline{\mathsf{nil}} \triangledown \mathsf{comp} \circ \mathsf{swap} \circ (\overline{\mathsf{plus}} \times k)|\!)$$

if there exists a function k such that $\overline{\oplus} \circ \mathsf{cons} \circ \underline{\mathsf{zero}} \triangle \mathsf{id} = k \circ \overline{\oplus}$ (the derived constant combinator $\underline{\cdot}$ is defined in the appendix. The following calculation allows to identify $k = \mathsf{cons}^\bullet \circ \mathsf{split} \circ \underline{\mathsf{id}} \triangle \mathsf{id}$.

$$
\begin{array}{cl}
 & \overline{\oplus} \circ \mathsf{cons} \circ \underline{\mathsf{zero}} \triangle \mathsf{id} \\
= & \{\,\mathsf{isums\text{-}Aux}\,\} \\
 & \mathsf{cons}^\bullet \circ \mathsf{split} \circ (\overline{\mathsf{plus}} \times \overline{\oplus}) \circ \underline{\mathsf{zero}} \triangle \mathsf{id} \\
= & \{\,\times\text{-}\mathsf{Absor}, \mathsf{zero}\ \text{is a left-identity of plus}\,\} \\
 & \mathsf{cons}^\bullet \circ \mathsf{split} \circ \underline{\mathsf{id}} \triangle \overline{\oplus} \\
= & \{\,\mathsf{const\text{-}Fusion}\,\} \\
 & \mathsf{cons}^\bullet \circ \mathsf{split} \circ \underline{\mathsf{id}} \circ \overline{\oplus} \triangle \overline{\oplus} \\
= & \{\,\times\text{-}\mathsf{Fusion}\,\} \\
 & \mathsf{cons}^\bullet \circ \mathsf{split} \circ \underline{\mathsf{id}} \triangle \mathsf{id} \circ \overline{\oplus}
\end{array}
$$

This uses a new split combinator that internalizes $(\cdot \triangle \cdot)$ in the point-free language, as well as an auxiliary law proved elsewhere [4].

$$\mathsf{split} : \dfrac{(B^A \times C^A) \rightarrow (B \times C)^A}{\mathsf{split} = (\mathsf{ap} \times \mathsf{ap}) \circ \pi_1 \times \mathsf{id} \triangle \pi_2 \times \mathsf{id}} \qquad \mathsf{split\text{-}Def}$$

$$\overline{\oplus} \circ \mathsf{cons} = \mathsf{cons}^\bullet \circ \mathsf{split} \circ (\overline{\mathsf{plus}} \times \overline{\oplus}) \qquad \mathsf{isums\text{-}Aux}$$

Substituting k and converting the resulting definition back to pointwise, one obtains at last the following linear time definition (isums runs in quadratic time).

```
isums_t :: [Int] -> Int -> [Int]
isums_t [] y    = []
isums_t (x:xs) y = (x+y) : isums_t xs (x+y)
```

4   Pointless Haskell: Programming Without Variables

This section describes our implementation of a Haskell library for point-free programming.

Implementing the Basic Combinators. It is well known that the semantics of a real functional programming language like Haskell differs from the standard domain-theoretic characterization, since all data types are by default pointed and lifted (every type has a distinct bottom element). This means that Haskell does not have true categorical products because $(\bot, \bot) \neq \bot$, nor true categorical exponentials because $(\lambda x. \bot) \neq \bot$. For instance, any function defined using pattern-matching, such as `\(_,_) -> 0`, can distinguish between $(\bot, \bot)$ and $\bot$. This problem does not occur with sums because the separated sum also has a distinguished least element.

As discussed in [6], this fact complicates equational reasoning because the standard laws about products and functions no longer hold. In point-free however, as will be shown later, pairs can only be inspected using a standard set of combinators that cannot distinguish both elements, and thus Haskell pairs can safely be used to model products. If we prohibit the use of `seq`, the same applies to functions. Sums are modeled by the standard Haskell data type `Either`.

```
data Either a b = Left a | Right b
```

Concerning the implementation of the terminal object 1, the special predefined unit data type () is not appropriate, because it has two inhabitants () and `undefined`. The same applies to any isomorphic data type with a single constructor without parameters. 1 can however be defined as the following data type, whose only inhabitant is `undefined` (to be denoted by _L).

```
newtype One = One One
_L = undefined
```

The definition of the point-free combinators in the Pointless library is trivial (see [3] for details). Equipped with these definitions, non-recursive point-free expressions can be directly translated to Haskell. For example, the `swap` and `distr` functions can be encoded as follows.

```
swap :: (a,b) -> (b,a)
swap = snd /\ fst
distr :: (c, Either a b) -> Either (c,a) (c,b)
distr = (swap -|- swap) . app . ((curry inl \/ curry inr) >< id) . swap
```

Implementing Functors and Data Types. The implementation of recursive types in Pointless is based on the generic programming library PolyP [15]. This library also views data types as fixed points of functors, but instead of using an explicit fixpoint operator, a non-standard multi-parameter type class with a functional dependency [10] is used to relate a data type `d` with its base functor `f`.

```
class (Functor f) => FunctorOf f d | d -> f
   where inn' :: f d -> d
         out' :: d -> f d
```

The dependency `d -> f` means that different data types can have the same base functor, but each data type can have at most one. The main advantage of using `FunctorOf` is that predefined Haskell types can be viewed as fixed points of functors (the use of the primes will be clarified later). A relevant subset of PolyP was reimplemented in Pointless according to our own design principles.

To avoid the explicit definition of the map functions, regular functors are described using a fixed set of combinators, according to the definitions

```
newtype Id x          = Id {unId :: x}
newtype Const t x     = Const {unConst :: t}
data (g :+: h) x      = Inl (g x) | Inr (h x)
data (g :*: h) x      = g x :*: h x
newtype (g :@: h) x = Comp {unComp :: g (h x)}
```

The `Functor` instances for these combinators are trivial and omitted here. Given this set of basic functors and functor combinators, the recursive structure of a data type can be captured without declaring new functor data types. For example, the standard Haskell type for lists can be declared as the fixed point

```
instance FunctorOf (Const One :+: (Const a :*: Id)) [a]
    where inn' (Inl (Const _))          = []
          inn' (Inr (Const x :*: Id xs)) = x:xs
          out' []      = Inl (Const _L)
          out' (x:xs) = Inr (Const x :*: Id xs)
```

Naturally, it is still possible to work with data types declared explicitly as fixed points. The fixpoint operator can be defined at the type level using `newtype`.

```
newtype Functor f => Mu f = Mu {unMu :: f (Mu f)}
```

The corresponding instance of `FunctorOf` can be defined once and for all.

```
instance (Functor f) => FunctorOf f (Mu f)
    where inn' = Mu
          out' = unMu
```

The following multi-parameter type class is used to convert values declared using the functor combinators into standard Haskell types and vice-versa.

```
class Rep a b | a -> b
    where to :: a -> b
          from :: b -> a
```

The first parameter should be a type declared using the basic set of functor combinators, and the second is the type that results after evaluating those combinators. The functional dependency imposes a unique result to evaluation. Unfortunately, a functional dependency from b to a does not exist because, for example, a type A can be the result of evaluating both Id A and $\underline{A}$ B.

The instances of `Rep` are rather trivial. For the case of products and sums, the types of the arguments should be computed prior to the resulting type. This evaluation order is guaranteed by using class constraints. We give as examples the identity, constant, and product functors:

```
instance Rep (Id a) a
    where to (Id x) = x
          from x = Id x
instance Rep (Const a b) a
    where to (Const x) = x
          from x = Const x
instance (Rep (g a) b, Rep (h a) c) => Rep ((g :*: h) a) (b, c)
    where to (x :*: y) = (to x, to y)
          from (x, y) = from x :*: from y
```

To ensure that context reduction terminates, standard Haskell requires that the context of an instance declaration must be composed of simple type variables. In this example, although that condition is not verified, reduction necessarily terminates because contexts always get smaller. In order to force the compiler to accept these declarations, a non-standard type system extension must be activated with the option `-fallow-undecidable-instances`.

A possible interaction with a Haskell interpreter could now be

```
> to (Id 'a' :*: Const 'b')
('a','b')
> from ('a','b') :: (Id :*: Const Char) Char
Id 'a' :*: Const 'b'
> from ('a','b') :: (Id :*: Id) Char
Id 'a' :*: Id 'b'
```

Note the annotations are compulsory since the same standard Haskell type can represent different functor combinations. This type-checking problem can be avoided by annotating the polytypic functions with the functor to which they should be specialized (similarly to the theoretical notation). Types cannot be passed as arguments to functions, and so this is achieved indirectly through the use of a "dummy" argument. By using the type class `FunctorOf`, together with its functional dependency, it suffices to pass as argument a value of a data type that is the fixed point of the desired functor.

To achieve an implicit coercion mechanism it suffices to insert the conversions in the functions that refer to functors, namely `inn'`, `out'`, and `fmap` (thus the use of primes). The following functions should be used instead.

```
inn :: (FunctorOf f d, Rep (f d) fd) => fd -> d
inn = inn' . from
out :: (FunctorOf f d, Rep (f d) fd) => d -> fd
out = to . out'
pmap :: (FunctorOf f d, Rep (f a) fa, Rep (f b) fb) =>
        d -> (a -> b) -> (fa -> fb)
pmap (_::d) (f::a->b) =
    to . (fmap f :: FunctorOf f d => f a -> f b) . from
```

Implementing Recursion. A polytypic hylomorphism operator can be defined:

```
hylo :: (FunctorOf f d, Rep (f b) fb, Rep (f a) fa) =>
        d -> (fb -> b) -> (a -> fa) -> a -> b
hylo mu g h = g . pmap mu (hylo mu g h) . h
```

Due to the use of implicit coercion it is now possible to program with hylomorphisms in a truly point-free style. For example, the definition of factorial from Section 2 can now be transcribed directly to Haskell. The same applies to derived recursion patterns. Notice the use of bottom as the dummy argument to indicate the type to which a polytypic function should be instantiated.

```
fact :: Int -> Int
fact = hylo (_L :: [Int]) f g    where g = (id -|- succ /\ id) . out
                                       f = one \/ mult
fold   (_::d) g = hylo (_L::d) g out
unfold (_::d) g = hylo (_L::d) inn g
```

5   DrHylo: Deriving Point-Free Hylomorphisms

DrHylo is a tool for deriving point-free definitions for a subset of Haskell. The resulting definitions can be executed with the Pointless library. It is based on the well-known equivalence between the simply-typed λ-calculus and cartesian closed categories, first stated by Lambek [12]. One half of this correspondence is testified by a translation from pointwise terms to categorical combinators, later used by Curien to study a new implementation technique for functional languages – the *categorical abstract machine* [5]. We show here how the translation can be extended to handle sums and recursion.

This translation is the starting point for our point-free derivation mechanism. The way variables are eliminated resembles the translation of the lambda calculus into *de Bruijn notation*, where variables are represented by integers that measure the distance to their binding abstractions. Typing contexts are represented by left-nested pairs, as defined by the grammar $\Gamma ::= \star \mid \langle \Gamma, x : A \rangle$, with x a variable and A a type. The translation Φ operates on typing judgments, translated as $\Phi(\Gamma : B \vdash M : A) : B \to A$ according to the rules (typing information omitted)

$$
\begin{aligned}
\Phi(\Gamma \vdash \star) &= \mathsf{bang} \\
\Phi(\Gamma \vdash x) &= \mathsf{path}(\Gamma, x) \\
\Phi(\Gamma \vdash MN) &= \mathsf{ap} \circ (\Phi(\Gamma \vdash M) \vartriangle \Phi(\Gamma \vdash N)) \\
\Phi(\Gamma \vdash \lambda x.M) &= \overline{\Phi(\langle \Gamma, x \rangle \vdash M)} \\
\Phi(\Gamma \vdash \langle M, N \rangle) &= \Phi(\Gamma \vdash M) \vartriangle \Phi(\Gamma \vdash N) \\
\Phi(\Gamma \vdash \mathsf{fst}\ M) &= \mathsf{fst} \circ \Phi(\Gamma \vdash M) \\
\Phi(\Gamma \vdash \mathsf{snd}\ M) &= \mathsf{snd} \circ \Phi(\Gamma \vdash M) \\
\Phi(\Gamma \vdash \mathsf{inl}\ M) &= \mathsf{inl} \circ \Phi(\Gamma \vdash M) \\
\Phi(\Gamma \vdash \mathsf{inr}\ M) &= \mathsf{inr} \circ \Phi(\Gamma \vdash M) \\
\Phi(\Gamma \vdash \mathsf{case}\ L\ M\ N) &= \mathsf{ap} \circ (\mathsf{either} \circ (\Phi(\Gamma \vdash M) \vartriangle \Phi(\Gamma \vdash N)) \vartriangle \Phi(\Gamma \vdash L)) \\
\Phi(\Gamma \vdash \mathsf{in}\ M) &= \mathsf{in} \circ \Phi(\Gamma \vdash M) \\
\Phi(\Gamma \vdash \mathsf{out}\ M) &= \mathsf{out} \circ \Phi(\Gamma \vdash M) \\
\mathsf{path}(\langle c, y \rangle, x) &= \begin{cases} \mathsf{snd} & \text{if } x = y \\ \mathsf{path}(c, x) \circ \mathsf{fst} & \text{otherwise} \end{cases}
\end{aligned}
$$

Each variable is replaced by the path to its position in the context tuple, given by function path. The translation of a closed term $M : A \to B$ is a point of type $1 \to (A \to B)$, which can be converted into the expected function of type $A \to B$ as $\mathsf{ap} \circ (\Phi(\star \vdash M) \circ \mathsf{bang} \bigtriangleup \mathsf{id})$.

Concerning the translation of the case construct, first notice that case $L\ M\ N$ is equivalent to $(M \bigtriangledown N)\ L$. This equivalence exposes the fact that a case is just an instance of application, and as such its translation exhibits the same top level structure $\mathsf{ap} \circ (\Phi(\Gamma \vdash M \bigtriangledown N) \bigtriangleup \Phi(\Gamma \vdash L))$. The question remains of how to combine $\Phi(\Gamma \vdash M) : \Gamma \to (A \to C)$ and $\Phi(\Gamma \vdash N) : \Gamma \to (B \to C)$ into a function of type $\Gamma \to (A + B \to C)$. Our solution is based on the internalization of the uncurried version of the either combinator, that can be defined in point-free as follows.

$$\frac{\mathsf{either}\ :\ (A \to C) \times (B \to C) \to (A + B) \to C}{\mathsf{either} = \overline{(\mathsf{ap} \bigtriangledown \mathsf{ap}) \circ (\mathsf{fst} \times \mathsf{id} + \mathsf{snd} \times \mathsf{id}) \circ \mathsf{distr}}}$$

We give as examples the translations of the swap and coswap functions. The former is translated as the following closed term of functional type, which we then convert to a function of type $A \times B \to B \times A$ and simplify as expected.

$$\Phi(\star \vdash \mathsf{swap}) = \overline{\mathsf{snd} \circ \mathsf{snd} \bigtriangleup \mathsf{fst} \circ \mathsf{snd}} : 1 \to (A \times B \to B \times A)$$

$$
\begin{array}{cl}
& \mathsf{ap} \circ (\overline{\mathsf{snd} \circ \mathsf{snd} \bigtriangleup \mathsf{fst} \circ \mathsf{snd}} \circ \mathsf{bang} \bigtriangleup \mathsf{id}) \\
= & \{\,\times\text{-}\textsc{Absor}\,\} \\
& \mathsf{ap} \circ (\overline{\mathsf{snd} \circ \mathsf{snd} \bigtriangleup \mathsf{fst} \circ \mathsf{snd}} \times \mathsf{id}) \circ (\mathsf{bang} \bigtriangleup \mathsf{id}) \\
= & \{\,\wedge\text{-}\textsc{Cancel}\,\} \\
& (\mathsf{snd} \circ \mathsf{snd} \bigtriangleup \mathsf{fst} \circ \mathsf{snd}) \circ (\mathsf{bang} \bigtriangleup \mathsf{id}) \\
= & \{\,\times\text{-}\textsc{Fusion}\,\} \\
& \mathsf{snd} \circ \mathsf{snd} \circ (\mathsf{bang} \bigtriangleup \mathsf{id}) \bigtriangleup \mathsf{fst} \circ \mathsf{snd} \circ (\mathsf{bang} \bigtriangleup \mathsf{id}) \\
= & \{\,\times\text{-}\textsc{Cancel}\,\} \\
& \mathsf{snd} \bigtriangleup \mathsf{fst}
\end{array}
$$

Consider now the translation of the function coswap defined as

$$
\begin{aligned}
\mathsf{coswap}\ &:\ A + B \to B + A \\
\mathsf{coswap}\ &= \lambda x.\mathsf{case}\ x\ (\lambda y.\ \mathsf{inr}\ y)\ (\lambda y.\ \mathsf{inl}\ y)
\end{aligned}
$$

The following result is obtained, which (given some additional facts about either) can be easily simplified into the expected definition $\mathsf{inr} \bigtriangledown \mathsf{inl}$.

$$\overline{\mathsf{ap} \circ (\mathsf{either} \circ \overline{(\mathsf{inr} \circ \mathsf{snd} \bigtriangleup \mathsf{inl} \circ \mathsf{snd})} \bigtriangleup \mathsf{snd})} : 1 \to (A + B \to B + A)$$

It can be shown that the translation Φ is sound [5], i.e, all equivalences proved with an equational theory for the λ-calculus can also be proved using the equations that characterize the point-free combinators. Soundness of the translation of sums is proved in [3].

Translating Recursive Definitions. Two methods can be used for translating recursive definitions into hylomorphisms. The first is based on the direct encoding of fix by a hylomorphism, first proposed in [14]. The insight to this result is that fix f is determined by the infinite application $f\ (f\ (f\ \ldots))$, whose recursion tree is a stream of functions f, subsequently consumed by application. Streams can be defined as Stream $A\ =\ \mu(\underline{A} \otimes \mathsf{Id})$ with a single constructor in : $A \times$ Stream $A \to$ Stream A. Given a function f, the hylomorphism builds the recursion tree in $(f, \mathsf{in}\ (f, \mathsf{in}\ (f, \ldots)))$, and then just replaces in by ap. The operator and its straightforward translation are given as follows

$$\mathsf{fix}\ :\ (A \to A) \to A \qquad\qquad \Phi(\Gamma \vdash \mathsf{fix}\ M) = \mathsf{fix} \circ \Phi(\Gamma \vdash M)$$
$$\mathsf{fix} = \mathsf{hylo}_{\mathsf{Stream}\ (A \to A)}\ \mathsf{ap}\ (\mathsf{id} \bigtriangleup \mathsf{id})$$

Although complete, this translation yields definitions that are difficult to manipulate by calculation. Ideally, one would like the resulting hylomorphisms to be more informative about the original function definition, in the sense that the intermediate data structure should model its recursion tree. An algorithm that derives such hylomorphisms from explicitly recursive definitions has been proposed [9]. In the present context, the idea is to use this algorithm in a stage prior to the point-free translation: first, a pointwise hylomorphism is derived, and then the translation is applied to its parameter functions. DrHylo incorporates this algorithm, adapted to the setting where data types are declared as fixed points, and pattern matching is restricted to sums. Although restrictions are imposed on the syntax of recursive functions, most useful definitions are covered.

Given a single-parameter recursive function defined as a fixpoint, three transformations are produced by the algorithm: one to derive the functor that generates the recursion tree of the hylomorphism ($\mathcal{F}$), a second one to derive the function that is invoked after recursion ($\mathcal{A}$), and a third one for the function that is invoked prior to recursion ($\mathcal{C}$). In general, the function fix $(\lambda f.\ \lambda x.\ L) : A \to B$ is translated as the following hylomorphism.

$$\mathsf{hylo}_{\mu(\mathcal{F}(L))}\ (\lambda x.\ \mathcal{A}(L))\ (\lambda x.\ \mathcal{C}(L)) : A \to B$$

For example, the length function is converted into the following hylomorphism, which can easily be shown to be equal to the expected definition.

$$\mathsf{length}\ :\ \mathsf{List}\ A \to \mathsf{Nat}$$
$$\mathsf{length} = \mathsf{hylo}_{\mu(\underline{1} \oplus \mathsf{Id})}\ (\lambda x.\ \mathsf{case}\ x\ (\lambda y.\mathsf{in}\ (\mathsf{inl}\ \star))\ (\lambda y.\ \mathsf{in}\ (\mathsf{inr}\ y)))$$
$$(\lambda x.\ (\mathsf{out}\ x)\ (\lambda y.\ \mathsf{inl}\ \star)\ (\lambda y.\ \mathsf{inr}\ (\mathsf{snd}\ y)))$$

Pattern Matching. In order to apply this translation to realistic Haskell code, we still need to accommodate in our λ-calculus some form of pattern-matching, and data types defined by collections of constructors. It is well-known how to implement an algorithm for defining FunctorOf instances for most user-defined data types [15]. This algorithm is incorporated in DrHylo, and since it replaces constructors by their equivalent fixpoint definitions, it suffices to have pattern-matching over the generic constructor in, sums, pairs, and the constant $\star$.

We will now introduce a new construct that implements such a mechanism, but with some limitations: there can be no repeated variables in the patterns, no overlapping, and the patterns must be exhaustive. It matches an expression against a set of patterns, binds all the variables in the matching pattern, and returns the respective right-hand side.

$$P ::= \star \mid x \mid \langle P, P \rangle \mid \text{in } P \mid \text{inl } P \mid \text{inr } P$$
$$M, N ::= \ldots \mid \text{match } M \text{ with } \{P \to N; \ldots; P \to N\}$$

Instead of directly translating this new construct to point-free, a rewriting system is defined that eliminates generalized pattern-matching, and simplifies expressions back into the core λ-calculus previously defined [3]. We remark that since Haskell does not have true products, this rewrite relation can sometimes produce expressions whose semantic behaviour is different from the original.

Consider the Haskell function \ (x,y) -> 0. It diverges when applied to _L, but returns zero if applied to (_L,_L). This function can be encoded using match and translated into the core λ-calculus using the following rewrite sequence.

$$\lambda z.\text{match } z \text{ with } \{\langle x, y \rangle \to \text{in } (\text{inl } \star)\}$$
$$\rightsquigarrow \lambda z.\text{match } (\text{fst } z) \text{ with } \{x \to \text{match } (\text{snd } z) \text{ with } \{y \to \text{in } (\text{inl } \star)\}\}$$
$$\rightsquigarrow \lambda z.\text{match } (\text{fst } z) \text{ with } \{x \to \text{in } (\text{inl } \star)\}$$
$$\rightsquigarrow \lambda z.\text{in } (\text{inl } \star)$$

The resulting function is different from the original since it never diverges. Apart from this problem, with this pattern-matching construct it is now possible to translate into point-free many typical Haskell functions, using a syntax closer to that language. For example, distr and the length function can be defined as

distr : $A \times (B + C) \to (A \times B) + (A \times C)$
distr $= \lambda x.\text{match } x \text{ with } \{\langle y, \text{inl } z \rangle \to \text{inl } \langle y, z \rangle; \langle y, \text{inr } z \rangle \to \text{inr } \langle y, z \rangle\}$
length : List $A \to$ Nat
length $= \text{fix}(\lambda f.\lambda l.\text{match } l \{\text{in } (\text{inl } \star) \to \text{in } (\text{inl } \star); \text{in } (\text{inr } \langle h, t \rangle) \to \text{in } (\text{inr } (f\ t))\})$

6 SimpliFree: Implementing Program Transformations

This section presents SimpliFree, a tool to transform Haskell programs written in the point-free style using Pointless. This tool can be used both to simplify point-free expressions, namely those generated by DrHylo, and to perform some program transformations using fold fusion. For full details on the tool and its implementation the reader is directed to [16].

Basic Principles. SimpliFree is based on the concept of *strategic rewriting*: there is a clear distinction between *rewrite rules*, that just dictate how an equational law should be oriented in order to transform a full term, and *rewriting strategies*, that specify how the basic rules should be applied inside a term and combined in order to produce a full rewrite system.

Likewise to other program transformation tools, such as MAG [7], SimpliFree is based on the notion of *active source*: inside a Pointless program one can also define the rules and strategies that will be used to transform it. When the tool runs with such a program as input, a new Haskell file is produced where:

- Point-free expressions are parsed into an abstract syntax data type `Term`.
- Rewrite rules are converted into functions of type `Term -> m Term`, that try to use Haskell's own pattern matching mechanism to apply a rewrite step to a term (`m` must be a monad belonging to class `MonadPlus`).
- Strategies are built using a basic set of strategy combinators defined in the SimpliFree library, which in turn are defined using the strategic programming library Strafunski [11].

When the resulting file is compiled and executed it returns the transformed Pointless program. Alternatively, it can also be interpreted, allowing the user to inspect the full sequence of rewrite rules applied to a particular expression. Notice that the SimpliFree library already implements some powerful strategies that can be used to effectively simplify most point-free expressions.

Implementing Rules. Rules and strategies are defined in a special annotated block inside the program to be transformed. In particular, rules have a name, and a definition that uses the same concrete syntax of the Pointless library. For example, ×-CANCEL, applied to the first argument of a split, and ×-FUSION, applied from right to left, can be defined as follows.

```
{- Rules:
prodCancel1 : fst . (f /\ g) -> f
prodFusionInv : (f . h) /\ (g . h) -> (f/\g) . h
-}
```

One of the fundamental problems to be solved when converting these rules into Haskell functions is how to handle the associativity of composition. In order to avoid implementing matching modulo associativity from scratch, a basic completion procedure had to be implemented on rewrite rules. Sequences of compositions are kept right-associated, and when the left hand side of a rule is a composition, it should be matched not only against a single composition, but also against a *prefix* of a sequence of compositions. For example, the first rule above is translated into the following function.

```
prodCancel1 (FST :.: (f :/\: g)) = return (f)
prodCancel1 (FST :.: ((f :/\: g) :.: x)) = return (f :.: x)
prodCancel1 _ = fail "rule prodCancel1 not applied"
```

Completion is not always this trivial. For example, when a variable is the left argument of a composition there might be the need to try different associations before finding a successful matching. Another problem arises when non-linear patterns are used in the left-hand side of a rule. Since the Haskell matching mechanism cannot handle these patterns, fresh identifiers must be generated to replace repeated variables, and appropriate equality tests have to be introduced in the function bodies. If a rule combines both these problems (such as `prodFusionInv` above) its implementation becomes rather complex.

Strategies. As mentioned above, Strafunski was used in the implementation of strategies and strategy combinators. Strafunski supports two kinds of strategies:

type-preserving strategies, of type `TP m` for a given monad `m`, that given a term of type `t` return a term of type `m t`; and *type-unifying* strategies, of type `TU a m`, where the result is always of type `m a` regardless of the type of the input. In SimpliFree all strategies are type-unifying. To be more specific they have type `TU Computation m`, where `Computation` is a data type containing both the resulting point-free term, and the list of all intermediate steps in the rewriting sequence. For each step, both the name of the applied rule and the resulting term is recorded.

First of all, there is a basic function that promotes a rule into a strategy:

```
rulePF :: (MonadPlus m)=>String -> (Term -> m Term) -> TU Computation m
```

Given a rule, it tries to apply it at most once anywhere inside a term. If successful, it applies an auxiliary type preserving strategy to the full term that associates all compositions to the right. The first argument of `rulePf` is the name of the rule to be recorded.

The library also provides a series of strategy combinators, such as **and**, that given two strategies tries to apply the first and, if successful, applies the second to the result of the first; **or**, that given two strategies tries to apply the first and, if not successful, tries to apply the second; **many**, that repeatedly tries to apply a strategy until it fails; **oneOrMore**, that tries to apply a strategy at least once; and **opt**, that tries to apply a strategy at most once.

Using these strategy combinators we could define the following strategy in a specially annotated block inside a Pointless program.

```
{- Strategies:
simplestrat : compute and (many fold_macros)
compute : simplify and (opt ((oneOrMore unfold_macros) and compute))
simplify : many base_rules

base_rules :  natId1 or natId2 or prodCancel1 or prodCancel2 ...
unfold_macros : exp_unfold or swap_unfold ...
fold_macros : exp_fold or swap_fold ...
-}
```

Each strategy has a name and definition that can refer to rules (defined inside the Rules block) or use strategy combinators to build complex rewriting systems. In this example, `simplestrat` tries to apply as many as possible rules from a set of base rules (that encode most of the laws presented in the appendix) in order to simplify a term. When these rules can no longer be applied, it tries to expand one or more macros (such as the definition of common functions like swap, or derived combinators like exponentiation) and returns to the simplification process. If no macros remain to be expanded the simplification stops. In the end it tries to rebuild macros in order to return a more understandable point-free expression to the user. Notice that the translation of strategies to Haskell is trivial: it is only necessary to replace rule invocation by the application of `rulePF` to the respective name.

Example. The SimpliFree tool has a predefined strategy advstrat that can be used to effectively simplify the point-free expressions derived by DrHylo. This strategy is an elaboration of the strategy simplstrat presented above. In a Pointless program we can specify which of the defined or predefined strategies should be used to transform each point-free declaration. After applying the tool to such a program, the resulting Haskell file contains for each declaration an additional function whose invocation produces the specified transformation, printing at the same time all intermediate steps. The name of this function is just the concatenation of the point-free declaration name and the strategy name (separated by an underscore). For example, after specifying that the swap definition returned by DrHylo should be transformed using the strategy advstrat, the following result can be obtained in the Haskell interpreter.

```
*Main> swap_advstrat
app . ((curry ((snd . snd) /\ (fst . snd)) . bang) /\ id)
  = { expCancel }
((snd . snd) /\ (fst . snd)) . (bang /\ id)
  = { prodFusion }
(snd . snd . (bang /\ id)) /\ (fst . snd . (bang /\ id))
  = { prodCancel2 }
(snd . id) /\ (fst . snd . (bang /\ id))
  = { natId2 }
snd /\ (fst . snd . (bang /\ id))
  = { prodCancel2 }
snd /\ (fst . id)
  = { natId2 }
snd /\ fst
```

More elaborate examples, in particular involving the conditional fusion law, can be found in [16].

7   Conclusions and Future Work

We have focused on the most important aspects of each component of the framework; more documentation can be found at the **UMinho Haskell Software** pages:

http://wiki.di.uminho.pt/wiki/bin/view/PURe/PUReSoftware

While Pointless has reached a stable stage of development, there are still many points for improvement in the other components. In DrHylo, the translation of recursive functions must be improved with the automatic translation to other standard recursion patterns such as folds, unfolds, and paramorphisms, rather than always resorting to the all-encompassing hylomorphisms.

In SimpliFree, we plan to incorporate other laws for recursive functions, such as unfold-fusion. An immediate goal is to make the fusion mechanism more powerful, to cover at least all the transformations that can be done in state-of-the-art tools such as MAG.

A significant improvement will be the introduction of truly generic laws: in the current version of SimpliFree different fold fusion laws are used for different data types. This is an unfortunate mismatch with the theoretical notation, where recursion patterns and laws are generically defined once and for all.

References

1. John Backus. Can programming be liberated from the von Neumann style? a functional style and its algebra of programs. *Communications of the ACM*, 21(8): 613–641, 1978.
2. Richard Bird. The promotion and accumulation strategies in transformational programming. *ACM Transactions on Programming Languages and Systems*, 6(4): 487–504, October 1984.
3. Alcino Cunha. *Point-free Program Calculation*. PhD thesis, Departamento de Informática, Universidade do Minho, 2005.
4. Alcino Cunha and Jorge Sousa Pinto. Point-free program transformation. *Fundamenta Informaticae*, 66(4):315–352, 2005. Special Issue on Program Transformation.
5. Pierre-Louis Curien. *Categorical Combinators, Sequential Algorithms, and Functional Programming*. Birkhuser, 2nd edition, 1993.
6. Nils Anders Danielsson and Patrik Jansson. Chasing bottoms, a case study in program verification in the presence of partial and infinite values. In Dexter Kozen, editor, *Proceedings of the 7th International Conference on Mathematics of Program Construction (MPC'04)*, volume 3125 of *LNCS*. Springer-Verlag, 2004.
7. Oege de Moor and Ganesh Sittampalam. Generic program transformation. In D. Swierstra, P. Henriques, and J. Oliveira, editors, *Proceedings of the 3rd International Summer School on Advanced Functional Programming*, volume 1608 of *LNCS*, pages 116–149. Springer-Verlag, 1999.
8. Jeremy Gibbons. Calculating functional programs. In R. Backhouse, R. Crole, and J. Gibbons, editors, *Algebraic and Coalgebraic Methods in the Mathematics of Program Construction*, volume 2297 of *LNCS*, chapter 5, pages 148–203. Springer-Verlag, 2002.
9. Zhenjiang Hu, Hideya Iwasaki, and Masato Takeichi. Deriving structural hylomorphisms from recursive definitions. In *Proceedings of the ACM SIGPLAN International Conference on Functional Programming (ICFP'96)*, pages 73–82. ACM Press, 1996.
10. Mark Jones. Type classes with functional dependencies. In *Proceedings of the 9th European Symposium on Programming*, volume 1782 of *LNCS*. Springer-Verlag, 2000.
11. Ralf Laemmel and Joost Visser. Typed combinators for generic traversal. In *PADL '02: Proceedings of the 4th International Symposium on Practical Aspects of Declarative Languages*, pages 137–154, London, UK, 2002. Springer-Verlag.
12. Joachim Lambek. From lambda calculus to cartesian closed categories. In J. P. Seldin and J. R. Hindley, editors, *To H. B. Curry: Essays on Combinatory Logic*, pages 375–402. Academic Press, 1980.
13. Erik Meijer, Maarten Fokkinga, and Ross Paterson. Functional programming with bananas, lenses, envelopes and barbed wire. In J. Hughes, editor, *Proceedings of the 5th ACM Conference on Functional Programming Languages and Computer Architecture (FPCA'91)*, volume 523 of *LNCS*. Springer-Verlag, 1991.

14. Erik Meijer and Graham Hutton. Bananas in space: Extending fold and unfold to exponential types. In *Proceedings of the 7th ACM Conference on Functional Programming Languages and Computer Architecture (FPCA'95)*. ACM Press, 1995.
15. Ulf Norell and Patrik Jansson. Polytypic programming in haskell. In *Draft proceedings of the 15th International Workshop on the Implementation of Functional Languages (IFL'03)*, 2003.
16. José Proença. Point-free simplification. Technical Report DI-PURe-05.06.01, Universidade do Minho, 2005.

A   Laws of the Calculus

$$\pi_1 \vartriangle \pi_2 = \mathsf{id} \qquad\qquad \times\text{-Reflex}$$

$$\mathsf{fst} \circ (f \vartriangle g) = f \ \wedge\ \mathsf{snd} \circ (f \vartriangle g) = g \qquad\qquad \times\text{-Cancel}$$

$$(f \vartriangle g) \circ h = f \circ h \vartriangle g \circ h \qquad\qquad \times\text{-Fusion}$$

$$(f \times g) \circ (h \vartriangle i) = f \circ h \vartriangle g \circ i \qquad\qquad \times\text{-Absor}$$

$$(f \times g) \circ (h \times i) = f \circ h \times g \circ i \qquad\qquad \times\text{-Functor}$$

$$f \vartriangle g = h \vartriangle i \ \Leftrightarrow\ f = h \ \wedge\ g = i \qquad\qquad \times\text{-Equal}$$

$$f \vartriangle g \ \text{strict} \ \Leftrightarrow\ f \ \text{strict} \ \wedge\ g \ \text{strict} \qquad\qquad \times\text{-Strict}$$

$$\mathsf{inl} \triangledown \mathsf{inr} = \mathsf{id} \qquad\qquad +\text{-Reflex}$$

$$(f \triangledown g) \circ \mathsf{inl} = f \ \wedge\ (f \triangledown g) \circ \mathsf{inr} = g \qquad\qquad +\text{-Cancel}$$

$$f \circ (g \triangledown h) = f \circ g \triangledown f \circ h \ \Leftarrow\ f \ \text{strict} \qquad\qquad +\text{-Fusion}$$

$$(f \triangledown g) \circ (h + i) = f \circ h \triangledown g \circ i \qquad\qquad +\text{-Absor}$$

$$(f + g) \circ (h + i) = f \circ h + g \circ i \qquad\qquad +\text{-Functor}$$

$$f \triangledown g = h \triangledown i \ \Leftrightarrow\ f = h \ \wedge\ g = i \qquad\qquad +\text{-Equal}$$

$$f \triangledown g \ \text{strict} \qquad\qquad +\text{-Strict}$$

$$\overline{\mathsf{ap}} = \mathsf{id} \qquad\qquad \wedge\text{-Reflex}$$

$$f = \mathsf{ap} \circ (\overline{f} \times \mathsf{id}) \qquad\qquad \wedge\text{-Cancel}$$

$$\overline{f \circ (g \times \mathsf{id})} = \overline{f} \circ g \qquad\qquad \wedge\text{-Fusion}$$

$$f^A \circ \overline{g} = \overline{f \circ g} \qquad\qquad \wedge\text{-Absor}$$

$$(f \circ g)^A = f^A \circ g^A \qquad\qquad \wedge\text{-Functor}$$

$$\overline{f} = \overline{g} \ \Leftrightarrow\ f = g \qquad\qquad \wedge\text{-Equal}$$

$$\overline{f} \ \text{strict} \ \Leftrightarrow\ f \ \text{left-strict} \qquad\qquad \wedge\text{-Strict}$$

$$\underline{f} = \overline{f \circ \pi_2} \qquad\qquad \text{const-Def}$$

$$\underline{f} \circ g = \underline{f} \qquad\qquad \text{const-Fusion}$$

Encoding Strategies in the Lambda Calculus with Interaction Nets

Ian Mackie[1,2]

[1] King's College London, Department of Computer Science,
Strand, London WC2R 2LS, UK
[2] CNRS & École Polytechnique, LIX (UMR 7161), 91128 Palaiseau Cedex, France[*]

Abstract. Interaction nets are a graphical paradigm of computation based on graph rewriting. They have proven to be both useful and enlightening in the encoding of linear logic and the λ-calculus. This paper offers new techniques for the theory of interaction nets, with applications to the encoding of specific strategies in the λ-calculus. In particular we show how to recover the usual call-by-value and call-by-name reduction strategies from general encodings.

1 Introduction

Graph rewriting has long been considered as the right implementation technique for functional programming languages, with one of the main motivations being that it captures *sharing* [27, 21, 24]. The general idea of graph transformation is to represent a functional program using a graph. Reduction is then expressed by replacing one sub-graph by another, in some context. However, such a formalism is potentially non-confluent, and a general pattern-match to identify a reduction can be highly costly. To encode a specific strategy, we need also to find the next redex to reduce.

Thus, to compute efficiently with graphs, we need to be able to identify redexes easily, and also remove the non-determinism to obtain a confluent system. Interaction nets [9] are one such formalism that are specific forms of graph rewrite systems, and they are well engineered for implementation. The main features of interaction nets are that:

- The left-hand side of all rewrite rules consist of just two nodes, which makes pattern matching a very simple operation.
- A number of constraints are placed upon the rewrite rules which makes the reduction confluent by construction (thus we do not need to look for confluent sub-systems of the general formalism). In fact reductions commute, which means that all reduction sequences are simply permutations of each other.

---

[*] Projet Logical, Pôle Commun de Recherche en Informatique du plateau de Saclay, CNRS, École Polytechnique, INRIA, Université Paris-Sud.

A. Butterfield, C. Grelck, and F. Huch (Eds.): IFL 2005, LNCS 4015, pp. 19–36, 2006.

- Further, a graph rewrite step can neither copy nor erase another redex, and thus they are local rewrite rules.

If we consider a system, such as the λ-calculus, compiled into interaction nets, then:

- the strategy is fixed by the compilation;
- the next redex is easy to find;
- reduction is local, and can be potentially implemented in parallel (even if there is no parallelism in the original program) [22].

For these reasons, we believe that interaction nets are a solid foundation for graph reduction systems for functional languages. Over the last few years, we have seen a number of systems of interaction nets for encoding linear logic (proofs and the cut-elimination process), and the λ-calculus (terms and the β-reduction process, which includes the substitution process), as well as other formalisms, for example term rewriting systems. See for instance [2, 7, 8, 17, 18, 19].

Perhaps one of the most interesting aspects of these works is that the encodings have offered new efficient strategies for reduction: examples include β-optimal reduction [13] and closed reduction [4], amongst others. This is related to the fact that interaction nets naturally capture sharing: no active pair (the interaction nets analogue of a redex) can ever be duplicated.

However, on the other side of the coin, interaction nets have not appeared to lend themselves to encoding existing strategies, for instance lazy cut-elimination in linear logic, call-by-value and call-by-name evaluation in the λ-calculus, as well as strategies for term rewriting systems. This is directly related to the above point, that active pairs can never be duplicated, and moreover interaction nets are free from strategies (they can be externally imposed, see for instance [3], but we can only place an order on the permutations possible for reduction).

The purpose of this paper is to show a general framework for interaction nets which will allow strategies to be encoded. The main are:

- We give an encoding of lazy cut-elimination in linear logic in interaction nets. This strategy, given in [6], has been frequently studied in the computational understandings of linear logic, and states that the exponential of linear logic (!) is a constructor, and since we do not know whether we need the contents of the box (it can be erased, duplicated or opened) we should wait before evaluating inside. This corresponds to reduction to *weak head normal form* (WHNF) in the λ-calculus. This interpretation of the exponential has been widely used in the literature, including Abramsky's proof expressions [1], which we can now encode faithfully in interaction nets.
- As a further development of the encoding of linear logic, we show how the different encodings of the λ-calculus into linear logic take on their usual meanings (i.e. the "call-by-value" translation gives call-by-value evaluation, the "call-by-name" translation gives call-by-name evaluation, etc.), which has never been the case, and is often a point of confusion with previous systems (i.e. the interaction net system encoding β-optimal reduction in the

λ-calculus offers the same strategy (β-optimal) whether we use the "call-by-value" or "call-by-name" translation).

Related work. Several works have investigated encoding strategies standard reduction strategies. Lippi [14] has given an encoding for head reduction; Sinot [25] has given an encoding for call-by-name and call-by-value using a synchronising mechanism (there is a unique token that travels through the net to initiate reduction). The work reported in this paper is a continuation of the work started in [5] and [20].

Structure. The rest of this paper is structured as follows: in the next section, we recall interaction nets, and some of the basic results that we need for the rest of the paper. In Section 3 we give our first contribution which is a general notion of a net in normal form, and give some examples. In Section 4 we show how to encode lazy reduction in linear logic. Section 5 is devoted to the λ-calculus, and the call-by-name and call-by-value translations (and a combination of the two). In Section 6 we discuss the results and compare the approach with other interaction net encodings of strategies. Finally, we conclude the paper in Section 7.

2 Background

Here we recall interaction nets and justify why we consider them useful for functional language implementation. An interaction net system [9] is specified by giving a set Σ of symbols, and a set $\mathcal{R}$ of interaction rules. Each symbol $\alpha \in \Sigma$ has an associated (fixed) *arity*. An occurrence of a symbol $\alpha \in \Sigma$ will be called an *agent*. If the arity of α is n, then the agent has $n + 1$ *ports*: a distinguished one called the *principal port* depicted by an arrow, and n *auxiliary ports* labelled $x_1, \ldots, x_n$ corresponding to the arity of the symbol. Such an agent will be drawn in the following way:

A net N built on Σ is a graph (not necessarily connected) with agents at the vertices. The edges of the graph connect agents together at the ports such that there is only one edge at every port. The ports of an agent that are not connected to another agent are called the free ports of the net. There are two special instances of a net: a wiring (no agents), and the empty net.

A pair of agents $(\alpha, \beta) \in \Sigma \times \Sigma$ connected together on their principal ports is called an *active pair*; the interaction net analog of a redex. An interaction rule $((\alpha, \beta) \Longrightarrow N) \in \mathcal{R}$ replaces an occurrence of the active pair (α, β) by a net N. The rule has to satisfy two conditions: all the free ports are preserved during reduction, and there is at most one rule for each pair of agents. The following diagram illustrates the idea, where N is any net built from Σ.

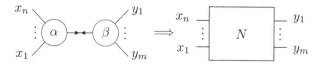

If a net does not contain any active pairs then we say that it is in normal form. We use the notation $\Longrightarrow$ for a one step reduction and $\Longrightarrow^*$ for the transitive and reflexive closure.

We consider interaction nets as an important model of computation for several reasons:

1. *All* aspects of a computation are captured by the rewriting rules—no external machinery such as copying a chunk of memory, or a garbage collector, are needed. Interaction nets are amongst the few formalisms which model computation where this is the case, and consequently they can serve as both a low level operational semantics and an object language for compilation, in addition to being well suited as a high-level programming language.
2. Interaction nets naturally capture *sharing*—interaction steps can never be duplicated. Thus only normal forms can be duplicated, and this must be done incrementally. Using interaction nets as an *object* language for a compiler offers strong evidence that this sharing will be passed on to the programming language being implemented. One of the most spectacular instances of this is the work by Gonthier, Abadi and Lévy, who gave a system of interaction nets to capture both β-optimal reduction [13] in the λ-calculus [7] (Lamping's algorithm [12]), and optimal reduction for cut-elimination in linear logic [8].
3. There is growing evidence that interaction nets can provide a platform for the development of parallel implementations, specifically parallel implementations of sequential programming languages. Using interaction nets as an *object* language for a compiler offers strong evidence that the programming language being implemented may be executed in parallel (*even if there was no parallelism in the original program*).

Lafont's interaction combinators [11] are a fixed system of interaction nets which consists of just three agents and six rewrite rules. Lafont demonstrated that this extremely simple system of rewriting is *universal*—any other system of interaction nets can be encoded (we also note that interaction nets are Turing complete: they can simulate a Turing machine). This important result in interaction nets is analogous to the functional completeness of **S** and **K** in Combinatory Logic. Below we give the three interaction combinators γ (a constructor), δ (a duplicator) and ϵ (an eraser), and in Figure 1 we give the six interaction rules for this system.

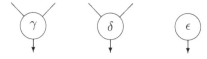

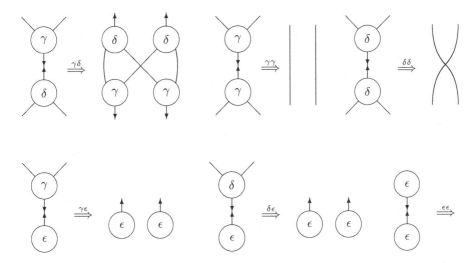

Fig. 1. Interaction Rules

The constructor agent γ can be used as a binary multiplexing/demultiplexing agent: it groups two edges (the auxiliary ports) into one (the principal port). The interaction rule for $\gamma\gamma$ can then be understood as removing the shared edge. This idea can be generalised to n-ary multiplexing nets using pairs of nets (M_n, M_n^*), where M_n is a multiplexing net of size n, and M_n^* is the corresponding demultiplexing net. Both M_n and M_n^* are constructed using only the agents γ and ϵ, and the pair (M_n, M_n^*) must satisfy the condition that the following reduction sequence is satisfied:

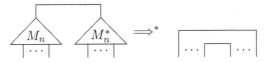

There are many possible ways of building these nets, one such way is given in Figure 2, where the duality between M_n and M_n^* is clear. An important point for this paper is that the nets M_n and M_n^* do not contain δ agents. Note also that for $n > 0$ the ϵ agent is not necessary since we can construct the nets from $n - 1$ γ agents. These nets are instances of *principal nets* (see [11]) and thus can be fully erased with ϵ agents, and fully duplicated with δ agents, as shown below:

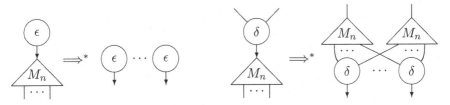

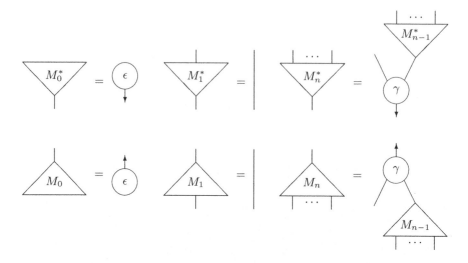

Fig. 2. Constructing Multiplexing Nets

This example system will in fact be heavily used in the rest of this paper: δ agents will always be used to duplicate, ϵ agents will be used to erase a net, and γ agents will be used to construct multiplexing nets which will be used in the compilation later.

3   Normal Form Nets

Here we present the first contribution of the paper, which is a general notion of a construction of a net in normal form. To motivate the ideas, consider that we want to do the following:

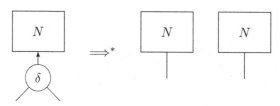

That is, we want to duplicate a net N, using a sequence of interactions with the δ agent. To achieve this with the standard rules for δ given above, N must satisfy the following conditions:

1. N must be free from δ agents, because the interaction rule for two δ agents causes an annihilation (i.e. δ cannot copy δ). This issue has had a lot of attention, and is in fact a main difficulty in encoding both linear logic and the λ-calculus in interaction nets. There are several solutions to

this problem in the literature: indexing agents (as used in the interaction net implementation of Lamping's β-optimal algorithm [12]), two different δ agents (called δ and c) together with a mechanism for introducing δ agents in a well-balanced discipline (as given by Abramsky for the so-called synchronous box encoding of linear logic [16]), and finally a general solution to the problem using a package which extracts δ agents from a given net, which is due to Lafont [11].

In this paper all the nets that we duplicate will be δ-free by virtue of the encoding.

2. N must be in *normal form*, otherwise the duplication process will force a normalisation. This of course is an advantage, in that redexes are not duplicated, but a disadvantage if we want to duplicate active pairs which is required if we want to simulate standard reduction strategies. The main idea of this paper is that for any net, we can cut edges corresponding to active pairs, which leaves us with a net in normal form.

3. N must be *deadlock-free*, which means that there cannot be any cycles of principal ports in the net. In this paper we ignore this case, as all the nets that we build are deadlock-free.

The purpose of this section is to show a general way of allowing the above reduction sequence, for *any* net. Thus we need a mechanism which allows active pairs to be duplicated and erased, and moreover, this should be possible for all nets, even nets not having a normal form. The approach that we adopt is to provide a net transformation, which will be called a *cut-net*, with the following two properties:

1. A cut-net, called $C(N)$, can be duplicated and erased, and
2. N can be recovered from $C(N)$.

Example. The example below shows the general construction. Consider the following net, which is built with agents $+$ and Z (representing addition and zero) containing two active pairs:

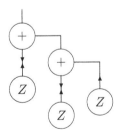

If we cut the active pairs, and connect the free edges from the Z agents together to an M_2, and the free edges from the $+$ agents to an M_2^*, then we obtain a net with three free edges. This completes the construction of an active-pair-free package. This net, and the corresponding decoder net are shown below.

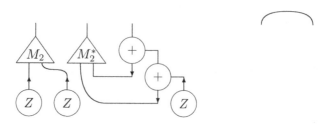

The decoder net (which is just an edge) is connected to the nets M_2 and M_2^* for decoding. This recovers the edges of the original net, and thus recovers the active pairs.

We now formalise this process, and prove some properties of the encoding.

Definition 1 (Active Pair Extraction). *Let N be a net built using agents with the signature Σ. Active pairs can be cut giving the net N^-, and grouped with a multiplexing pair. The result of this packing of N is denoted $C(N)$, where we assume that n ($n > 0$) edges have been cut.*

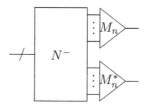

The resulting system has agents in $\Sigma \cup \{\gamma\}$ and an additional rule for $\gamma\gamma$ needs to be added.

Definition 2 ($C(N)$ Decoding). *The corresponding decoder for edge extraction is simply an edge connecting the two additional free edges together.*

Lemma 1 (Unpack). *Let $C(N)$ be a cut-net of the net N, then the following reduction sequence exists which recovers N from the $C(N)$:*

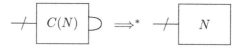

Lemma 2 (Duplicate). *For any net N, if $C(N)$ is a net without deadlocks, and without δ agents, then:*

Lemma 3 (Erase). *For any net N, if $P_e(N)$ is a terminating net free from deadlocks, then it can be completely erased:*

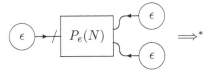

As a consequence of the above Lemmas, cut-nets can be erased, duplicated and unpacked. In the following two sections we look at two applications of this result for the encoding of lazy reduction in linear logic, and reduction strategies in the λ-calculus.

4   Lazy Cut-Elimination in Linear Logic

In this section we show how cut-nets can be used to encode boxes in linear logic [6], in such a way as not to allow any internal reductions. Thus, we obtain an interaction net implementation of lazy cut-elimination for linear logic. We refer the reader to [10] for the lazy cut-elimination strategy. Here we only show the encoding of the multiplicative exponential fragment of linear logic, the additives can also be encoded but will not be used for the λ-calculus that we give as the main application in the next section. We base our encoding on the system presented in [16], but in fact any interaction system encoding linear logic can be adapted to work with lazy reduction.

Let π be a proof with conclusion Γ. Our translation $T(\pi)$ into interaction nets will have the following general form:

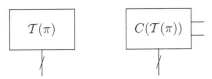

The free edges at the bottom correspond to Γ (one edge for each formula, in the correct order, to avoid labelling the free edges). $C(T(\pi))$ is the cut-net, i.e. all active pairs have been abstracted.

Axiom, Cut and Multiplicatives. If π is an axiom, then $T(\pi)$ is simply translated into an edge. The proof and the corresponding net are given by:

$$\frac{\quad\quad\quad\quad}{A^\perp, A}\text{ (Axiom)}$$

If π ends with a cut rule, then let π_1 be a proof of Γ, A and π_2 a proof of $A^\perp, \Delta$, then $T(\pi)$ is built by connecting the ports A and $A^\perp$ together with an edge. The rule and the corresponding net are given by:

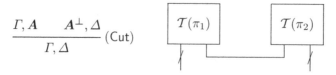

$$\frac{\Gamma, A \qquad A^{\perp}, \Delta}{\Gamma, \Delta} \text{ (Cut)}$$

If π ends with the Tensor rule, then let π_1 be a proof of Γ, A and π_2 a proof of B, Δ. $\mathcal{T}(\pi)$ is then built in the following way by introducing an agent $\otimes$, which connects the edges A and B together to form a single edge. The rule and the corresponding net are given by:

$$\frac{\Gamma, A \qquad B, \Delta}{\Gamma, A \otimes B, \Delta} \text{ ($\otimes$)}$$

The principal port of the $\otimes$ agent corresponds to the conclusion $A \otimes B$ in the rule, and the auxiliary ports correspond to the premises A and B respectively.

If π_1 is a proof of Γ, A, B then we can build a proof π of $\Gamma, A \otimes B$ using the Par rule. $\mathcal{T}(\pi)$ is then built by introducing an agent $\otimes$, which connects the edges A and B together to form a single edge. The rule and the corresponding net are given by:

$$\frac{\Gamma, A, B}{\Gamma, A \otimes B} \text{ ($\otimes$)}$$

The principal port of the $\otimes$ agent corresponds to the conclusion $A \otimes B$ in the rule, and the auxiliary ports correspond to the premises A and B respectively.

Cut-elimination is simulated for the multiplicatives by the following rule, which is nothing more than the proof net reduction rule:

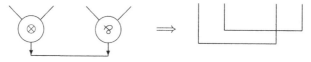

Promotion rule. Let π_1 be a proof of $?\Gamma, A$, and π the proof of $?\Gamma, !A$ built from π_1 using the promotion rule (!). The rule and the corresponding net $\mathcal{T}(\pi)$ are then given by:

$$\frac{?\Gamma, A}{?\Gamma, !A} \text{ (!)}$$

where we have introduced an n-ary agent ! which groups the edges corresponding to the context $?\Gamma$, the main conclusion A, and the additional two edges derived from the construction. The principal port of the ! agent corresponds to the main conclusion $!A$ in the proof. We remark that $C(T(\pi))$ is a net in normal form, and is also a net free from δ agents and deadlocks.

Dereliction rule. Let π_1 be a proof of Γ, A, and π the proof of $\Gamma, ?A$ built from π_1 using the dereliction rule (D). The rule and the corresponding net $T(\pi)$ are then given as follows, where we have introduced a new agent d corresponding to the rule.

$$\frac{\Gamma, A}{\Gamma, ?A}\,(D)$$

The dereliction cut-elimination step is the following, which "opens" an exponential box:

$$\frac{\dfrac{\dfrac{\pi_1}{?\Delta, A}}{?\Delta, !A}\,(!) \quad \dfrac{\dfrac{\pi_2}{A^\perp, \Gamma}}{?A^\perp, \Gamma}\,(D)}{?\Delta, \Gamma}\,(\text{Cut}) \quad \rightarrow \quad \dfrac{\dfrac{\pi_1}{?\Delta, A} \quad \dfrac{\pi_2}{A^\perp, \Gamma}}{?\Delta, \Gamma}\,(\text{Cut})$$

This rule suggests the following net transformation, which is simply the translation of the left and right-hand sides of the rule:

The following is the only rule that we need, which will make all the connections required, and moreover connect the additional edges for the package together which, by the Unpack Lemma 1, easily shows that this cut-elimination step is correctly simulated.

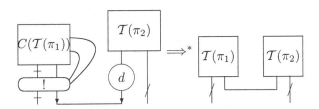

Contraction rule. Let π_1 be a proof of $\Gamma, ?A, ?A$, and π the proof of $\Gamma, ?A$ built from π_1 using the contraction rule (C). The rule and the corresponding net $\mathcal{T}(\pi)$ are then given by the following, where we have introduced a new agent c corresponding to contraction.

$$\frac{\Gamma, ?A, ?A}{\Gamma, ?A}\,(C)$$

In Figure 3 we show the cut-elimination step, which causes duplication of the proof π_1. To implement this in interaction nets, we require that c will copy the ! agent, and introduce δ agents to duplicate the package. In the same figure, we also give the interaction rule which implements the cut-elimination step.

$$\frac{\dfrac{\dfrac{\pi_1}{?\Delta, A}}{?\Delta, !A}\,(!) \quad \dfrac{\dfrac{\pi_2}{?A^\perp, ?A^\perp, \Gamma}}{?A^\perp, \Gamma}\,(C)}{?\Delta, \Gamma}\,(\text{Cut})$$

$$\rightarrow$$

$$\frac{\dfrac{\dfrac{\pi_1}{?\Delta, A}}{?\Delta, !A}\,(!) \quad \dfrac{\dfrac{\dfrac{\pi_1}{?\Delta, A}}{?\Delta, !A}\,(!) \quad \dfrac{\pi_2}{?A^\perp, ?A^\perp, \Gamma}}{?\Delta, ?A^\perp, \Gamma}\,(\text{Cut})}{\dfrac{?\Delta, ?\Delta, \Gamma}{?\Delta, \Gamma}\,(C)}\,(\text{Cut})$$

Fig. 3. Contraction cut-elimination step and interaction rule

With this rule and the addition of rules for δ with all the other agents of the system (δ simply duplicates all agents except another δ, cf. Figure 1 for the combinators), together with the Duplicate Lemma 2, we see that the cut-elimination step is correctly implemented.

Weakening rule. Let π_1 be a proof of Γ, and π the proof of $\Gamma, ?A$ built from π_1 using the weakening rule (W). The rule and the corresponding net $\mathcal{T}(\pi)$ are then given by the following, where we have used the ϵ agent to represent weakening.

$$\frac{\Gamma}{\Gamma, ?A}\,(W)$$

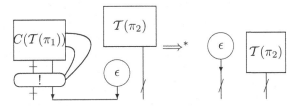

The weakening cut-elimination step is given by the following rule:

$$\frac{\dfrac{\pi_1}{\dfrac{?\Delta, A}{?\Delta, !A}\,(!)} \quad \dfrac{\pi_2}{\dfrac{\Gamma}{?A^\perp, \Gamma}\,(W)}}{?\Delta, \Gamma}\,(\mathsf{Cut}) \quad \rightarrow \quad \dfrac{\dfrac{\pi_2}{\Gamma}}{?\Delta, \Gamma}\,(W)$$

which corresponds to the following net transformation:

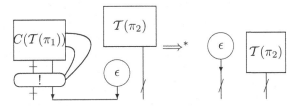

In words, we erase completely the promoted proof, and weakenings are introduced for each formula in Δ. With the addition of rules for ϵ to erase each agent in the system, and then by the Erase Lemma 3 the net can be completely erased, and we see that this cut-elimination step is correctly implemented.

This completes the lazy cut-elimination procedure for linear logic:

Theorem 1. *Let π be a proof with conclusion Γ, then if π reduces to π' by lazy cut-elimination, then $\mathcal{T}(\pi)$ reduces to $\mathcal{T}(\pi')$.*

Proof. Direct consequence of the above simulations.

We remark that this system is one of the simplest encodings of linear logic, and moreover, the correctness is established without any of the usual complications generally encountered. One application of this encoding of lazy cut-elimination is for the implementation of proof expressions [1] (for the multiplicative exponential part) as a system of interaction nets, and thus offers an alternative implementation technique for the parallel implementation of proof expressions.

5   Application to λ-Calculus Translations

In this section we briefly outline how three translations of the λ-calculus into linear logic offer very different systems of interaction nets when using the encoding for lazy cut-elimination. We remark that this is not at all the case with other encodings, for instance, the interaction system for encoding β-optimal reduction gives the same strategy (β-optimal reduction) for any of the translations used. The following table summarises the results that we present in this section:

	WHNF	HNF
Call-by-value	$!(A \multimap B)$	N/A
Call-by-name	$!(!A \multimap B)$	$!A \multimap B$

We recall that (closed) weak head normal forms (WHNF) are terms of the form $\lambda x.t$, for any t, and (closed) head normal forms (HNF) are terms of the form $\lambda x.x_i t$, where x_i is the head variable. We begin with a general remark. A packed net, which is the encoding of a promotion rule, is a net in normal form which can be erased and duplicated. Thus an encoding which uses promotion for the function will immediately give a reduction strategy to weak head normal form. Similarly, if a promotion is used for the argument, then we cannot perform any reduction on that argument and thus obtain call-by-name reduction. These basic observations will now be spelled out for each case below.

The call-by-value translation. Recall that the call-by-value translation of the λ-calculus into linear logic (also known as the $!(A \multimap B)$ translation) places an exponential box around the function, which will be packaged, thus no reduction inside an abstraction is possible. For this reason, we see easily that we obtain reduction to weak head normal form. We begin by giving the translation. Variables are translated into a connecting edge (no agents), and abstraction $\lambda x.t$ and application tu are given by the following two nets:

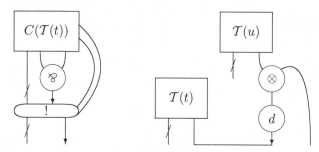

Remark that for the abstraction, if there is no occurrence of the variable x in t, then we must use an ϵ agent connected to the left auxiliary port of the $\invamp$ agent, and if an application shares a common free variable, then we must use a contraction (c) agent.

Proposition 1.   *1. Let t be a WHNF, then $\mathcal{T}(t)$ is a net in normal form.*
  2. If t reduces to a WHNF v by the call-by-value strategy, then $\mathcal{T}(t) \Longrightarrow^* \mathcal{T}(v)$.

The call-by-name translation. The call-by-name translation, also known as the $!A \multimap B$ translation, is distinguished by the placing of the box around the argument. Thus we see immediately that no reduction inside an argument is possible.

The translation is straightforward: a variable becomes a dereliction agent, and abstraction $\lambda x.t$ and application tu are given by the following two nets, where again we may have to use ϵ and c in the same way as the previous case.

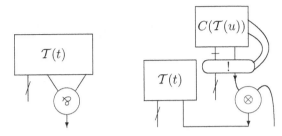

Proposition 2.   *1. Let t be a* HNF, *then $\mathcal{T}(t)$ is a net in normal form.*
2. If t reduces to a HNF v *by the call-by-name strategy, then $\mathcal{T}(t) \Longrightarrow^* \mathcal{T}(v)$.*

The combined call-by-name/value translation. Finally, we look at the combined translation, also known as the $!(!A \multimap B)$ translation, which is nothing more than a superposition of the above two translations. Therefore, variables become dereliction agents, abstraction is promoted, and the application uses a dereliction and a promotion. Since there is now a box around the function and the argument, we obtain call-by-name to weak head normal form.

Proposition 3.   *1. Let t be a* WHNF, *then $\mathcal{T}(t)$ is a net in normal form.*
2. If t reduces to a WHNF v *by the call-by-name strategy, then $\mathcal{T}(t) \Longrightarrow^* \mathcal{T}(v)$.*

6   Evaluation of the Results

The idea of encoding a specific strategy in interaction nets is not a new one. As we stated in the introduction, there are other approaches that have been previously studied. Here we briefly compare these, and also state some further applications of the technique introduced in this paper.

One of the first attempts to encode a specific reduction strategy in the λ-calculus was through encodings of abstract machines into term rewriting systems. From this a system of interaction nets can be obtained through the interaction net encoding of the term rewriting system [2]. Using this approach it is possible to write different abstract machines, performing different reduction strategies, in a uniform way to simulate a variety of different strategies. However, this translation works on the syntax of the system, and therefore we find a collection of interaction rules which are doing nothing else but manipulating the syntax (for instance, lists need to be encoded for some environment machines, and operations are needed to manipulate these lists—these interactions have nothing to do with the actual computation). It is a therefore a general approach to simulating existing reduction strategies in interaction nets, where efficiency is not a concern.

Lippi [14, 15] gave an interaction net encoding of a specific reduction strategy in the λ-calculus. His approach is very powerful: nets can be encoded (frozen) and decoded (unfrozen) dynamically, whereas our approach only allows nets to be decoded (encoding is done only at compile time). However, there is a cost to this, in that nets need to be traversed with specific coding/decoding agents to perform these operations. Such a cost is dependent on the size of the net, which has an effect on the overall performance.

More recently, Sinot [25, 26] has investigated ways of controlling the evaluation order of λ-terms represented as interaction nets. This is achieved by a single control node that traverses the net to identify the next redex. Incorporating such control mechanisms in the same framework is quite an achievement, but each specific strategy needs a new set of rules for the control agents. Moreover, the natural parallelism of interaction nets is disturbed through this level of control, but is perhaps the best approach to simulate a specific reduction strategy.

Finally, we should also remark that Pinto [23] has studied weak reduction in interaction nets. This approach is quite different in that the evaluation of interaction nets is constrained to follow a particular reduction order. There are cases when one can do this to achieve a specific strategy in the underlying system, and of course there is no overhead in the interaction system (no need to introduce any new agents or rules).

Our goal is to simulate a specific reduction strategy the most efficient way, by taking an efficient implementation of the λ-calculus and block some of the β-reductions. Packing nets in this way has relatively little overhead. It is also worth remarking that all the proofs for correctness are obtained directly from the rewriting system, and thus are quite straightforward to obtain.

The ideas of this paper can also work beyond the λ-calculus. In particular, they can be used for any system of interaction nets where some order of evaluation is required. When encoding functional languages, with a given reduction semantics, then we are forced to find some way to control the evaluation order. This is particularly pertinent when side-effects are available in the language. We have also experimented with the approach for encoding other programming paradigms, and we will report on this more completely in the future.

7   Conclusions

In this paper we have put forward interaction nets as an implementation formalism for functional programming languages. In particular, to capture standard, existing reduction strategies. This has been achieved using encoding techniques from interaction nets. Although this paper has focused on the λ-calculus (through linear logic), the way forward to cover richer languages is already quite well developed.

One of the most striking features of the encodings is the simplicity of the system: the proofs of correctness are far simpler than any other system of interaction. Additionally, we have shown that the different embeddings of the

λ-calculus into linear logic allow us to obtain interaction net evaluators for the λ-calculus which offer different strategies for reduction.

References

1. S. Abramsky. Computational Interpretations of Linear Logic. *Theoretical Comput. Sci.*, 111:3–57, 1993.
2. M. Fernández and I. Mackie. Interaction nets and term rewriting systems. *Theoretical Computer Science*, 190(1):3–39, January 1998.
3. M. Fernández and I. Mackie. A calculus for interaction nets. In G. Nadathur, editor, *Proceedings of the International Conference on Principles and Practice of Declarative Programming (PPDP'99)*, volume 1702 of *Lecture Notes in Computer Science*, pages 170–187. Springer-Verlag, September 1999.
4. M. Fernández and I. Mackie. Closed reduction in the λ-calculus. In J. Flum and M. Rodríguez-Artalejo, editors, *Proceedings of Computer Science Logic (CSL'99)*, volume 1683 of *Lecture Notes in Computer Science*, pages 220–234. Springer-Verlag, September 1999.
5. M. Fernández and I. Mackie. Packing interaction nets: Applications to linear logic and the lambda calculus. In M. Frias and J. Heintz, editors, *Proceedings of the 5th Argentinian Workshop of Theoretical Computer Science (WAIT2001)*, volume 30 of *Anales JAIIO*, pages 91–107, September 2001.
6. J.-Y. Girard. Linear Logic. *Theoretical Computer Science*, 50(1):1–102, 1987.
7. G. Gonthier, M. Abadi, and J.-J. Lévy. The geometry of optimal lambda reduction. In *Proceedings of the 19th ACM Symposium on Principles of Programming Languages (POPL'92)*, pages 15–26. ACM Press, Jan. 1992.
8. G. Gonthier, M. Abadi, and J.-J. Lévy. Linear logic without boxes. In *Proceedings of the 7th IEEE Symposium on Logic in Computer Science (LICS'92)*, pages 223–234. IEEE Press, 1992.
9. Y. Lafont. Interaction nets. In *Proceedings of the 17th ACM Symposium on Principles of Programming Languages (POPL'90)*, pages 95–108. ACM Press, Jan. 1990.
10. Y. Lafont. From proof nets to interaction nets. In J.-Y. Girard, Y. Lafont, and L. Regnier, editors, *Advances in Linear Logic*, number 222 in London Mathematical Society Lecture Note Series, pages 225–247. Cambridge University Press, 1995.
11. Y. Lafont. Interaction combinators. *Information and Computation*, 137(1):69–101, 1997.
12. J. Lamping. An algorithm for optimal lambda calculus reduction. In *Proceedings of the 17th ACM Symposium on Principles of Programming Languages (POPL'90)*, pages 16–30. ACM Press, Jan. 1990.
13. J.-J. Lévy. *Réductions Correctes et Optimales dans le Lambda-Calcul*. Thèse d'état, Université Paris VII, Jan. 1978.
14. S. Lippi. λ-calculus left reduction with interaction nets. *Mathematical Structures in Computer Science*, 12(6), 2002.
15. S. Lippi. *Théorie et pratique des réseaux d'interaction*. PhD thesis, Université de la Méditerranée, June 2002.
16. I. Mackie. *The Geometry of Implementation*. PhD thesis, Department of Computing, Imperial College of Science, Technology and Medicine, September 1994.
17. I. Mackie. YALE: Yet another lambda evaluator based on interaction nets. In *Proceedings of the 3rd International Conference on Functional Programming (ICFP'98)*, pages 117–128. ACM Press, 1998.

18. I. Mackie. Interaction nets for linear logic. *Theoretical Computer Science*, 247(1):83–140, September 2000.
19. I. Mackie. Efficient λ-evaluation with interaction nets. In V. van Oostrom, editor, *Proceedings of the 15th International Conference on Rewriting Techniques and Applications (RTA'04)*, volume 3091 of *Lecture Notes in Computer Science*, pages 155–169. Springer-Verlag, June 2004.
20. I. Mackie and J. S. Pinto. Encoding linear logic with interaction combinators. *Information and Computation*, 176(2):153–186, August 2002.
21. S. L. Peyton Jones. *The Implementation of Functional Programming Languages*. Prentice Hall International, 1987.
22. J. S. Pinto. *Parallel Implementation with Linear Logic*. PhD thesis, École Polytechnique, February 2001.
23. J. S. Pinto. Weak reduction and garbage collection in interaction nets. In *Proceedings of the 3rd International Workshop on Reduction Strategies in Rewriting and Programming*, Valencia, Spain, 2003.
24. R. Plasmeijer and M. Eekelen. *Functional Programming and Parallel Graph Rewriting*. Addison Wesley, 1993.
25. F.-R. Sinot. Call-by-name and call-by-value as token-passing interaction nets. In P. Urzyczyn, editor, *TLCA*, volume 3461 of *Lecture Notes in Computer Science*, pages 386–400. Springer, 2005.
26. F.-R. Sinot. Token-passing nets: Call-by-need for free. *Electronic Notes in Theoretical Computer Science*, 135(5):129–139, March 2006.
27. C. P. Wadsworth. *Semantics and Pragmatics of the Lambda-Calculus*. PhD thesis, Oxford University, 1971.

Proof Tool Support for Explicit Strictness

Marko van Eekelen and Maarten de Mol

Institute for Computing and Information Sciences
Radboud University Nijmegen
The Netherlands
marko@cs.ru.nl, maartenm@cs.ru.nl

Abstract. In programs written in lazy functional languages such as for example Clean and Haskell, the programmer can choose freely whether particular subexpressions will be evaluated lazily (the default) or strictly (must be specified explicitly). It is widely known that this choice affects resource consumption, termination and semantics in several ways. However, functional programmers tend to be less aware of the consequences for logical program properties and formal reasoning.

This paper aims to give a better understanding of the concept of explicit strictness and its impact on properties and reasoning. It will be shown that explicit strictness may make reasoning more cumbersome, due to the introduction of additional definedness conditions.

Fortunately, these definedness conditions can be handled quite effectively by proof assistants. This paper describes the specific support that is offered by Sparkle for expressing and proving definedness conditions. This support makes reasoning with explicit strictness almost appear like reasoning without explicit strictness. To our knowledge, Sparkle is currently the only proof assistant with such strictness specific support.

1 Introduction

Lazy functional programming languages, such as for example Clean and Haskell, are excellent for developing readable and reliable software. One of their key features is lazy evaluation, which makes it possible to adopt a natural, almost mathematical, programming style. The downside of lazy evaluation, however, is lack of control; it becomes very difficult to predict when subexpressions will be evaluated, which makes resource management a non-trivial task.

This issue has been addressed by the introduction of *explicit strictness*, with which a functional programmer can enforce the evaluation of a subexpression by hand. Adding explicit strictness can indeed change the resource consumption of programs significantly, and it is therefore used a lot in practice. Moreover, explicit strictness can easily be incorporated in the semantics of functional languages, and is therefore theoretically sound as well.

Not all is well, however. In this paper, we will show that the addition (or removal) of strictness to programs may also give rise to many unexpected (and undesirable) effects. Of course, some effects are already widely known, such as for example the possible introduction of non-termination. However, less widely known to programmers, is that explicit strictness may:

A. Butterfield, C. Grelck, and F. Huch (Eds.): IFL 2005, LNCS 4015, pp. 37–54, 2006.

- break program properties, forcing them to be reformulated by adding (or removing) definedness conditions;
- break proof rules that are based on reduction, adding a new definedness precondition to them that has to be shown to be satisfied in order for the rule to be applicable.

In other words: changing strictness properties can have serious consequences for formal reasoning. In general, the addition of explicit strictness makes reasoning more cumbersome and forces one to pay attention to technical details that are not so interesting. Fortunately, exactly these kinds of details can be dealt with effectively by means of a proof assistant.

We will demonstrate the facilities that Sparkle, the proof assistant for Clean, offers for dealing with definedness conditions. Sparkle has been introduced in [6], but its specific definedness facilities have not yet been addressed in any publication. The definedness facilities of Sparkle include:

1. a dedicated proof rule for proving definedness conditions;
2. an upgraded reduction system that takes advantage of available definedness information; and
3. a mechanism to conveniently denote definedness conditions.

With these facilities, definedness conditions are often handled in the background and are hidden from the user completely, making reasoning with strictness look like reasoning without strictness.

This paper is structured as follows. First, in Section 2 the concept of explicit strictness is introduced, both informally and formally. Also, its effects on program semantics and program transformations are discussed. Then, in Section 3 the effects of explicit strictness on program properties and reasoning will be examined. The three kinds of support that Sparkle offers for this purpose will be introduced in Section 4. Finally, Sections 5 and 6 discuss related work and conclusions.

2   The Concept of Explicit Strictness

Although it is seldom mentioned in publications, explicit strictness is present in almost every real-world lazy program. Explicit strictness is used for:

- improving the *efficiency of data structures* (e.g. strict lists),
- improving the *efficiency of evaluation* (e.g. functions that are made strict in arguments that always have to be evaluated),
- *enforcing the evaluation order* in interfacing with the outside world (e.g. an interface to an external C-call is defined to be strict in order to ensure that the arguments are fully evaluated before the external call is issued).

Language features that are used to explicitly enforce strictness include:

- type annotations (in functions: Clean and in data structures: Clean, Haskell),
- special data structures (unboxed arrays: Clean, Haskell),
- special primitives (seq: Haskell),
- special language constructs (let!, #!: Clean).

Implementers of real-world applications make it their job to know about explicit strictness, because without it essential parts of their programs would not work properly. The compiler generates code that takes strictness annotations into account by changing the order of evaluation. It is often thought that the only effects of changes in evaluation order can be on the termination properties of the program as a whole and on the program's resource consumption (with respect to space or time). Therefore, strictness is usually considered an implementation issue only.

However, in the following subsections we will show that explicit strictness is far from an implementation issue only. In Section 2.1 it is illustrated that strictness has a fundamental influence on program semantics, because explicit strictness is not just an 'option' that may be ignored by the reduction system, but a 'must' that changes reduction order. An example of how radical this influence can be, is given in Section 2.2. Finally, to deal with that influence, formal semantics are extended with strictness in Section 2.3.

2.1   When Strictness Is Not an Option but a Must

With explicit strictness, performing an evaluation is not anymore just an option. Instead each explicit strictness annotation constitutes an evaluation obligation that has to be fulfilled before proceeding further. We will illustrate the consequences of this changed evaluation with the following example.

Consider the following Clean definition of the function f, which by means of the !-annotation in the type is made explicitly strict in its first argument. In Haskell a similar effect can be obtained using an application of seq.

```
f :: !Int -> Int
f x = 5
```

Without the strictness annotation, the property $\forall_x[f\ x = 5]$ would hold unconditionally by definition. Now consider the effects of the strictness annotation in the type which makes the function f strict in its argument. Clearly, the proposition f 3 = 5 still holds. However, f undef = 5 does not hold, because f undef does not terminate due to the enforced evaluation of undef. Therefore, $\forall_x[f\ x = 5]$ does not hold unconditionally. The property can be fixed by adding a definedness condition using the special symbol $\perp$, denoting undefined. This results in $\forall_x[x \neq \perp\ \rightarrow f\ x = 5]$, which *does* hold for the annotated function f.

Another consequence is that the definition of f cannot just be substituted in all its occurrences. Instead it is only allowed to substitute f when it is **known** that its argument x is **not undefined**. This has a fundamental impact on the semantics of function application.

The addition of an exclamation mark by a programmer is therefore more than just a harmless annotation. It also has an effect on the logical properties of functions. Changes in logical properties are not only important for the programmer but also for those who work on the compiler. Of course, it is obvious that code has to be generated to accommodate the strictness. Less obvious however, is the consequences adding strictness may have on the correctness of program transformations. There can be far-reaching consequences on various kinds of program transformations. An example of such a far-reaching consequence is given in the next subsection.

2.2   A Dramatic Case of the Influence of Explicit Strictness

The Clean compiler uses term graph rewriting semantics [3] to incorporate pattern matching, sharing and cycles. With term graph rewriting semantics, on right-hand sides of definitions those parts that are not *connected* to the root cannot have any influence on the outcome. These definitions are thrown away in a very early stage of the compilation process. Consequently, possible syntactic and semantic errors in such disconnected definitions may not be spotted by the compiler. This can be annoying but it is consistent with the term graph rewriting semantics. When strictness comes into the picture, however, this early connectedness program transformation of the compiler is no longer semantically valid.

This is illustrated by the following example. Take the following Clean programs with definition K x y = x:

```
Start                Start
  #! y = undef         #! y = undef
  = K 42 y             = 42
```

The programs use the #!-notation of Clean which denotes a strict let. The strict let will be formally defined in Section 2.3. It forces y to be evaluated before the result of Start is computed. In Haskell the same effect can be achieved using a seq.

For the left program, due to the #! y must be evaluated first. So, the result of the program is: "Error: undefined!".

For the right program one would expect the same result. But, the result is *different* since the compiler removes unconnected nodes before any analysis is done, transforming the right program into Start = 42. So, the result of the right program is 42. This makes the right program a *wrong* program and the left program the *right* program. Clearly, this is an unwanted situation.

Due to the combination of connectedness and explicit strictness Clean programs are not always referentially transparent anymore. The meaning is not always preserved during reduction and it is not always sound to substitute a definition. Of course, this situation is acknowledged as a bug in the compiler for several years now. The consequences of removing this bug, however, are so drastic for the structure of the compiler that at this point in time this bug still remains to be present.

It may be a relief to the reader that Sparkle's mixed lazy/strict semantics are not based on connectedness.

2.3   Incorporating Explicit Strictness in Formal Semantics

The semantics of lazy functional languages have been described elegantly in practice in various ways: both operationally and denotationally, in terms of a term-graph rewrite system, in [12]; or just operationally, in terms of a graph rewrite-system, in [14]. All these semantics are well established, are widely known and accepted in the functional language community, and have been used for various kinds of theoretical purposes.

The basic forms of all these semantics, however, are limited to lazy expressions in which no explicit strictness is allowed to occur. If one wants to include strictness, an upgrade is required, because the introduction of strictness in an expression has an effect on its meaning that cannot be described in terms of existing concepts. In other words, strictness has to be accounted for on the semantic level as well.

As a starting point we will use the operational semantics of Launchbury [12]. We extend this to a *mixed lazy/strict semantics*, which is able to cope with laziness as well as with strictness. In this paper, we will limit ourselves to the basic definitional components of the mixed semantics. The formal proofs that our extension is correct are therefore not included; however, these proofs can be built analogously to the proofs in [12].

We will choose to extend expressions with the *strict let*, which is the basic primitive for denoting strictness in Clean. The strict let is a variation of the normal let, which only allows the actual sharing to take place after the expression to be shared has first successfully been reduced to weak head normal form. Moreover, it only allows a single non-recursive expression to be shared at a time; this keeps the strict let as simple as possible, yet still sufficiently powerful.

In the base set of expressions, we will include basic values ($b \in BasicValue$), constructors ($c \in Constructor$) and case distinctions in the same manner as in [12]. Furthermore, we will also include a constant expression '$\perp$' that denotes the undefined computation. This $\perp$ can simply be regarded as an abbreviation for let x = x in x. Adding the strict let to this set of expressions leads to:

$$
\begin{array}{lll}
e \in Exp ::= & \lambda\, x.\, e & \textit{(lambda expressions)} \\
| & x & \textit{(variables)} \\
| & e\, x & \textit{(applications)} \\
| & let\ x_1 = e_1 \ \cdots\ x_n = e_n\ in\ e & \textit{(let expressions)} \\[4pt]
| & b & \textit{(basic values)} \\
| & c\, x_1 \ldots x_n & \textit{(constructor applications)} \\
| & case\ e\ of\ \{c_i\ y_1 \cdots y_{m_i} \to e_i\}_{i=1}^{n} & \textit{(case distinctions)} \\
| & \perp & \textit{(undefined expression)} \\[4pt]
| & let!\ x = e_1\ in\ e & \textit{(strict let expressions)}
\end{array}
$$

Due to its similarity with the normal let, the strict let is a convenient primitive that can be added to the semantical level with minimal effort. Naturally, all forms of explicit strictness can easily be expressed in terms of the strict let. This also goes for the basic Haskell primitive, *seq*:

for all expressions e_1, e_2 and fresh variables x,

$seq\ e_1\ e_2$ is equivalent to $let!\ x = e_1\ in\ e_2$.

Launchbury describes both an operational and a denotational semantics, which both have to be updated to cope with the strict let. Here, we treat the extension of the operational semantics only. This semantics is given by means of a multi-step term-graph rewrite system which has to be extended with a rule for the strict let. The new rule is much like the rule for the normal let, but also demands the reduction of the shared expression to weak head normal form as an additional precondition:

$$\frac{(\Gamma, x_1 \mapsto e_1 \cdots x_n \mapsto e_n) : e \Downarrow \Delta : z}{\Gamma : let\ x_1 = e_1 \cdots x_n = e_n\ in\ e \Downarrow \Delta : z} \quad \text{Let}$$

$$\frac{\Gamma : e_1 \Downarrow \Theta : z_1 \qquad (\Theta, x_1 \mapsto z_1) : e \Downarrow \Delta : z}{\Gamma : let!\ x_1 = e_1\ in\ e\ \Downarrow \Delta : z} \quad \text{StrictLet}$$

(for the technical details of this definition: see [12])

The addition of this single StrictLet rule is sufficient to incorporate the concept of explicit strictness in a formal semantics. Our extension is equivalent to the one that is introduced in [2] for dealing formally with parallelism. In [2] *seq* is used as the basic primitive to denote explicit strictness. Using the equivalence of *seq* and *let!* sketched above, the proofs of soundness and computational adequacy that were given in [2] can be applied to our mixed semantics as well.

3   Reasoning in the Context of Strictness

In the previous sections, a general introduction to the concept of explicit strictness has been provided and its, more or less obvious, effects on programs and semantics have been discussed. In this section, the effect of strictness on *reasoning* will be described. We will show that adding or removing strictness requires program properties to be reformulated. As a consequence, the proofs of the reformulated properties may have to be redone from scratch. In addition, certain proof rules may no longer be applicable and have to be replaced as well.

The effects of strictness on reasoning are not so commonly known, mainly because programming and reasoning are usually separate activities that are not carried out by the same person. With this paper, we strive to show that the effects of strictness on reasoning are quite profound and should not be ignored.

3.1   Strictness and Logical Properties

A logical (equational) property about a program is constructed by means of logical operators ($\forall, \exists, \wedge, \vee, \rightarrow, \neg$) out of basic equations of the form $E_1[x_1 \ldots x_n] = E_2[x_1 \ldots x_n]$, where $x_1 \ldots x_n$ are the variables that have been introduced by the quantors. The equations in a property can be divided into a number of conditions that precede a single obligatory conclusion. A property with conclusion

$E_1 = E_2$ denotes that E_1 may safely be replaced by E_2 in all contexts, if properly instantiated and if all conditions are satisfied.

Semantically, two expressions may only be replaced by each other if either: (1) they both compute the exact same value; or (2) they both do not compute any value at all. Note that this is a total semantics, and an expression that does not terminate, or terminates erroneously, may not be replaced by an expression that successfully computes a value, nor vice versa.

If explicit strictness is added to or removed from a program, the value that it computes on success is not affected, but the conditions under which it produces this defined value are. Unfortunately, if the *definedness conditions* of an expression E_1 are changed, but the definedness conditions of E_2 stay the same, then a previously valid equation $E_1 = E_2$ will become invalid, because the replacement of E_1 by E_2 is no longer allowed.

In other words: the addition or removal of strictness to programs may cause previously valid logical properties to be broken. From a proving point of view this is a real problem: suppose one has successfully proved a difficult property by means of a sequence of lemmata, then the invalidation of even a single lemma may cause a ripple effect throughout the entire proof! The adaptation to such a ripple effect is both cumbersome and resource-intensive.

Unfortunately, the invalidation of logical properties due to changed strictness annotations is quite common. This invalidation can usually be fixed, either by the addition or, quite surprisingly, by the *removal* of definedness conditions. This is illustrated briefly by the following two examples:

Example of the addition of a condition:
$$\forall_{f,g}\forall_{xs}[\texttt{map}\ (f\ \texttt{o}\ g)\ xs = \texttt{map}\ f\ (\texttt{map}\ g\ xs)]$$
Affected by strictness:

This property is valid for lazy lists, but invalid for element-strict lists.

Note that no assumptions can be made about the possible strictness of f or g. Instead, the property must hold for all possible functions f and g.

Invalid in the strict case because:

Suppose $xs = [12]$, $g\ 12 = \bot$ and $f\ (g\ 12) = 7$.

Then $\texttt{map}\ (f\ \texttt{o}\ g)\ xs = [7]$, both in the lazy and in the strict case.

However, $\texttt{map}\ f\ (\texttt{map}\ g\ xs) = [7]$ in the lazy case, but $\bot$ in the strict case.

Extra definedness condition for the lazy case:

The problematic case can be excluded by demanding that for all elements of the list $g\ x$ can be evaluated successfully.

Reformulated property for the strict case:
$$\forall_{f,g,xs}[\forall_{x\in xs}[g\ x \neq \bot] \rightarrow \texttt{map}\ (f\ \texttt{o}\ g)\ xs = \texttt{map}\ f\ (\texttt{map}\ g\ xs)].$$

Example of the removal of a condition:
$$\forall_{xs}[\textit{finite}\ xs \rightarrow \texttt{reverse}\ (\texttt{reverse}\ xs) = xs]$$
Affected by strictness:

This property is valid both for lazy lists and for spine-strict lists. However, the condition *finite xs* is satisfied automatically for spine-strict lists. In the spine-strict case, the property can therefore safely be reformulated (or, rather, optimized) by removing the *finite xs* condition.

Invalid without finite condition in the lazy case because:

Suppose $xs = [1, 1, 1, \ldots]$.

Then reverse (reverse xs) $= \perp$, both in the lazy and in the strict case.

However, $xs = \perp$ in the strict case, while it is unequal to $\perp$ in the lazy case.

Reformulated property for the strict case:

$\forall_{xs}[\text{reverse (reverse } xs) = xs]$

In Section 4.3 it will be shown how mathematical conditions such as *finite xs* and $\forall_x[g \; x \neq \perp]$ can be expressed within the Sparkle framework.

In principle, all invalidated properties can be fixed this way. The definedness conditions to be added can be obtained by carefully considering the consequences of components of quantified variables to be undefined. Such an analysis is far from easy, however, and it is easy to forget certain conditions. On paper, this may lead to incorrect proofs; when using a proof assistant, this makes it impossible to prove the property at all.

An automatic analysis to obtain definedness conditions would be helpful. This does not seem too far-fetched. An idea is to extend the GAST-system (see [11]) for this purpose. With GAST, it is possible to automatically generate valid values for the quantified variables and test the property on these values. However, GAST currently is not able to cope with undefinedness.

3.2   Strictness and Formal Reasoning

Formal reasoning is the process in which formal proofs are constructed for logical program properties. These proofs are constructed by the repeated application of proof steps. Each proof step can be regarded as a function from a single property to a list of new properties. The conjunction of the produced properties must be logically stronger, and hopefully also easier to prove, than the input property.

In the previous section, it has been shown that the addition or removal of strictness to programs often requires a reformulation of the associated logical properties. This is not the only cumbersome effect of strictness on reasoning, however. A second problem is that strictness changes the behavior of reduction, and consequently also of proof steps that make use of reduction. This in turn may cause existing proofs to become invalid.

A proof step that makes use of reduction is based on the observation that if e_1 reduces to e_2, then e_1 is also semantically equal to e_2, and therefore e_1 may safely be replaced with e_2 within a logical property to be proved. It is clear that this relation is changed by the introduction of strictness. It is not intuitively clear where this change is problematic for the actual proof process.

The hidden reason is the availability of *logical expression variables* within propositions. Such a variable denotes an 'open position', to be replaced with a concrete expression later. It is introduced and bound by means of a (existential or universal) quantor. When reduction is forced, due to explicit strictness, to reduce such a variable to weak head normal form, the following problem occurs:

Suppose that e is an expression in which the variable x occurs lazily.

Suppose that e reduces to e'.

Suppose that within e, x is now marked as explicitly strict.
Then, the strict version cannot be reduced at all, because the required
preparatory reduction of x to weak head normal fails.

In other words: the introduction of explicit strictness causes a previously valid
reduction to become invalid. This in turn causes proof steps that depend on it
to become invalid. That in turn causes the proof as a whole to become invalid.
This effect is illustrated in the following basic example:

Property: $\forall_x[\text{id } x = x]$.
Proof: Introduce x. Reduce $(\text{id } x)$ to x. Use reflexivity. QED.
Validity: This proof is only valid if the first argument of id is not explicitly
    marked as strict. If it is, then the strictness annotation forces x to be reduced
    to weak head normal form before the application $(\text{id } x)$ may be expanded.
    Because x cannot be brought into weak head normal form, $(\text{id } x)$ cannot be
    reduced at all, and the proof sketched above becomes invalid.

This effect actually occurs quite frequently, which is a big nuisance. It causes
many previously valid proof steps to become invalid, and therefore requires the
proofs themselves to be revised. Fortunately, this revision is often easily realized.
A general solution, which usually suffices, is to distinguish explicitly between
$x = \bot$ and $x \neq \bot$. In the first case, the whole expression reduces to $\bot$. In the
second case, it is statically known that x has a weak head normal form, and
reduction is therefore allowed to continue in the same way as in the lazy case.

Nevertheless, the introduction of explicit strictness makes reasoning more difficult. To deal with this problem, the proof assistant Sparkle offers specific support
to deal with explicit strictness. The following section is devoted to explaining
this support.

4   Tool Support for Explicit Strictness in Sparkle

Sparkle [6] is Clean's dedicated proof-assistant. Apart from its location of origin
Sparkle is used rather intensively in Budapest (Object Abstraction [16]) and
Dublin (I/O models [7]). Sparkle works directly on a desugared version of Clean,
called Core-Clean. Sparkle allows properties of functions to be expressed using a
first-order logic. Predicates are not supported. Sparkle offers the usual operators
and quantors with the restriction that quantification is only allowed over typed
expressions and propositions.

> *Basic units: True, False, $e_1 = e_2$, x*
> *Operators:* $\neg, \wedge, \vee, \rightarrow, \leftrightarrow$
> *Quantors:* $\forall, \exists$

Sparkle is aimed towards making proving possible for the programmer. It contains many features to lower the threshold to start with proving theorems about
programs, such as:

- it can be called from within the Clean Integrated Development Environment;
- it can load a complete Clean project including all the modules of the project;
- the proof environment is highly interactive and allows a wide range of information to be displayed in separate windows at the user's will;
- the proof tactics are dedicated to the programming language.

Sparkle's reduction semantics are based on term graph rewriting. Sparkle has a total semantics. The constant expression $\bot$ is used to represent the "undefined" value. Both non-terminating reductions and erroneous reductions are equal to $\bot$. For example: hd [ ] reduces to $\bot$ on Sparkle's semantic level. Error values propagate stepwise to the outermost level. For example: (hd [ ]) + 7 reduces to $\bot$ + 7 reduces to $\bot$.

Sparkle's semantics of equality are based on reduction in a manner which is independent of the reduction strategy. The equality copes with infinite reductions and equalities between infinite structures using the concept of an observation of an expression. The *observation* of an expression is obtained by replacing all its redexes by $\bot$. What remains is the fully evaluated part. Two expressions e_1 and e_2 are equal if: (1) for all reducts r_1 of e_1, there exists a reduct r_2 of e_2 such that the observation of r_1 is smaller than the observation of r_2; and (2) also the analogue property holds for all reducts of e_2. The observational ordering is such that an expression r_1 is smaller than r_2 if r_2 can be obtained by substituting subexpressions for $\bot$'s in r_1.

Being dedicated to the use of a lazy programming language, Sparkle generates on the one hand definedness conditions for extensionality ($f = g$ not only requires $f\ x = g\ x$ for all x, but also $f = \bot \leftrightarrow g = \bot$), induction (base case for $\bot$) and case-distinction (base case for $\bot$ as well). On the other hand Sparkle also offers specific support for reasoning with definedness conditions in the context of explicit strictness. To our knowledge, Sparkle is currently the only proof assistant that fully supports explicit strictness in the context of a lazy functional programming language. The specific support consists of three components:

1. a specific 'Definedness' tactic; and
2. a smart reduction proof step: the 'Reduce' tactic;
3. using an 'eval' function to denote definedness conditions.

These three kinds of support are explained in detail in the following sections.

4.1   The 'Definedness' Tactic of Sparkle

Definedness conditions on variables and expressions occur frequently in proofs. They are introduced by various tactics that take explicit strictness into account, such as 'Induction', 'Case' and 'Assume'. These conditions usually appear in parts of the proof that are not in the main line of reasoning. Therefore, one wishes to get rid of them as soon as possible with as little effort as possible.

Unfortunately, proving definedness conditions often involves several small reasoning steps as is illustrated by the following example:

Example of proving a definedness condition:

$$\forall_{x,y}[\neg(x = \bot) \rightarrow y = (\texttt{let!}\ z = x\ \texttt{in}\ \texttt{Cons}\ 7\ z) \rightarrow \neg(y = \bot)].$$

Proof without the Definedness tactic:

Introduce x and y.

Assume H1: $\neg(x = \bot)$ and H2: $y = (\texttt{let!}\ z = x\ \texttt{in}\ \texttt{Cons}\ 7\ z)$.

Using H1, reduce H2 to H2': $y = \texttt{Cons}\ 7\ x$.

Rewrite H2' in the goal, which leaves $\neg(\texttt{Cons}\ 7\ x = \bot)$ to be proved.

This follows from the injectivity of $\texttt{Cons}$.

QED.

In Sparkle the 'Definedness' tactic is introduced to remove the burden of all such small proofs from the user. This tactic analyzes all subexpressions that occur in the hypotheses that have been introduced, and attempts to determine if they are 'defined' (statically known to be unequal to $\bot$) or 'undefined' (statically known to be equal to $\bot$). If the tactic finds any overlap between the defined expressions and the undefined ones, it then proves any goal by contradiction.

The tactic is implemented by the following algorithm, which assumes that it is activated in a goal with hypotheses $H_1 \ldots H_n$ and a statement to prove of the form $\forall_{x_1 \ldots x_i}[P_1 \rightarrow (P_2 \rightarrow \ldots (P_j \rightarrow Q) \ldots)]$ (note that i and j can be zero for no top-level quantors or implications, making the form universal):

1. Collect as many known equalities as possible in the set Eq as follows:
   - for all $1 \leq i \leq n$, if H_i states $e_1 = e_2$, then add $(e_1 = e_2)$ to Eq;
   - for all $1 \leq j \leq n$, if P_j states $e_1 = e_2$, then add $(e_1 = e_2)$ to Eq;
   - if Q states $\neg(e_1 = e_2)$, then add $(e_1 = e_2)$ to Eq.

   Note that $\neg Q$ can be used as a hypothesis here, because Q and $(\neg Q \rightarrow False)$ are logically equivalent.
2. Collect as many known inequalities as possible in the set Eq as follows:
   - for all $1 \leq i \leq n$, if H_i states $\neg(e_1 = e_2)$, then add $(e_1 \neq e_2)$ to Eq;
   - for all $1 \leq j \leq n$, if P_j states $\neg(e_1 = e_2)$, then add $(e_1 \neq e_2)$ to Eq;
   - if Q states $e_1 = e_2$, then add $(e_1 \neq e_2)$ to Eq.
3. Determine X, the set of all subexpressions that occur in the goal as a whole.
4. Compute $D = \{e \in X \mid Eq \vdash Defined(e)\}$ and
   $$U = \{e \in X \mid Eq \vdash Undefined(e)\}.$$
5. If D and U overlap, then the tactic proves the goal.

In Tables 1 and 2, two derivation systems are defined, one for statically computing $Eq \vdash Undefined(e)$ and one for statically computing $Eq \vdash Defined(e)$. The derivation rules are described formally using the representation of expressions given in Section 2.3. In practice, Sparkle implements procedural variations of the derivation systems that have been lifted to Core-Clean. Proving the *soundness* of the derivation systems (meaning that expressions in D have a weak head normal form, while those in U have not) is left as future work.

The special tactic 'Definedness' is quite powerful and very useful in practice. It can be used to automatically get rid of almost all kinds of valid definedness conditions that have been stated in order to keep reduction going in strict contexts. The proof of the example can be simplified with it as follows:

Table 1. Derivation system for statically computing undefinedness

$$\overline{Eq \vdash Undefined(\bot)}$$

$$\frac{(e_1 = e_2) \in Eq \quad Eq \vdash Undefined(e_2)}{Eq \vdash Undefined(e_1)} \qquad \frac{(e_1 = e_2) \in Eq \quad Eq \vdash Undefined(e_1)}{Eq \vdash Undefined(e_2)}$$

$$\frac{Eq, (x_i = e_i), \ldots, (x_n = e_n) \vdash Undefined(e)}{Eq \vdash Undefined(let\ x_1 = e_1 \ldots x_n = e_n\ in\ e)}$$

$$\frac{Eq \vdash Defined(e_1) \quad Eq, (x = e_1) \vdash Undefined(e)}{Eq \vdash Undefined(let!\ x = e_1\ in\ e)}$$

$$\frac{Eq \vdash Undefined(e)}{Eq \vdash Undefined(case\ e\ of\ \{c_i\ y_1 \cdots y_{m_i} \to e_i\}_{i=1}^n)} \qquad \frac{Eq \vdash Undefined(e_1)}{Eq \vdash Undefined(let!\ x = e_1\ in\ e)}$$

Example of proving a definedness condition (2):

$\forall_{x,y}[\neg(x = \bot) \to y = (\texttt{let!}\ z = x\ \texttt{in}\ \texttt{Cons}\ 7\ z) \to \neg(y = \bot)]$.

Proof with the Definedness tactic:

Apply Definedness.

Q.E.D.

Explanation:

Eq is computed to be $\{(x \neq \bot), (y = (\texttt{let!}\ z = x\ \texttt{in}\ \texttt{Cons}\ 7\ z)), (y = \bot)\}$.

Derive(1) $Eq \vdash Undefined(\bot)$ (base case)

Derive(2) $Eq \vdash Undefined(y)$ (from 1, with equality)

Derive(3) $Eq \vdash Defined(x)$ (from 1, with inequality)

Derive(4) $Eq, z = x \vdash Defined(\texttt{Cons}\ 7\ z)$ (base case)

Derive(5) $Eq \vdash Defined(\texttt{let!}\ z = x\ \texttt{in}\ \texttt{Cons}\ 7\ z)$ (from 3+4, with let! rule)

Derive(6) $Eq \vdash Defined(y)$ (from 5, with equality)

Contradiction between 2 and 6.

4.2   The 'Reduce' Tactic of Sparkle

One of the proof steps (or *tactics*, as they are usually called in the context of mechanized proof assistants) that is made available by Sparkle is 'Reduce'. This tactic applies reduction within the current logical property to be proved.

Sparkle operates on a basic functional language with a reduction mechanism similar to the one given in Section 2.3. The reduction tactic of Sparkle does *not necessarily* have to correspond completely to the formal reduction relation of this language; instead, it suffices that it is *sound*, meaning that it may only transform e_1 to e_2 if $e_1 = e_2$ formally holds. Of course, the tactic does have to be *based on* reduction, because it must look like normal reduction to the end-user.

This degree of freedom is used by Sparkle to offer specific support for the reduction of explicitly strict subexpressions that contain logical expression variables.

Table 2. Derivation system for statically computing definedness

$$\overline{Eq \vdash Defined(b)} \qquad \overline{Eq \vdash Defined(\lambda\ x.\ e)} \qquad \overline{Eq \vdash Defined(c\ x_1 \ldots x_n)}$$

$$\frac{(e_1 = e_2) \in Eq \quad Eq \vdash Defined(e_2)}{Eq \vdash Defined(e_1)} \qquad \frac{(e_1 = e_2) \in Eq \quad Eq \vdash Defined(e_1)}{Eq \vdash Defined(e_2)}$$

$$\frac{(e_1 \neq e_2) \in Eq \quad Eq \vdash Undefined(e_2)}{Eq \vdash Defined(e_1)} \qquad \frac{(e_1 \neq e_2) \in Eq \quad Eq \vdash Undefined(e_1)}{Eq \vdash Defined(e_2)}$$

$$\frac{Eq, (x_i = e_i), \ldots, (x_n = e_n) \vdash Defined(e)}{Eq \vdash Defined(let\ x_1 = e_1 \ldots x_n = e_n\ in\ e)}$$

$$\frac{Eq \vdash Defined(e_1) \quad Eq, (x = e_1) \vdash Defined(e)}{Eq \vdash Defined(let!\ x = e_1\ in\ e)}$$

The aim of this support is to hide the cumbersome effects of strictness to the user, allowing the same proof style and the same proof rules to be used both for the lazy and for the strict case.

The support offered by Sparkle manifests itself in the following customized behavior when reduction encounters explicit strictness of the form *let!* $x = e_1$ *in* e:

- First, reduction is recursively applied to e_1 as usual.
- If this results in either $\perp$ or a weak head normal form, then reduction continues as usual.
- Suppose that, due to logical expression variables, the recursive reduction cannot be completed and instead results in some expression e_1' that is neither $\perp$ nor a weak head normal form.
- Then, and this is new, apply the same definedness analysis that was described in Section 4.1. If this analysis determines that e_1 is defined ($e_1 \in D$), then reduction is allowed to continue by expanding the strict let.
  This expansion is semantically sound, because the definedness analysis shows that $\neg(e_1 = \perp)$, which implies that e_1 has a weak head normal form, even though it is not known at this point what it actually looks like.
- If this fails, then add $x = \perp$ as hypothesis and perform another definedness analysis. If this analysis shows that e is undefined ($e \in U$), then reduction is allowed to continue by expanding the strict let.
  This expansion is semantically sound, because the definedness analysis shows that $x = \perp \rightarrow e = \perp$, which means that the explicit strictness annotation has no effect on semantics and may safely be ignored.

If either of the two 'escape clauses' succeed, then it seems to the user as if reduction has the same effect in the strict case as in the lazy case. In other words: by silently checking for additional conditions, Sparkle can sometimes hide the cumbersome effects of explicit strictness on reduction altogether.

To illustrate the additional power of the reduction mechanism, consider the following two basic examples:

Example of continuation of reduction:

Suppose that datatype (`Tree a`) is defined as follows:

```
:: Tree a = Leaf | Edge !a !(Tree a) !(Tree a)
```

Suppose that the function `treeDepth` has the following signature:

```
treeDepth :: !(Tree a) -> Int
```

Suppose that the logical expression variable x (of type `Tree Int`) and the hypothesis $\neg(x = \bot)$ have both been introduced earlier in the proof.

Then, Sparkle allows the function application `treeDepth (Edge 7 Leaf x)` to be expanded, because by means of recursive analysis Sparkle is able to determine that `Edge 7 Leaf x` is unequal to $\bot$.

Note that: this example uses strict constructors and strict functions, which can be considered as notational sugar for the strict let.

Example of increased stability of proofs:

Suppose that the identify function is defined as follows:

```
id :: !a -> a
id x = x
```

Sparkle determines statically that if the argument of the function is undefined, then the result of the function will be undefined as well. Therefore, Sparkle allows applications of `id` to be expanded, regardless of its argument. The proof of Section 3.2, which was shown to be *invalid* with a standard reduce tactic, in fact becomes *valid* when the powerful strictness specific 'Reduce' tactic of Sparkle is used.

Note that: this example uses strict functions as well.

4.3   Using an 'eval' Function to Denote Definedness Conditions

In many cases, it may seem impossible to express definedness conditions just using the first-order logic of Sparkle. For instance, spine evaluation of datastructures is very hard to express. However, the possibility to define functions in the higher-order programming language and the possibility to use these functions as predicates gives unexpected expressive power. The higher-order of the programming language can be combined with the Sparkle's first order logic.

On the programming level we define a function `eval`. The purpose of this function is to fully reduce its argument and return `True` afterwards. Such an 'eval' function is usually used to express evaluation strategies in the context of parallelism [4,17]. We use `eval` for expressing definedness conditions.

In the standard program library of Sparkle (`StdSparkle`), the function `eval` is defined by means of overloading. The instance on characters is defined by:

```
class eval a :: !a -> Bool

instance eval Char
where    eval :: !Char -> Bool
         eval x = True
```

Now, in a logical property, (eval x) can be used as termination condition. As is usual in proof assistants, this is equivalent to (eval x = True). The meaning of this condition is as follows:

- If (it is known that) x can be successfully reduced to an arbitrary character, then eval x will produce True and the condition will be satisfied, since True = True is *True*.
- If (it is known that) x cannot successfully be reduced to a character, then eval x does not terminate and is equal to $\perp$ on the semantic level. Therefore, the condition is not satisfied, because $\perp$ = True is *False*.
- Note that eval is defined in such a way that eval x *never* reduces to False. So, all cases are covered in the previous reasoning.

The same principle can be used for lists, making use of overloading to assume the presence of 'eval' on the element type. This leads to the following definition:

```
instance eval [a] | eval a
where     eval :: ![a] -> Bool | eval a
          eval [x:xs] = eval x && eval xs
          eval []     = True
```

This instance of eval fully evaluates both the list itself and all its elements. It can therefore be used to express the condition that a list must be fully evaluated. Below we give a few examples of the use of eval in properties of functions:

- $\forall_n [\text{eval } n \rightarrow n < n = \textit{False}]$
- $\forall_{n,xs} [\text{eval } n \rightarrow \text{take } n \text{ } xs \text{ ++ drop } n \text{ } xs = xs]$
- $\forall_{p,xs} [\text{eval (map } p \text{ } xs) \rightarrow \text{takeWhile } p \text{ } xs \text{ ++ dropWhile } p \text{ } xs = xs]$
- $\forall_{x,p,xs} [\text{eval } x \rightarrow \text{eval } xs \rightarrow \text{eval (map } p \text{ } xs) \rightarrow$
  $\text{isMember } x \text{ (filter } p \text{ } xs) = \text{isMember } x \text{ } xs \text{ && } p \text{ } x]$

The conditions in the examples of Section 3.1 can be expressed using 'eval'. The property of the first example is then expressed as follows (using isMember instead of the mathematical $\in$):

$$\forall_{f,g,xs} [\forall_x [\text{isMember } x \text{ } xs \rightarrow \text{eval}(g \text{ } x)] \rightarrow \text{map } (f \text{ o } g) \text{ } xs = \text{map } f \text{ (map } g \text{ } xs)]$$

To express the definedness condition of the second example of Section 3.1 we need another variant of 'eval' that does not evaluate its argument fully but that evaluates only the 'spine' of the argument. This is given below.

Expressing Spine Evaluation and List Finiteness. Spine evaluation can be expressed easily by means of an 'eval' variant. However, if already an instance for full evaluation is given, then a new function must be defined since the type class system allows only one instance per type.

```
evalSpine :: ![a] -> Bool
evalSpine [x:xs]   = evalSpine xs
evalSpine []       = True
```

This same function `evalSpine` also expresses finiteness of lists, as when the spine of a list is fully evaluated, the list is evidently finite.

Some valid properties that are defined using `evalSpine`:

- $\forall_{xs}[\text{eval }(\text{length } xs) \rightarrow \text{evalSpine } xs]$
- $\forall_{xs}[\text{evalSpine } xs \rightarrow \text{evalSpine }(\text{reverse } xs)]$

The second example of Section 3.1 can now be reformulated to:

$$\forall_{xs}[\text{evalSpine } xs \rightarrow \text{reverse }(\text{reverse } xs) = xs]$$

Properties of 'eval'. All instances of the class 'eval' have to share certain properties. To prove properties of *all* members of a certain type class, the recently added tool support for general type classes can be used [10]. With this tool, the following properties of 'eval' can be stated and proven in Sparkle.

- $\forall_x[\text{eval } x \rightarrow x \neq \bot]$
- $\forall_x[\text{eval } x \neq \text{False}]$

5   Related Work

In [5] Danielsson and Jansson perform a case study in program verification using partial and undefined values. They assume proof rules to be valid for the programming language. They do not use a formal semantics. We expect that our formal semantic approach can be used as a basis to prove their proof rules.

With the purpose of deriving a lazy abstract machine Sestoft [15] has revised Launchbury's semantics. Launchbury's semantics require global inspection (which is unwanted for an abstract machine) for preserving the Distinct Names property. When an abstract machine is to be derived from the semantics used in this paper, analogue revisions will be required. As is further pointed out by Sestoft [15] the rules given by Launchbury are not *fully lazy*. Full laziness can be achieved by introducing new let-bindings for every maximal free expression [8].

An equivalent extension of Launchbury's semantics can be found in [2]. In this paper, a formal semantics for Glasgow Parallel Haskell is constructed on top of the standard Launchbury's semantics. Interestingly, not only parallellism is added, but enforced strictness in terms of a seq-construct as well. Furthermore, it is formally shown that this extension is sound. However, no properties are proven that are specific for the seq, such as the relation between 'lazy' and 'strict' terms. It is possible to translate seq's to let!s (and vice versa) and shown properties can be compared directly.

Andrew Pitts [13] discusses non-termination issues of logical relations and operational equivalence in the context of the presence of existential types in a strict language. He provides some theory that might also be used to address the problems that arise in a mixed lazy/strict context. That would require a combination of his work and the work of Patricia Johann and Janis Voigtländer [9] who use a denotational approach to present some "free" theorems in the presence of Haskell's seq.

At Chalmers University of Technology for the language Haskell a proof assistant Agda [1] has been developed in the context of the CoVer project. As with Sparkle the language is translated to a core-version on which the proofs are performed. Being geared towards facilitating the 'average' functional programmer Sparkle uses dedicated tactics and proof rules based on standard proof theory. Agda uses constructive type theory on λ-terms enabling independent proof checking. However, in contrast to Sparkle, Agda has no facilities to prove properties that are related to changed strictness properties.

Another project that aims to integrate programming, properties and validation is the Programatica project (www.cse.ogi.edu/PacSoft/projects/programatica) of the Pacific Software Research Center in Oregon. A wide range of validation techniques for programs written in different languages is intended to be supported. For functional languages they use a logic (P-logic) based on a modal μ-calculus (in which also undefinedness can be expressed). In the Programatica project properties are mixed with the Haskell source. So, reasoning is bound to take place on the more complex syntactical source level instead of on a simpler core-language.

6   Conclusions / Future Work

The impact of changes in strictness properties on logical program properties is shown to be quite significant. It is illustrated how program properties can be adapted to reflect these changes. Furthermore, it is explained what the influence of explicit changes in strictness is on the semantics and on the reasoning steps.

We have shown that the special combination of several techniques, that have been made available in the proof assistant Sparkle to deal with definedness aspects, is well suited to assist the programmer in constructing the required proofs. We do not know of any other proof assistant with such a combined set of techniques to help dealing with these kinds of proofs.

Future work could be to study the relation of our approach to an approach which only aims to prove partial correctness.

References

1. A. Abel, M. Benke, A. Bove, J. Hughes, and U. Norell. Verifying Haskell programs using constructive type theory. In D. Leijen, editor, *Proceedings of the ACM SIGPLAN 2005 Haskell Workshop*, pages 62 – 74. Tallinn, Estonia, ACM Press, 2005.
2. C. Baker-Finch, D. King, and P. Trinder. An operational semantics for parallel lazy evaluation. In *ACM-SIGPLAN International Conference on Functional Programming (ICFP'00)*, pages 162–173, Montreal, Canada, 2000.
3. H. P. Barendregt, M. C. J. D. van Eekelen, J. R. W. Glauert, R. Kennaway, M. J. Plasmeijer, and M. R. Sleep. Term graph rewriting. In J. W. de Bakker, A. J. Nijman, and P. C. Treleaven, editors, *PARLE (2)*, volume 259 of *Lecture Notes in Computer Science*, pages 141–158. Springer, 1987.

4. G. L. Burn. Evaluation transformers a model for the parallel evolution of functional languages. In *Proc. of a conference on Functional programming languages and computer architecture*, pages 446–470, London, UK, 1987. Springer-Verlag.

5. N. A. Danielsson and P. Jansson. Chasing bottoms: A case study in program verification in the presence of partial and infinite values. In *Prcoeedings of the 7th International Conference on Mathematics of Program Construction*, pages 85–109.

6. M. de Mol, M. van Eekelen, and R. Plasmeijer. Theorem proving for functional programmers - Sparkle: A functional theorem prover. In T. Arts and M. Mohnen, editors, *Selected Papers from the 13th International Workshop on Implementation of Functional Languages, IFL 2001*, volume 2312 of *Lecture Notes in Computer Science*, pages 55–72, Stockholm, Sweden, 2001. Springer Verlag.

7. M. Dowse, A. Butterfield, and M. van Eekelen. A language for reasoning about concurrent functional i/o. In T. Arts and M. Mohnen, editors, *Selected Papers from the 16th International Workshop on Implementation and Application of Functional Languages, IFL 2004*, volume 3074 of *Lecture Notes in Computer Science*, pages 177–195, Lbeck, Germany, 2004. Springer Verlag.

8. J. Gustavsson and D. Sands. Possibilities and limitations of call-by-need space improvement. In *Proceedings of the sixth ACM SIGPLAN International Conference on Functional Programming*, pages 265–276. ACM Press, 2001.

9. P. Johann and J. Voigtländer. Free theorems in the presence of seq. In *Proceedings of the 31st ACM SIGPLAN-SIGACT Symposium on Principles of Programming Languages*, pages 99–110, Venice, Italy, 2004.

10. Kesteren, R. van and Eekelen, M. van and Mol, M. de. *Proof Support for General Type Classes*. Intellect, 2004. to appear.

11. P. Koopman, A. Alimarine, J. Tretmans, and R. Plasmeijer. Gast: Generic automated software testing. In R. Peña and T. Arts, editors, *The 14th International Workshop on the Implementation of Functional Languages, IFL'02, Selected Papers*, volume 2670 of *LNCS*, pages 84–100. Springer, 2003.

12. J. Launchbury. A natural semantics for lazy evaluation. In *Proceedings of the 20th Annual ACM SIGPLAN-SIGACT Symposium on Principles of Programming Languages*, pages 144–154, Charleston, South Carolina, 1993.

13. A. M. Pitts. Existential types: Logical relations and operational equivalence. In *Proceedings of the 25th International Conference on Automata Languages and Programming, ICALP'98*, volume 1443 of *Lecture Notes in Computer Science*, pages 309–326. Springer-Verlag, Berlin, 1998.

14. R. Plasmeijer and M. van Eekelen. *Functional Programming and Parallel Graph Rewriting*. 1993. ISBN 0-201-41663-8.

15. P. Sestoft. Deriving a lazy abstract machine. *Journal of Functional Programming*, 7(3):231–264, 1997.

16. M. Tejfel, Z. Horváth, and T. Kozsik. Extending the sparkle core language with object abstraction. *Acta Cybernetica*, 17(2), 2005.

17. P. W. Trinder, K. Hammond, H.-W. Loidl, and S. L. P. Jones. Algorithm + strategy = parallelism. *J. Funct. Program.*, 8(1):23–60, 1998.

A Rational Deconstruction
of Landin's J Operator

Olivier Danvy and Kevin Millikin

BRICS*, Department of Computer Science, University of Aarhus
IT-parken, Aabogade 34, DK-8200 Aarhus N, Denmark
{danvy, kmillikin}@brics.dk

Abstract. Landin's J operator was the first control operator for functional languages, and was specified with an extension of the SECD machine. Through a series of meaning-preserving transformations (transformation into continuation-passing style (CPS) and defunctionalization) and their left inverses (transformation into direct style and refunctionalization), we present a compositional evaluation function corresponding to this extension of the SECD machine. We then characterize the J operator in terms of CPS and in terms of delimited-control operators in the CPS hierarchy. Finally, we present a motivated wish to see Landin's name added to the list of co-discoverers of continuations.

1 Introduction

Forty years ago, Peter Landin unveiled the first control operator, J, to a heretofore unsuspecting world [24, 23, 25]. He did so to generalize the notion of jumps and labels and showed that the resulting notion of 'program closure' makes sense not just in an imperative setting, but also in a functional one. He specified the J operator by extending the SECD machine [22].

At IFL'04, Danvy presented a 'rational deconstruction' of Landin's SECD machine into a compositional evaluation function [9]. The goal of this work is to extend this rational deconstruction to the J operator.

1.1 Deconstruction of the SECD Machine with the J Operator

Let us outline our deconstruction of the SECD machine before substantiating it in Section 2. We essentially follow the order of Danvy's deconstruction [9], though with a twist: in the middle of the derivation, we abandon the stack-threading, callee-save features of the SECD machine for the more familiar register-based, caller-save features of traditional definitional interpreters [18, 28, 31].

The SECD machine is defined as the transitive closure of a transition function over a quadruple—a data stack containing intermediate values (of type S), an environment (of type E), a control stack (of type C), and a dump (of type D):

---

* Basic Research in Computer Science (www.brics.dk), funded by the Danish National Research Foundation.

A. Butterfield, C. Grelck, and F. Huch (Eds.): IFL 2005, LNCS 4015, pp. 55–73, 2006.

```
run : S * E * C * D -> value
```

The definition of this transition function is complicated because it has several induction variables, i.e., it dispatches on several components of the quadruple.

- We disentangle it into four transition functions, each of which has one induction variable, i.e., dispatches on one component of the quadruple:

```
run_c :        S * E * C * D -> value
run_d :              value * D -> value
run_t : term * S * E * C * D -> value
run_a :        S * E * C * D -> value
```

  The first function, run_c, dispatches towards run_d if the control stack is empty, run_t if the top of the control stack contains a term, and run_a if the top of the control stack contains an apply directive. This disentangled specification is in defunctionalized form: the control stack and the dump are defunctionalized data types, and run_c and run_d are the corresponding apply functions.

- Refunctionalization eliminates the two apply functions:

```
run_t : term * S * E * C * D -> value
run_a :        S * E * C * D -> value
where C = S * E * D -> value and D = value -> value
```

  As identified in the first rational deconstruction [9], the resulting program is a stack-threading, callee-save interpreter in continuation-passing style (CPS).

- In order to focus on the nature of the J operator, we eliminate the data stack and adopt the more familiar caller-save evaluation strategy:

```
run_t :        term * E * C * D -> value
run_a : value * value * C * D -> value
where C = value * D -> value and D = value -> value
```

  The interpreter is still in CPS.

- The direct-style transformation eliminates the dump continuation:

```
run_t :        term * E * C -> value
run_a : value * value * C -> value
where C = value -> value
```

  The clause for the J operator and the main evaluation function are expressed using the delimited-control operators shift and reset [10]. The resulting evaluator still threads an explicit continuation, even though it is not tail-recursive.

- The direct-style transformation eliminates the control continuation:

```
run_t :        term * E -> value
run_a : value * value -> value
```

  The clauses catering for the non-tail-recursive uses of the control continuation are expressed using the delimited-control operators $shift_1$, $reset_1$, $shift_2$, and $reset_2$ [4, 10, 14, 21, 30]. The resulting evaluator is in direct style. It is also in closure-converted form: the applicable values are a defunctionalized data type and run_a is the corresponding apply function.

- Refunctionalization eliminates the apply function:

```
run_t : term * E -> value
```

  The resulting evaluator is compositional.

There is plenty of room for variation in the present reconstruction. The path we are taking seems reasonably pedagogical—in particular, the departure from threading a data stack and managing the environment in a callee-save fashion. Each of the steps is reversible: one can CPS-transform and defunctionalize an evaluator into an abstract machine [1, 2, 3, 4, 9].

1.2   Prerequisites and Domain of Discourse

Up to Section 2.4, we use pure ML as a meta-language. We assume a basic familiarity with Standard ML and with reasoning about ML programs as well as an elementary understanding of defunctionalization [13, 31], the CPS transformation [10, 11, 18, 28, 31, 34], and delimited continuations [4, 10, 14, 16, 21]. From Section 2.5, we use pure ML with delimited-control operators.

The Source Language of the SECD Machine. The source language is the λ-calculus, extended with literals (as observables) and the J operator. A program is a closed term.

```
datatype term = LIT of int
              | VAR of string
              | LAM of string * term
              | APP of term * term
              | J
type program = term
```

The Control Directives. A directive is a term or the tag APPLY:

```
datatype directive = TERM of term | APPLY
```

The Environment. We use a structure Env with the following signature:

```
signature ENV = sig
                  type 'a env
                  val empty : 'a env
                  val extend : string * 'a * 'a env -> 'a env
                  val lookup : string * 'a env -> 'a
                end
```

The empty environment is denoted by Env.empty. The function extending an environment with a new binding is denoted by Env.extend. The function fetching the value of an identifier from an environment is denoted by Env.lookup.

Values. There are five kinds of values: integers, the successor function, function closures, program closures, and "state appenders" [6, page 84]:

```
datatype value = INT of int
               | SUCC
               | FUNCLO of E * string * term
               | PGMCLO of value * D
               | STATE_APPENDER of D
```

```
withtype S = value list                              (* stack *)
    and E = value Env.env                      (* environment *)
    and C = directive list                        (* control *)
    and D = (S * E * C) list                         (* dump *)
```

A function closure pairs a λ-abstraction (i.e., its formal parameter and its body) and its lexical environment. A program closure is a first-class continuation. A state appender is an intermediate value; applying it yields a program closure.

The Initial Environment. The initial environment binds the successor function:

```
val e_init = Env.extend ("succ", SUCC, Env.empty)
```

1.3 Overview

We first detail the deconstruction of the SECD machine into a compositional evaluator in direct style (Section 2). We then analyze the J operator (Section 3), review related work (Section 4), and conclude (Sections 5 and 6).

2 Deconstruction of the SECD Machine with the J Operator

2.1 The Starting Specification

Several formulations of the SECD machine with the J operator have been published [6,15,24]. We take the most recent one, i.e., Felleisen's [15], as our starting point, and we consider the others in Section 4.

```
(*  run : S * E * C * D -> value                                    *)
(*  where S = value list, E = value Env.env, C = directive list,    *)
(*    and D = (S * E * C) list                                      *)
fun run (v :: nil, e, nil, nil)
    = v
  | run (v :: nil, e', nil, (s, e, c) :: d)
    = run (v :: s, e, c, d)
  | run (s, e, (TERM (LIT n)) :: c, d)
    = run ((INT n) :: s, e, c, d)
  | run (s, e, (TERM (VAR x)) :: c, d)
    = run ((Env.lookup (x, e)) :: s, e, c, d)
  | run (s, e, (TERM (LAM (x, t))) :: c, d)
    = run ((FUNCLO (e, x, t)) :: s, e, c, d)
  | run (s, e, (TERM (APP (t0, t1))) :: c, d)
    = run (s, e, (TERM t1) :: (TERM t0) :: APPLY :: c, d)
  | run (s, e, (TERM J) :: c, d)                             (* 1 *)
    = run ((STATE_APPENDER d) :: s, e, c, d)
  | run (SUCC :: (INT n) :: s, e, APPLY :: c, d)
    = run ((INT (n+1)) :: s, e, c, d)
  | run ((FUNCLO (e', x, t)) :: v :: s, e, APPLY :: c, d)
    = run (nil, Env.extend (x, v, e'), (TERM t) :: nil, (s, e, c) :: d)
```

```
  | run ((PGMCLO (v, d')) :: v' :: s, e, APPLY :: c, d)              (* 2 *)
     = run (v :: v' :: nil, e_init, APPLY :: nil, d')
  | run ((STATE_APPENDER d') :: v :: s, e, APPLY :: c, d)            (* 3 *)
     = run ((PGMCLO (v, d')) :: s, e, c, d)

fun evaluate0 t                            (*  evaluate0 : program -> value  *)
   = run (nil, e_init, (TERM t) :: nil, nil)
```

The SECD machine does not terminate for divergent source terms. If it becomes
stuck, an ML pattern-matching error is raised (alternatively, the codomain of
run could be made value option and a fallthrough else clause could be added).
Otherwise, the result of the evaluation is v for some ML value v : value. The
clause marked "1" specifies that the J operator, at any point, denotes the current
dump; evaluating it captures this dump and yields a state appender that, when
applied (in the clause marked "3"), yields a program closure. Applying a program
closure (in the clause marked "2") restores the captured dump.

2.2 A Disentangled Specification

In the definition of Section 2.1, all the possible transitions are meshed together in
one recursive function, run. As in the first rational deconstruction [9], we factor
run into four mutually recursive functions, each of them with one induction
variable. In this disentangled definition,

- run_c interprets the list of control directives, i.e., it specifies which transition
  to take according to whether the list is empty, starts with a term, or starts
  with an apply directive. If the list is empty, it calls run_d. If the list starts
  with a term, it calls run_t, caching the term in an extra component (the first
  parameter of run_t). If the list starts with an apply directive, it calls run_a.
- run_d interprets the dump, i.e., it specifies which transition to take according
  to whether the dump is empty or non-empty, given a valid data stack.
- run_t interprets the top term in the list of control directives.
- run_a interprets the top value in the current data stack.

```
(*  run_c :          S * E * C * D -> value                          *)
(*  run_d :              value * D -> value                          *)
(*  run_t : term * S * E * C * D -> value                            *)
(*  run_a :          S * E * C * D -> value                          *)
(*  where S = value list, E = value Env.env, C = directive list,     *)
(*    and D = (S * E * C) list                                       *)
fun run_c (v :: nil, e, nil, d)
    = run_d (v, d)
  | run_c (s, e, (TERM t) :: c, d)
    = run_t (t, s, e, c, d)
  | run_c (s, e, APPLY :: c, d)
    = run_a (s, e, c, d)
and run_d (v, nil)
    = v
  | run_d (v, (s, e, c) :: d)
    = run_c (v :: s, e, c, d)
```

```
and run_t (LIT n, s, e, c, d)
     = run_c ((INT n) :: s, e, c, d)
   | run_t (VAR x, s, e, c, d)
     = run_c ((Env.lookup (x, e)) :: s, e, c, d)
   | run_t (LAM (x, t), s, e, c, d)
     = run_c ((FUNCLO (e, x, t)) :: s, e, c, d)
   | run_t (APP (t0, t1), s, e, c, d)
     = run_t (t1, s, e, (TERM t0) :: APPLY :: c, d)
   | run_t (J, s, e, c, d)
     = run_c ((STATE_APPENDER d) :: s, e, c, d)
and run_a (SUCC :: (INT n) :: s, e, c, d)
     = run_c ((INT (n+1)) :: s, e, c, d)
   | run_a ((FUNCLO (e', x, t)) :: v :: s, e, c, d)
     = run_t (t, nil, Env.extend (x, v, e'), nil, (s, e, c) :: d)
   | run_a ((PGMCLO (v, d')) :: v' :: s, e, c, d)
     = run_a (v :: v' :: nil, e_init, nil, d')
   | run_a ((STATE_APPENDER d') :: v :: s, e, c, d)
     = run_c ((PGMCLO (v, d')) :: s, e, c, d)

fun evaluate1 t                           (* evaluate1 : program -> value *)
     = run_t (t, nil, e_init, nil, nil)
```

Proposition 1 (full correctness). *Given a program,* evaluate0 *and* evaluate1 *either both diverge or both yield values that are structurally equal.*

2.3   A Higher-Order Counterpart

In the disentangled definition of Section 2.2, there are two possible ways to construct a dump—nil and consing a triple—and three possible ways to construct a list of control directives—nil, consing a term, and consing an apply directive. (We could phrase these constructions as two data types rather than as two lists.)

These data types, together with run_d and run_c, are in the image of defunctionalization (run_d and run_c are the apply functions of these two data types). The corresponding higher-order evaluator reads as follows; it is higher-order because c and d now denote functions:

```
(* run_t : term * S * E * C * D -> value                              *)
(* run_a :         S * E * C * D -> value                             *)
(* where S = value list, E = value Env.env, C = S * E * D -> value    *)
(*   and D = value -> value                                           *)
fun run_t (LIT n, s, e, c, d)
     = c ((INT n) :: s, e, d)
   | run_t (VAR x, s, e, c, d)
     = c ((Env.lookup (x, e)) :: s, e, d)
   | run_t (LAM (x, t), s, e, c, d)
     = c ((FUNCLO (e, x, t)) :: s, e, d)
   | run_t (APP (t0, t1), s, e, c, d)
     = run_t (t1, s, e,
            fn (s, e, d) => run_t (t0, s, e,
                        fn (s, e, d) => run_a (s, e, c, d), d), d)
```

```
  | run_t (J, s, e, c, d)
    = c ((STATE_APPENDER d) :: s, e, d)
and run_a (SUCC :: (INT n) :: s, e, c, d)
    = c ((INT (n+1)) :: s, e, d)
  | run_a ((FUNCLO (e', x, t)) :: v :: s, e, c, d)
    = run_t (t, nil, Env.extend (x, v, e'), fn (v :: nil, e'', d) => d v,
          fn v => c (v :: s, e, d))
  | run_a ((PGMCLO (v, d')) :: v' :: s, e, c, d)
    = run_a (v :: v' :: nil, e_init, fn (v :: nil, e, d) => d v, d')
  | run_a ((STATE_APPENDER d') :: v :: s, e, c, d)
    = c ((PGMCLO (v, d')) :: s, e, d)

fun evaluate2 t                          (* evaluate2 : program -> value  *)
    = run_t (t, nil, e_init, fn (v :: nil, e, d) => d v, fn v => v)
```

The resulting evaluator is in CPS, with two layered continuations c and d. It threads a stack of intermediate results (s), an environment (e), a control continuation (c), and a dump continuation (d). Except for the environment being callee-save, the evaluator follows a traditional eval–apply schema: run_t is eval and run_a is apply. Defunctionalizing it yields the definition of Section 2.2.

Proposition 2 (full correctness). *Given a program,* evaluate1 *and* evaluate2 *either both diverge or both yield values that are structurally equal.*

2.4   A Stack-Less, Caller-Save Counterpart

We want to focus on J, and the non-standard aspects of the evaluator of Section 2.3 (the data stack and the callee-save environment) are a distraction. We therefore transmogrify the evaluator into the more familiar register-based, caller-save form [18, 28, 31], renaming run_t as eval and run_a as apply. Intermediate values are explicitly passed instead of being stored on the data stack, and environments are no longer passed to apply and to the control continuation:

```
(*  eval :       term * E * C * D -> value                        *)
(*  apply : value * value * C * D -> value                        *)
(*  where E = value Env.env, C = value * D -> value,              *)
(*    and D = value -> value                                      *)
fun eval (LIT n, e, c, d)
    = c (INT n, d)
  | eval (VAR x, e, c, d)
    = c (Env.lookup (x, e), d)
  | eval (LAM (x, t), e, c, d)
    = c (FUNCLO (e, x, t), d)
  | eval (APP (t0, t1), e, c, d)
    = eval (t1, e,
          fn (v1, d) => eval (t0, e,
                          fn (v0, d) => apply (v0, v1, c, d), d), d)
  | eval (J, e, c, d)
    = c (STATE_APPENDER d, d)
```

```
and apply (SUCC, INT n, c, d)
    = c (INT (n+1), d)
  | apply (FUNCLO (e', x, t), v, c, d)
    = eval (t, Env.extend (x, v, e'), fn (v, d) => d v,
            fn v => c (v, d))
  | apply (PGMCLO (v, d'), v', c, d)
    = apply (v, v', fn (v, d) => d v, d')
  | apply (STATE_APPENDER d', v, c, d)
    = c (PGMCLO (v, d'), d)

fun evaluate3 t                          (*  evaluate3 : program -> value  *)
    = eval (t, e_init, fn (v, d) => d v, fn v => v)
```

The new evaluator is still in CPS, with two layered continuations.

Proposition 3 (full correctness). *Given a program,* evaluate2 *and* evaluate3 *either both diverge or both yield values that are structurally equal.*

2.5 A Dump-Less Direct-Style Counterpart

The evaluator of Section 2.4 is in continuation-passing style, and therefore it is in the image of the CPS transformation. The clause for J captures the current continuation (i.e., the dump), and therefore its direct-style counterpart naturally uses call/cc [11]. With an eye on our next step, we do not, however, use call/cc but its cousins shift and reset [10, 14] to write the direct-style counterpart.

Concretely, we use an ML functor to obtain an instance of shift and reset with value as the type of intermediate answers [14, 16]: reset delimits the (now implicit) dump continuation in evaluate, and corresponds to its initialization with the identity function; and shift captures it in the clauses where J is evaluated and where a program closure is applied:

```
structure SR = Shift_and_Reset (type intermediate_answer = value)

(*  eval  :       term * E * C -> value                              *)
(*  apply : value * value * C -> value                              *)
(*  where E = value Env.env and C = value -> value                  *)
fun eval (LIT n, e, c)
    = c (INT n)
  | eval (VAR x, e, c)
    = c (Env.lookup (x, e))
  | eval (LAM (x, t), e, c)
    = c (FUNCLO (e, x, t))

  | eval (APP (t0, t1), e, c)
    = eval (t1, e, fn v1 => eval (t0, e, fn v0 => apply (v0, v1, c)))
  | eval (J, e, c)
    = SR.shift (fn d => d (c (STATE_APPENDER d)))                    (* * *)
and apply (SUCC, INT n, c)
    = c (INT (n+1))
```

```
  | apply (FUNCLO (e', x, t), v, c)
     = c (eval (t, Env.extend (x, v, e'), fn v => v))              (* * *)
  | apply ((PGMCLO (v, d)), v', c)
     = SR.shift (fn d' => d (apply (v, v', fn v => v)))            (* * *)
  | apply (STATE_APPENDER d, v, c)
     = c (PGMCLO (v, d))

fun evaluate4 t                         (*   evaluate4 : program -> value   *)
     = SR.reset (fn () => eval (t, e_init, fn v => v))
```

The dump continuation is now implicit and is accessed using shift. CPS-transforming this evaluator yields the evaluator of Section 2.4.

Proposition 4 (full correctness). *Given a program,* evaluate3 *and* evaluate4
either both diverge or both yield values that are structurally equal.

2.6   A Control-Less Direct-Style Counterpart

The evaluator of Section 2.5 still threads an explicit continuation, the control
continuation. It however is not in continuation-passing style because of the non-
tail calls to c, eval, and apply (in the clauses marked "*") and for the occurrences
of shift and reset. This pattern of control is characteristic of the CPS hierarchy [4,
10, 14, 21]. We therefore use the delimited-control operators $shift_1$, $reset_1$, $shift_2$,
and $reset_2$ to write the direct-style counterpart of this evaluator ($shift_2$ and $reset_2$
are the direct-style counterparts of $shift_1$ and $reset_1$, and $shift_1$ and $reset_1$ are
synonyms for shift and reset).

Concretely, we use two ML functors to obtain layered instances of shift and
reset with value as the type of intermediate answers [14, 16]: $reset_2$ delimits
the (now twice implicit) dump continuation in evaluate; $shift_2$ captures it in
the clauses where J is evaluated and where a program closure is applied; $reset_1$
delimits the (now implicit) control continuation in evaluate and in apply, and
corresponds to its initialization with the identity function; and $shift_1$ captures
it in the clause where J is evaluated:

```
structure SR1 = Shift_and_Reset (type intermediate_answer = value)

structure SR2 = Shift_and_Reset_next (type intermediate_answer = value
                                      structure over = SR1)

(*   eval  :        term * E -> value                                   *)
(*   apply : value * value -> value                                     *)
(*   where E = value Env.env                                            *)

fun eval (LIT n, e)
     = INT n
  | eval (VAR x, e)
     = Env.lookup (x, e)
  | eval (LAM (x, t), e)
     = FUNCLO (e, x, t)
```

```
  | eval (APP (t0, t1), e)
    = let val v1 = eval (t1, e)
          val v0 = eval (t0, e)
      in apply (v0, v1) end
  | eval (J, e)
    = SR1.shift (fn c => SR2.shift (fn d => d (c (STATE_APPENDER d))))
and apply (SUCC, INT n)
    = INT (n+1)
  | apply (FUNCLO (e', x, t), v)
    = SR1.reset (fn () => eval (t, Env.extend (x, v, e')))
  | apply (PGMCLO (v, d), v')
    = SR1.shift (fn c' => SR2.shift (fn d' =>
      d (SR1.reset (fn () => apply (v, v')))))
  | apply (STATE_APPENDER d, v)
    = PGMCLO (v, d)

fun evaluate5 t                         (*  evaluate5 : program -> value  *)
    = SR2.reset (fn () => SR1.reset (fn () => eval (t, e_init)))
```

The control continuation is now implicit and is accessed using shift$_1$. The dump continuation is still implicit and is accessed using shift$_2$. CPS-transforming this evaluator yields the evaluator of Section 2.5.

Proposition 5 (full correctness). *Given a program,* evaluate4 *and* evaluate5 *either both diverge or both yield values that are structurally equal.*

2.7   A Compositional Counterpart

We now turn to the data flow of the evaluator of Section 2.6. As for the SECD machine without J [9], this evaluator is in defunctionalized form: each of the values constructed with SUCC, FUNCLO, PGMCLO, and STATE_APPENDER are constructed at one place and consumed at another (the apply function). We therefore refunctionalize them into the function space value -> value:

```
datatype value = INT of int
               | FUN of value -> value

val e_init = Env.extend ("succ",
                         FUN (fn (INT n) => INT (n+1)),
                         Env.empty)

structure SR1 = Shift_and_Reset (type intermediate_answer = value)

structure SR2 = Shift_and_Reset_next (type intermediate_answer = value
                                      structure over = SR1)

(*  eval  : term * E -> value                                          *)
(*  where E = value Env.env                                            *)
fun eval (LIT n, e)
    = INT n
```

```
| eval (VAR x, e)
  = Env.lookup (x, e)
| eval (LAM (x, t), e)
  = FUN (fn v => SR1.reset (fn () => eval (t, Env.extend (x, v, e))))
| eval (APP (t0, t1), e)
  = let val v1      = eval (t1, e)
        val (FUN f) = eval (t0, e)
    in f v1 end
| eval (J, e)
  = SR1.shift (fn c => SR2.shift (fn d =>
    d (c (FUN (fn (FUN f) => FUN (fn v' => SR1.shift (fn c' =>
                                           SR2.shift (fn d' =>
                                           d (SR1.reset (fn () =>
                                              f v')))))))))))

fun evaluate5' t                      (* evaluate5' : program -> value *)
  = SR2.reset (fn () => SR1.reset (fn () => eval (t, e_init)))
```

Defunctionalizing this evaluator yields the evaluator of Section 2.6.

Proposition 6 (full correctness). *Given a program,* evaluate5 *and* evaluate5' *either both diverge or both yield values that are related by defunctionalization.*

2.8   Summary

We graphically summarize the derivations as follows. The evaluators in the top row are the defunctionalized counterparts of the evaluators in the bottom row.

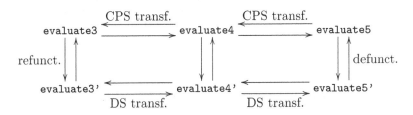

3   Three Simulations of the J Operator

The evaluator of Section 2.7 and the refunctionalized counterparts of the evaluators of Sections 2.5 and 2.4 are compositional. They can be viewed as syntax-directed encodings into their meta-language, as embodied in the first Futamura projection [19]. Below, we state these encodings as three simulations of J: one in direct style, one in CPS with one layer of continuations, and one in CPS with two layers of continuations.

We assume a call-by-value meta-language with right-to-left evaluation.

– In direct style, using shift_2 ($\mathcal{S}_2$), reset_2 ($\langle\!\langle\cdot\rangle\!\rangle_2$), shift_1 ($\mathcal{S}_1$), and reset_1 ($\langle\!\langle\cdot\rangle\!\rangle_1$):L

$$[\![n]\!] = n$$
$$[\![x]\!] = x$$
$$[\![t_0\ t_1]\!] = [\![t_0]\!]\ [\![t_1]\!]$$
$$[\![\lambda x.t]\!] = \lambda x.\langle\!\langle [\![t]\!]\rangle\!\rangle_1$$
$$[\![\mathbf{J}]\!] = \mathcal{S}_1\lambda c.\mathcal{S}_2\lambda d.d\ (c\ \lambda x.\boxed{\lambda x'.\mathcal{S}_1\lambda c'.\mathcal{S}_2\lambda d'.d\ \langle\!\langle x\ x'\rangle\!\rangle_1})$$

A program p is translated as $\langle\!\langle [\![p]\!]\rangle\!\rangle_1\rangle\!\rangle_2$.

– In CPS with one layer of continuations, using shift ($\mathcal{S}$) and reset ($\langle\!\langle\cdot\rangle\!\rangle$):

$$[\![n]\!]' = \lambda c.c\ n$$
$$[\![x]\!]' = \lambda c.c\ x$$
$$[\![t_0\ t_1]\!]' = \lambda c.[\![t_1]\!]'\ \lambda x_1.[\![t_0]\!]'\ \lambda x_0.x_0\ x_1\ c$$
$$[\![\lambda x.t]\!]' = \lambda c.c\ \lambda x.\lambda c.c\ ([\![t]\!]'\ \lambda x.x)$$
$$[\![\mathbf{J}]\!]' = \lambda c.\mathcal{S}\lambda d.d\ (c\ \lambda x.\lambda c.c\ \boxed{\lambda x'.\lambda c'.\mathcal{S}\lambda d'.d\ (x\ x'\ \lambda x''.x'')})$$

A program p is translated as $\langle [\![p]\!]'\ \lambda x.x\rangle$.

– In CPS with two layers of continuations (the outer continuation, i.e., the dump continuation, can be η-reduced in the first three clauses):

$$[\![n]\!]'' = \lambda c.\lambda d.c\ n\ d$$
$$[\![x]\!]'' = \lambda c.\lambda d.c\ x\ d$$
$$[\![t_0\ t_1]\!]'' = \lambda c.\lambda d.[\![t_1]\!]''\ (\lambda x_1.\lambda d.[\![t_0]\!]''\ (\lambda x_0.\lambda d.x_0\ x_1\ c\ d)\ d)\ d$$
$$[\![\lambda x.t]\!]'' = \lambda c.\lambda d.c\ (\lambda x.\lambda c.\lambda d.[\![t]\!]''\ (\lambda x.\lambda d.d\ x)\ \lambda x.c\ x\ d)\ d$$
$$[\![\mathbf{J}]\!]'' = \lambda c.\lambda d.c\ (\lambda x.\lambda c.\lambda d'''.c\ \boxed{(\lambda x'.\lambda c'.\lambda d'.x\ x'\ (\lambda x''.\lambda d''.d''\ x'')\ d)}\ d''')\ d$$

A program p is translated as $[\![p]\!]''\ (\lambda x.\lambda d.d\ x)\ \lambda x.x$.

Analysis: The simulation of literals, variables, and applications is standard. The control continuation of the body of each λ-abstraction is delimited, corresponding to it being evaluated with an empty control stack in the SECD machine. The J operator abstracts the control continuation and the dump continuation and immediately restores them, resuming the computation with a state appender which holds the abstracted dump continuation captive. Applying this state appender to a value v yields a program closure (boxed in the three simulations above). Applying this program closure to a value v' has the effect of discarding both the current control continuation and the current dump continuation, applying v to v', and resuming the captured dump continuation with the result.

The first rational deconstruction [9] already characterized the SECD machine in terms of the CPS hierarchy: the control stack is the first continuation, the dump is the second one (i.e., the meta-continuation), and abstraction bodies are evaluated within a control delimiter (i.e., an empty control stack). Our work further characterizes the J operator as capturing (a copy of) the meta-continuation.

4 Related Work

4.1 Landin and Burge

Landin [24] introduced the J operator as a new language feature motivated by three questions about labels and jumps:

- Can a language have jumps without having assignment?
- Is there some component of jumping that is independent of labels?
- Is there some feature that corresponds to functions with arguments in the same sense that labels correspond to procedures without arguments?

He gave the semantics of the J operator by extending the SECD machine. In addition to using J to model jumps in Algol 60 [23], he gave examples of programming with the J operator, using it to represent failure actions as program closures where it is essential that they abandon the context of their application.

In his textbook [6, Section 2.10], Burge adjusted Landin's original specification of the J operator. Indeed, in Landin's extension of the SECD machine, J could only occur in the context of an application. Burge adjusted the original specification so that J could occur in arbitrary contexts. To this end, he introduced the notion of a "state appender" as the denotation of J.

Thielecke [36] gave a detailed introduction to the J operator as presented by Landin and Burge. Burstall [7] illustrated the use of the J operator by simulating threads for parallel search algorithms, which in retrospect is the first simulation of threads in terms of first-class continuations.

4.2 Reynolds

Reynolds [31] gave a comparison of J to escape, the binder form of Scheme's call/cc [8][1]. He gave encodings of Landin's J (i.e., restricted to the context of an application) and escape in terms of each other.

His encoding of escape in terms of J reads as follows:

$$(\text{escape } k \text{ in } t)^* \; = \; \text{let } k = \mathbf{J} \, \lambda x.x \text{ in } t^*$$

As Thielecke notes [36], this encoding is only valid immediately inside an abstraction. Indeed, the dump continuation captured by J only coincides with the continuation captured by escape if the control continuation is the initial one (i.e., immediately inside a control delimiter). Thielecke generalized the encoding by adding a dummy abstraction:

$$(\text{escape } k \text{ in } t)^* \; = \; (\lambda().\text{let } k = \mathbf{J} \, \lambda x.x \text{ in } t^*) \, ()$$

From the point of view of the rational deconstruction, this dummy abstraction implicitly inserts a control delimiter.

---

[1] **escape** k **in** $t \equiv$ **call/cc** $\lambda k.t$.

Reynolds's converse encoding of J in terms of escape reads as follows:

$$(\text{let } d = \mathbf{J}\ \lambda x.t_1 \text{ in } t_0)^\circ\ =\ \mathbf{escape}\ k\ \mathbf{in}\ (\text{let } d = \lambda x.k\ t_1{}^\circ \text{ in } t_0{}^\circ)$$

where k does not occur free in t_0 and t_1. For the same reason as above, this encoding is only valid immediately inside an abstraction.

4.3   Felleisen

Felleisen showed how to embed Landin's extension of applicative expressions with J into the Scheme programming language [15]. The embedding is defined as Scheme syntactic extensions (i.e., macros). J is treated as a dynamic identifier that is bound in the body of every abstraction. Its control aspect is handled through Scheme's control operator call/cc.

As pointed out by Thielecke [36], Felleisen's simulation can be stated in direct style, assuming a call-by-value meta-language with right-to-left evaluation and call/cc. In addition, we present the corresponding simulations using $\mathcal{C}$ and reset, using shift and reset, and in CPS:

- In direct style, using either of call/cc, $\mathcal{C}$, or shift ($\mathcal{S}$), and one global control delimiter ($\langle\cdot\rangle$):

$$
\begin{aligned}
[\![x]\!] &= x\\
[\![t_0\ t_1]\!] &= [\![t_0]\!]\ [\![t_1]\!]\\
[\![\lambda x.t]\!] &= \lambda x.\mathbf{call/cc}\ \lambda d.\text{let } \mathbf{J} = \lambda x.\boxed{\lambda x'.d\ (x\ x')}\ \mathbf{in}\ [\![t]\!]\\
&= \lambda x.\mathcal{C}\lambda d.\text{let } \mathbf{J} = \lambda x.\boxed{\lambda x'.d\ (x\ x')}\ \mathbf{in}\ d\ [\![t]\!]\\
&= \lambda x.\mathcal{S}\lambda d.\text{let } \mathbf{J} = \lambda x.\boxed{\lambda x'.\mathcal{S}\lambda c'.d\ (x\ x')}\ \mathbf{in}\ d\ [\![t]\!]
\end{aligned}
$$

  A program p is translated as $\langle [\![p]\!] \rangle$.
- In CPS:

$$
\begin{aligned}
[\![x]\!]' &= \lambda c.c\ x\\
[\![t_0\ t_1]\!]' &= \lambda c.[\![t_1]\!]'\ \lambda x_1.[\![t_0]\!]'\ \lambda x_0.x_0\ x_1\ c\\
[\![\lambda x.t]\!]' &= \lambda c.c\ (\lambda x.\lambda d.\text{let } \mathbf{J} = \lambda x.\lambda c.c\ \boxed{\lambda x'.\lambda c'.x\ x'\ d}\ \mathbf{in}\ [\![t]\!]'\ d)
\end{aligned}
$$

A program p is translated as $[\![p]\!]'\ \lambda x.x$.

Analysis: The simulation of variables and applications is standard. The continuation of the body of each λ-abstraction is captured, and the identifier J is dynamically bound to a function closure (the state appender) which holds the continuation captive. Applying this function closure to a value v yields a program closure (boxed in the simulations above). Applying this program closure to a value v' has the effect of applying v to v' and resuming the captured continuation with the result, abandoning the current continuation.

4.4 Felleisen and Burge

Felleisen's version of the SECD machine with the J operator differs from Burge's. In the notation of Section 2.1, Burge's clause for applying program closures reads

```
| run ((PGMCLO (v, (s', e', c') :: d'')) :: v' :: s, e, APPLY :: c, d)
  = run (v :: v' :: s', e', APPLY :: c', d'')
```

instead of

```
| run ((PGMCLO (v, d')) :: v' :: s, e, APPLY :: c, d)
  = run (v :: v' :: nil, e_init, APPLY :: nil, d')
```

Felleisen's version delays the consumption of the dump until the function, in the program closure, completes, whereas Burge's version does not. The modification is unobservable because a program cannot capture the control continuation and because applying the argument of a state appender pushes the data stack, the environment, and the control stack on the dump. Felleisen's modification can be characterized as wrapping a control delimiter around the argument of a dump continuation, similarly to the simulation of static delimited continuations in terms of dynamic ones [5].

Burge's version, however, is not in defunctionalized form. In an extended version of this article [12], we put it in defunctionalized form without inserting a control delimiter and we outline the corresponding compositional evaluation functions and simulations.

5 Summary and Conclusion

We have extended the rational deconstruction of the SECD machine to the J operator, and we have presented a series of alternative implementations, including a compositional evaluation function in CPS. In passing, we have also presented new applications of defunctionalization and new examples of control delimiters and of both pushy and jumpy delimited continuations in programming practice.

6 On the Origin of First-Class Continuations

> *We have shown that jumping and labels are not essentially connected with strings of imperatives and in particular, with assignment. Second, that jumping is not essentially connected with labels. In performing this piece of logical analysis we have provided a precisely limited sense in which the "value of a label" has meaning. Also, we have discovered a new language feature, not present in current programming languages, that promises to clarify and simplify a notoriously untidy area of programming—that concerned with success/failure situations, and the actions needed on failure.*
>
> – Peter J. Landin, 1965 [24, page 133]

It was Strachey who coined the term "first-class functions" [35, Section 3.5.1][2]. In turn it was Landin who, through the J operator, invented what we know today as first-class continuations [17]. Indeed, like Reynolds for escape, Landin defined J in an unconstrained way, i.e., with no regard for it to be compatible with the last-in, first-out allocation discipline prevalent for control stacks since Algol 60[3].

Today, 'continuations' is an overloaded term, that may refer

- to the original semantic description technique for representing 'the meaning of the rest of the program' as a function, the continuation, as multiply co-discovered at the turn of the 1970's [32]; or
- to the programming-language feature of first-class continuations as typically provided by a control operator such as J, escape, or call/cc, as invented by Landin.

Whether a semantic description technique or a programming-language feature, the goal of continuations was the same: to formalize Algol's labels and jumps. But where Wadsworth and Abdali gave a continuation semantics to Algol, Landin translated Algol programs into applicative expressions in direct style. In turn, he specified the semantics of applicative expressions with the SECD machine, i.e., using first-order means. The meaning of an Algol label was an ISWIM 'program closure' as obtained by the J operator. Program closures were defined by extending the SECD machine, i.e., still using first-order means.

Landin did not use an explicit representation of the rest of the computation in his direct semantics of Algol 60, and so he is not listed among the co-discoverers of continuations [32]. Such an explicit representation, however, exists in the SECD machine, in first-order form: the dump, which represents the rest of the computation after returning from the current function call.

In this article, we have shown that, though it is first-order, the SECD machine directly corresponds to a compositional evaluation function in CPS—the tool of choice for specifying control operators since Reynolds's work [31]. As a corollary, the dump directly corresponds to a functional representation of control, since it is a defunctionalized continuation. Therefore, in the light of defunctionalization, we wish to see Landin's name added to the list of co-discoverers of continuations.

Acknowledgments. Thanks are due to Dariusz Biernacki, Julia L. Lawall, Kristian Støvring, and the anonymous reviewers of IFL'05 for comments. We are also grateful to Andrzej Filinski, Dan Friedman, Lockwood Morris, John Reynolds, Guy Steele, Carolyn Talcott, Bob Tennent, Hayo Thielecke, and Chris Wadsworth for their feedback on Section 6.

---

[2] *"Out of Quine's dictum: To be is to be the value of a variable, grew Strachey's 'first-class citizens'."* Peter J. Landin, 2000 [27, page 75].

[3] *"Dumps and program-closures are data-items, with all the implied latency for unruly multiple use and other privileges of first-class-citizenship."* Peter J. Landin, 1997 [26, Section 1].

This work was partly carried out while the two authors visited the TOPPS group at DIKU (http://www.diku.dk/topps). It is partly supported by the Danish Natural Science Research Council, Grant no. 21-03-0545 and by the ESPRIT Working Group APPSEM II (http://www.appsem.org).

References

[1] M. S. Ager, D. Biernacki, O. Danvy, and J. Midtgaard. A functional correspondence between evaluators and abstract machines. In D. Miller, editor, *Proceedings of the Fifth ACM-SIGPLAN International Conference on Principles and Practice of Declarative Programming (PPDP'03)*, pages 8–19. ACM Press, Aug. 2003.

[2] M. S. Ager, O. Danvy, and J. Midtgaard. A functional correspondence between call-by-need evaluators and lazy abstract machines. *Information Processing Letters*, 90(5):223–232, 2004. Extended version available as the technical report BRICS RS-04-3.

[3] M. S. Ager, O. Danvy, and J. Midtgaard. A functional correspondence between monadic evaluators and abstract machines for languages with computational effects. *Theoretical Computer Science*, 342(1):149–172, 2005. Extended version available as the technical report BRICS RS-04-28.

[4] M. Biernacka, D. Biernacki, and O. Danvy. An operational foundation for delimited continuations in the CPS hierarchy. *Logical Methods in Computer Science*, 1(2:5):1–39, Nov. 2005. A preliminary version was presented at the Fourth ACM SIGPLAN Workshop on Continuations (CW'04).

[5] D. Biernacki and O. Danvy. A simple proof of a folklore theorem about delimited control. Research Report BRICS RS-05-25, DAIMI, Department of Computer Science, University of Aarhus, Aarhus, Denmark, Aug. 2005. Theoretical Pearl to appear in the Journal of Functional Programming.

[6] W. H. Burge. *Recursive Programming Techniques*. Addison-Wesley, 1975.

[7] R. M. Burstall. Writing search algorithms in functional form. In D. Michie, editor, *Machine Intelligence*, volume 5, pages 373–385. Edinburgh University Press, 1969.

[8] W. Clinger, D. P. Friedman, and M. Wand. A scheme for a higher-level semantic algebra. In J. Reynolds and M. Nivat, editors, *Algebraic Methods in Semantics*, pages 237–250. Cambridge University Press, 1985.

[9] O. Danvy. A rational deconstruction of Landin's SECD machine. In C. Grelck, F. Huch, G. J. Michaelson, and P. Trinder, editors, *Implementation and Application of Functional Languages, 16th International Workshop, IFL'04*, number 3474 in Lecture Notes in Computer Science, pages 52–71, Lübeck, Germany, Sept. 2004. Springer-Verlag. Recipient of the 2004 Peter Landin prize. Extended version available as the technical report BRICS RS-03-33.

[10] O. Danvy and A. Filinski. Abstracting control. In M. Wand, editor, *Proceedings of the 1990 ACM Conference on Lisp and Functional Programming*, pages 151–160, Nice, France, June 1990. ACM Press.

[11] O. Danvy and J. L. Lawall. Back to direct style II: First-class continuations. In W. Clinger, editor, *Proceedings of the 1992 ACM Conference on Lisp and Functional Programming*, LISP Pointers, Vol. V, No. 1, pages 299–310, San Francisco, California, June 1992. ACM Press.

[12] O. Danvy and K. Millikin. A rational deconstruction of Landin's J operator. Research Report BRICS RS-06-04, DAIMI, Department of Computer Science, University of Aarhus, Aarhus, Denmark, Feb. 2006.

[13] O. Danvy and L. R. Nielsen. Defunctionalization at work. In H. Søndergaard, editor, *Proceedings of the Third International ACM SIGPLAN Conference on Principles and Practice of Declarative Programming (PPDP'01)*, pages 162–174, Firenze, Italy, Sept. 2001. ACM Press. Extended version available as the technical report BRICS RS-01-23.

[14] O. Danvy and Z. Yang. An operational investigation of the CPS hierarchy. In S. D. Swierstra, editor, *Proceedings of the Eighth European Symposium on Programming*, number 1576 in Lecture Notes in Computer Science, pages 224–242, Amsterdam, The Netherlands, Mar. 1999. Springer-Verlag.

[15] M. Felleisen. Reflections on Landin's J operator: a partly historical note. *Computer Languages*, 12(3/4):197–207, 1987.

[16] A. Filinski. Representing monads. In H.-J. Boehm, editor, *Proceedings of the Twenty-First Annual ACM Symposium on Principles of Programming Languages*, pages 446–457, Portland, Oregon, Jan. 1994. ACM Press.

[17] D. P. Friedman and C. T. Haynes. Constraining control. In M. S. V. Deusen and Z. Galil, editors, *Proceedings of the Twelfth Annual ACM Symposium on Principles of Programming Languages*, pages 245–254, New Orleans, Louisiana, Jan. 1985. ACM Press.

[18] D. P. Friedman, M. Wand, and C. T. Haynes. *Essentials of Programming Languages, second edition*. The MIT Press, 2001.

[19] Y. Futamura. Partial evaluation of computation process – an approach to a compiler-compiler. *Systems · Computers · Controls*, 2(5):45–50, 1971. Reprinted in Higher-Order and Symbolic Computation 12(4):381–391, 1999, with an interview [20].

[20] Y. Futamura. Partial evaluation of computation process, revisited. *Higher-Order and Symbolic Computation*, 12(4):377–380, 1999.

[21] Y. Kameyama. Axioms for delimited continuations in the CPS hierarchy. In J. Marcinkowski and A. Tarlecki, editors, *Computer Science Logic, 18th International Workshop, CSL 2004, 13th Annual Conference of the EACSL, Proceedings*, volume 3210 of *Lecture Notes in Computer Science*, pages 442–457, Karpacz, Poland, Sept. 2004. Springer.

[22] P. J. Landin. The mechanical evaluation of expressions. *The Computer Journal*, 6(4):308–320, 1964.

[23] P. J. Landin. A correspondence between Algol 60 and Church's lambda notation. *Commun. ACM*, 8:89–101 and 158–165, 1965.

[24] P. J. Landin. A generalization of jumps and labels. Research report, UNIVAC Systems Programming Research, 1965. Reprinted in Higher-Order and Symbolic Computation 11(2):125–143, 1998, with a foreword [36].

[25] P. J. Landin. The next 700 programming languages. *Commun. ACM*, 9(3):157–166, 1966.

[26] P. J. Landin. Histories of discoveries of continuations: Belles-lettres with equivocal tenses. In O. Danvy, editor, *Proceedings of the Second ACM SIGPLAN Workshop on Continuations (CW'97)*, Technical report BRICS NS-96-13, University of Aarhus, pages 1:1–9, Paris, France, Jan. 1997.

[27] P. J. Landin. My years with Strachey. *Higher-Order and Symbolic Computation*, 13(1/2):75–76, 2000.

[28] F. L. Morris. The next 700 formal language descriptions. *Lisp and Symbolic Computation*, 6(3/4):249–258, 1993. Reprinted from a manuscript dated 1970.

[29] P. D. Mosses. A foreword to 'Fundamental concepts in programming languages'. *Higher-Order and Symbolic Computation*, 13(1/2):7–9, 2000.

[30] C. R. Murthy. Control operators, hierarchies, and pseudo-classical type systems: A-translation at work. In O. Danvy and C. L. Talcott, editors, *Proceedings of the First ACM SIGPLAN Workshop on Continuations (CW'92)*, Technical report STAN-CS-92-1426, Stanford University, pages 49–72, San Francisco, California, June 1992.

[31] J. C. Reynolds. Definitional interpreters for higher-order programming languages. In *Proceedings of 25th ACM National Conference*, pages 717–740, Boston, Massachusetts, 1972. Reprinted in Higher-Order and Symbolic Computation 11(4):363–397, 1998, with a foreword [33].

[32] J. C. Reynolds. The discoveries of continuations. *Lisp and Symbolic Computation*, 6(3/4):233–247, 1993.

[33] J. C. Reynolds. Definitional interpreters revisited. *Higher-Order and Symbolic Computation*, 11(4):355–361, 1998.

[34] G. L. Steele Jr. Rabbit: A compiler for Scheme. Master's thesis, Artificial Intelligence Laboratory, Massachusetts Institute of Technology, Cambridge, Massachusetts, May 1978. Technical report AI-TR-474.

[35] C. Strachey. Fundamental concepts in programming languages. International Summer School in Computer Programming, Copenhagen, Denmark, Aug. 1967. Reprinted in Higher-Order and Symbolic Computation 13(1/2):11–49, 2000, with a foreword [29].

[36] H. Thielecke. An introduction to Landin's "A generalization of jumps and labels". *Higher-Order and Symbolic Computation*, 11(2):117–124, 1998.

A Dependently Typed Framework for Static Analysis of Program Execution Costs

Edwin Brady and Kevin Hammond

School of Computer Science,
University of St Andrews, St Andrews, Scotland
Tel: +44-1334-463253; Fax: +44-1334-463278
{eb,kh}@dcs.st-and.ac.uk

Abstract. This paper considers the use of dependent types to capture information about dynamic resource usage in a static type system. Dependent types allow us to give (explicit) proofs of properties with a program; we present a dependently typed core language TT, and define a framework within this language for representing size metrics and their properties. We give several examples of size bounded programs within this framework and show that we can construct proofs of their size bounds within TT. We further show how the framework handles recursive higher order functions and sum types, and contrast our system with previous work based on sized types.

1 Background and Motivation

Obtaining accurate information about the run-time time and space behaviour of computer software is important in a number of areas. One of the most significant of these is embedded systems. Embedded systems are becoming an increasingly important application area: today, more than 98% of *all* processors are used in embedded systems and the number of processors employed in such systems is increasing year on year. At the same time, the complexity of embedded software is growing apace. Assembly language, until recently the development language of choice, has consequently been supplanted by C/C++, and there is a growing trend towards the use of even higher-level languages. This trend towards increased expressivity is, however, in tension with the need to understand the dynamic run-time behaviour of embedded systems. Such understanding is critical for the construction of resource-bounded software.

Because there is a need for strong guarantees concerning the run-time behavior of embedded software to be available *at compile-time*, existing approaches have usually either focused on restricting the programming language so that only resource-bounded programs are expressible, or else relied on painstaking, and often manual and inaccurate, post-facto performance measurement and analysis. However, restricting the language deprives the programmer of many useful abstraction mechanisms (c.f. [22,27,28]). Conversely effective program analyses work at a low level of abstraction, and thus cannot deal effectively with high-level abstraction mechanisms, such as polymorphism, higher-order functions (e.g. `fold`), algebraic data types (e.g. `Either`), and general recursion.

A. Butterfield, C. Grelck, and F. Huch (Eds.): IFL 2005, LNCS 4015, pp. 74–90, 2006.

In this paper we develop a framework based on *dependent types* which is capable of expressing dynamic execution costs in the type system. We focus on a strict, purely functional expression language and exemplify our approach with reference to the size of a data structure. The approach is, however, general and should, in due course, be readily extensible to other metrics such as dynamic heap allocation, stack usage or time.

A key feature of a dependently typed setting is that it is possible to express more complex properties of programs than the usual simply typed frameworks in use in languages such as Standard ML or Haskell. In fact, computation is possible at the type level, and it is also possible to expose proof requirements that must be satisfied. These capabilities are exploited in the framework we present here to allow static calculation of cost bounds; we use type level computation to construct bounds on execution costs. In this way we can *statically* guarantee that costs lie within required limits.

1.1 Dependent Types

The characteristic feature of a dependent type system is that types may be predicated on values. Such systems have traditionally been applied to reasoning and program verification, as in the LEGO [17] and COQ [6] theorem provers. More recent research, however, has led to the use of dependent types in programming itself, for example Cayenne [2] and Epigram [20,19]. Our aim is to use dependent types to include explicit size information in programs, rather than as an external property. In this way, type checking subsumes checking of these properties.

1.2 Contributions

We have previously used sized type systems such as [15,24] to represent program execution cost; such systems seem attractive for this purpose because there is a clear link between, for example, data structure size and heap usage. However, there are limits to the expressivity of sized type systems. In particular, there is a limit to the form of expressions we can use to express size, leading to difficulty in giving accurate sizes to higher order functions. In this paper, we explore the benefits of using a dependently typed intermediate language to represent size constraints of a high level program:

- We can express more complex properties than those available in the sized type system; we are not restricted in the constraint language. Since we can write programs at the type level, we can extend the constraint language as we wish. In particular, this gives us more flexibility in expressing the cost of higher order functions. There need be no loss of size information — we can give each program as precise a size predicate as we need.
- With dependent types, we can verify the correctness of constraints given by an external inference system. A program with embedded size constraints is a complete, self-contained, checkable term; correctness of the constraints is verified by the typechecker, a small and well understood (and hence relatively straightforward to verify) program. We do not have to provide soundness or completeness proofs for our framework if we implement it entirely within a system already known to be sound and complete.

- In situations where a sized type inference system is not powerful enough to derive a size recurrence, or where the user requires a weaker constraint on the size, we can allow the user to specify the size constraint by hand and still be able to check it. Dependent types allow us to overcome the limitations of a sized type based inference system — it is always possible for the user to provide hints.
- Where an automated proof construction system is not powerful enough to solve a constraint, we can expose proof obligations to the user, either for the user to solve, or to show that a constraint cannot be satisfied.

It is important to note that we do not use a dependent type system to help *infer* size information; this is left to an external inference system, or to the programmer (or possibly to some extent both). Rather, we use dependent types to verify that the constraints we have are satisfiable.

2 Programming with Dependent Types

We use a strongly normalising type theory with inductive families [9], similar to Luo's UTT [16]. This language, which we call TT, is an enriched lambda calculus, with the usual properties of subject reduction, Church Rosser, and uniqueness of types. The strong normalisation property is guaranteed by allowing only primitive recursion over strictly positive inductive datatypes. This is a dependent type system, with *no syntactic distinction* between types and terms; hence we can have arbitrarily complex terms in types. Full details of TT are given in [4]. For clarity of the presentation here, we use a higher level notation similar to the Epigram notation of [20]. In this section, we give a brief introduction to programming and theorem proving with inductive families.

2.1 Inductive Families

Inductive families are simultaneously defined collections of algebraic data types which can be indexed over values as well as types. For example, we can define a "lists with length" (or vector) type; to do this we first declare a type of natural numbers to represent such lengths, using the natural deduction style notation proposed for Epigram in [20]:

$$\underline{\text{data}} \quad \frac{}{\mathbb{N} \,:\, \star} \quad \underline{\text{where}} \quad \frac{}{0 \,:\, \mathbb{N}} \quad \frac{n \,:\, \mathbb{N}}{\mathsf{s}\, n \,:\, \mathbb{N}}$$

It is straightforward to define addition and multiplication by primitive recursion. Then we may make the following declaration of vectors; note that nil only targets vectors of length zero, and cons x xs only targets vectors of length greater than zero:

$$\underline{\text{data}} \quad \frac{A \,:\, \star \quad n \,:\, \mathbb{N}}{\mathsf{Vect}\, A\, n \,:\, \star} \quad \underline{\text{where}} \quad \frac{}{\mathsf{nil} \,:\, \mathsf{Vect}\, A\, 0}$$
$$\frac{x \,:\, A \quad xs \,:\, \mathsf{Vect}\, A\, k}{\mathsf{cons}\, x\, xs \,:\, \mathsf{Vect}\, A\, (\mathsf{s}\, k)}$$

We leave A and k as implicit arguments to cons; their type can be inferred from the type of Vect. When the type includes explicit length information like this, it follows that a function over that type will express the invariant properties of the length. For example, the type of the following program **vPlus**, which adds corresponding numbers in each vector, expresses the invariant that the input vectors are the same length as the output:

$$\underline{\text{let}} \quad \frac{xs, ys \ : \ \mathsf{Vect}\ A\ n}{\mathbf{vPlus}\ xs\ ys \ : \ \mathsf{Vect}\ A\ n}$$

$$\mathbf{vPlus} \quad \mathsf{nil} \quad \mathsf{nil} \quad \mapsto \mathsf{nil}$$
$$\mathbf{vPlus}\ (\mathsf{cons}\ x\ xs)\ (\mathsf{cons}\ y\ ys) \mapsto \mathsf{cons}\ (x\ +\ y)\ (\mathbf{vPlus}\ xs\ ys)$$

Unlike in a simply typed language, we do not need to give error handling cases when the lengths of the vectors do not match; the typechecker verifies that these cases are impossible.

2.2 Theorem Proving

The dependent type system of TT also allows us to express properties directly. For example, the following heterogeneous definition of equality, due to McBride [18], is built in to TT (rather than introduced as a datatype, so we omit the <u>data</u> keyword):

$$\frac{a \ : \ A \quad b \ : \ B}{a\ =\ b \ : \ \star} \qquad \frac{A \ : \ \star \quad a \ : \ A}{\mathsf{refl}\ a \ : \ a\ =\ a}$$

This definition introduces an infix type constructor, $=$, parametrised over two types; we can declare equality between any two types, but can only construct an instance of equality between two definitionally equal values in the same type; e.g. $\mathsf{refl}\ (\mathsf{s}\ 0)$ is an instance of a proof that $\mathsf{s}0 = \mathsf{s}0$. Furthermore, since equality is an ordinary datatype just like $\mathbb{N}$ and Vect, we can also write programs by case analysis on instances of equality, such as the following program which can be viewed as a proof that s respects equality:

$$\underline{\text{let}} \quad \frac{p \ : \ n\ =\ m}{\mathbf{resp\_s}\ p \ : \ (\mathsf{s}\ n)\ =\ (\mathsf{s}\ m)}$$

$$\mathbf{resp\_s}\ (\mathsf{refl}\ n) \ \mapsto \ \mathsf{refl}\ (\mathsf{s}\ n)$$

We can also represent more complex properties, such as the less than or equal relation:

$$\underline{\text{data}} \quad \frac{x, y \ : \ \mathbb{N}}{x \leq y \ : \ \star} \quad \text{where} \quad \frac{}{\mathsf{leO} \ : \ 0 \leq y} \qquad \frac{p \ : \ x \leq y}{\mathsf{leS}\ p \ : \ \mathsf{s}\ x \leq \mathsf{s}\ y}$$

Note that x and y can be left implicit, as their types (and even their values) can be inferred from the type of the relation. For example, $\mathsf{leS}\ (\mathsf{leS}\ \mathsf{leO})$ could represent a proof of $\mathsf{s}\ (\mathsf{s}\ 0) \leq \mathsf{s}\ (\mathsf{s}\ (\mathsf{s}\ (\mathsf{s}\ 0)))$.

As with equality, given a proof, we can write programs by recursion over the proof. For example, we can write a safe subtraction function (i.e. the result is guaranteed to be non-negative) by primitive recursion over the proof that the second argument is less than or equal to the first:

$$\underline{\text{let}} \quad \frac{n, m \ : \ \mathbb{N} \quad p \ : \ m \leq n}{\mathbf{minus}\ n\ m\ p \ : \ \mathbb{N}}$$

$$\mathbf{minus} \quad n \quad 0 \quad (\mathsf{leO}\ n) \mapsto n$$
$$\mathbf{minus}\ (\mathsf{s}\ n)\ (\mathsf{s}\ m)\ (\mathsf{leS}\ p) \mapsto \mathbf{minus}\ n\ m\ p$$

The values for the arguments n and m are determined by the indices of leO and leS; no case analysis on the numbers themselves is required. The Curry-Howard isomorphism [8,13] describes this correspondence between proofs and programs. We will exploit this further in developing our framework; by expressing the size properties explicitly in a program's type, we know that a *type correct* program is also a *size correct* program.

3 Dependent Types for Resource Analysis

In previous work [24] we have extended the basic sized type system by incorporating notions of *time*, for time costs, and *latent costs* to capture cost information for higher-order functions. The notion of *size* is now used to obtain information about bounds on the size of function arguments and results. This can in turn be used to calculate time and space costs of executing a function. For example, given $map : (\alpha \xrightarrow{fc} \beta) \rightarrow [\alpha]^n \xrightarrow{mapc} [\beta]^n$, we can deduce that the latent cost for *map*, *mapc*, is proportional to $fc \times n$.

In this paper, we consider the use of dependent types to represent program size; thus we can use sized type inference to give size bounds where possible, and represent these bounds in a dependently typed framework. In this way we can check that both machine generated and user specified bounds are admissible.

3.1 Source Language

Our source language is a strict, higher order functional language with no partial application (to avoid additional complications such as currying, although in future work we may remove this restriction). The exact details are not important to the dependently typed framework we will develop — it suffices to say that the syntax is similar to Haskell. For the moment, we assume that functions are total, and recursion is primitive. Ultimately, we hope to apply the methods presented to multi-stage Hume programs [11], ensuring the resource properties we specify are preserved between stages.

Our aim is to describe a resource framework in which all source language programs can be represented *homogeneously* along with proofs of their resource bounds, in order to facilitate an automated translation into TT. There are two aspects to consider: representation of datatypes, and representation of functions.

3.2 Representing Datatypes

The key idea behind our framework is that each user defined type is represented within the framework by a type predicated on a natural number, $\mathbb{N}$. Thus we can embed size information explicitly within a type, and represent proofs of size properties directly in TT code via relations such as $=$ and $\leq$. e.g. Given the user defined type of lists ...

```
data List a = nil | cons a (List a)
```

... we can create a "sized list" type in our dependently typed framework as follows, where the size of the empty list is 0, and the size of the non-empty list is one more than the size of its tail:

$$\text{\underline{data}} \quad \frac{A \; : \; \mathbb{N} \to \star}{\text{Lists } A \; : \; \mathbb{N} \to \star} \quad \text{\underline{where}} \quad \frac{}{\text{nil}_\text{s} \; : \; \text{Lists } A \; 0}$$

$$\frac{x \; : \; A \; xn \qquad xs \; : \; \text{Lists } A \; xsn}{\text{cons}_\text{s} \; x \; xs \; : \; \text{Lists } A \; (\text{s } xsn)}$$

Note that the element type A, like all types within the framework, is also predicated on a size. We use the convention that sized types (and their constructors) generated from the source language are given the suffix s.

We can be flexible as to what the size information for a structure is; whether it be high level information such as the above length of list, or the total size of all elements in the list, or more low level information such as the number of heap cells required to store a structure. Within our framework, the *meaning* of the size index of a family is not important, what matters is that the index satisfies the required properties.

3.3 Representing Functions

With dependent types, we can ensure that the size index of a value satisfies the required properties of that value by specifying those properties in the types of functions. In our TT representation of functions, we would like to be able to capture such properties.

To this end, we define the following Size type, which pairs a sized value with a predicate describing the properties that value respects:

$$\text{\underline{data}} \quad \frac{A \; : \; \mathbb{N} \to \star \qquad P \; : \; \forall n{:}\mathbb{N}. \; A \; n \to \star}{\text{Size } A \; P \; : \; \star}$$

$$\text{\underline{where}} \quad \frac{val \; : \; A \; n \qquad p \; : \; P \; n \; val}{\text{size } val \; p \; : \; \text{Size } A \; P}$$

The size constructor takes a value of type $A \; n$, coupled with a proof that A satisfies the required property, specified by the predicate P.

We use $\mathcal{S}\,(n, v) \; : \; A. \; P$ as a shorthand for Size $A \; (\lambda n{:}\mathbb{N}. \; \lambda v{:}A \; n. \; P)$.

We translate[1] functions in the source language to a function in TT which returns a Size; to demonstrate this, let us consider the append function on lists, as shown above for Vect and defined in the source language as:

```
append nil ys = ys
append (cons x xs) ys = cons x (append xs ys)
```

Given the size of List, the size of the result is the sum of the sizes of the inputs. In our framework, we express the type of this function as follows:

$$\text{\underline{let}} \quad \frac{xs \; : \; \text{Lists } A \; xsn \qquad ys \; : \; \text{Lists } A \; ysn}{\mathbf{append} \; xs \; ys \; : \; (\mathcal{S}\,(n, v) \; : \; \text{Lists } A. \; n = xsn + ysn)}$$

The predicate given to Size requires that any result of this function must be paired with a proof that its size (n) is equal to the sum of the input sizes. In the definition of **append** we show that the return values satisfy the predicate by returning the value paired with a proof object. In many cases these proofs can be constructed automatically

---

[1] By hand, currently.

via the Omega decision procedure; in the following definition of **append**, we indicate where in the term there are proof objects to construct with the "hole" notation $\Box_n$. As a notational convenience, we allow pattern matching <u>let</u> definitions, in order to extract size information and the return value separately from the recursive call:

$$\textbf{append} \quad \text{nil}_{\text{S}} \quad ys \mapsto \text{size } ys \ \Box_1$$
$$\textbf{append} \ (\text{cons}_{\text{S}} \ x \ xs) \ ys \mapsto \underline{\text{let}} \ (\text{size } val \ p) \ = \ \textbf{append } xs \ ys \ \underline{\text{in}}$$
$$\text{size} \ (\text{cons}_{\text{S}} \ x \ val) \ \Box_2$$

Given val : $\text{List}_{\text{S}} \ A \ n$, xs : $\text{List}_{\text{S}} \ A \ xsn$ and y : $\text{List}_{\text{S}} \ A \ ysn$, the types of the holes are as follows:

$$\Box_1 \ : \ ysn \ = \ 0 + ysn$$
$$\Box_2 \ : \ \text{s} \ n \ = \ (\text{s} \ xsn) + ysn$$

Normalising the goals gives the following equalities to prove (note that in the case of $\Box_2$ reduction is possible because $+$ is defined by recursion on its first argument):

$$\Box_1 \ : \ ysn \ = \ ysn$$
$$\Box_2 \ : \ \text{s} \ n \ = \ \text{s} \ (xsn + ysn)$$

To prove $\Box_1$ is straightforward, by reflexivity (refl ysn). We can prove $\Box_2$ by induction, using p : n = $xsn + ysn$ and a lemma **resp_s** to show that s respects equality. The full definition of **append**, including these proofs, is as follows:

$$\underline{\text{let}} \quad \frac{xs \ : \ \text{List}_{\text{S}} \ A \ xsn \qquad ys \ : \ \text{List}_{\text{S}} \ A \ ysn}{\textbf{append } xs \ ys \ : \ (S \ (n, v) \ : \ \text{List}_{\text{S}} \ A. \ n = xsn + ysn)}$$

$$\textbf{append} \quad \text{nil}_{\text{S}} \quad ys \mapsto \text{size } ys \ (\text{refl } ysn)$$
$$\textbf{append} \ (\text{cons}_{\text{S}} \ x \ xs) \ ys \mapsto \underline{\text{let}} \ (\text{size } val \ p) \ = \ \textbf{append } xs \ ys \ \underline{\text{in}}$$
$$\text{size} \ (\text{cons}_{\text{S}} \ x \ val) \ (\textbf{resp\_s } p)$$

Although we have filled in the proof details explicitly here, in many cases this can be done automatically. We cannot do this in general, as the problem is the type inhabitation problem, to find a term a : A for any A — however, for certain classes of A, there is a method for constructing an appropriate a (if it exists). For the examples in this paper, all proof obligations can be discharged using COQ's omega tactic, based on Pugh's Omega calculator [23].

4 Examples

We present several examples of functions defined in our framework. These examples have all been implemented in the COQ theorem prover, using the omega tactic to solve *all* of the equational constraints. A COQ script implementing these examples can be found on the first author's web page.[2]

For these examples, we define representations of booleans and natural numbers. We give the size of a boolean as zero in both cases — if we are not interested in the size of a type, we can give all of its values a size of zero. We could also give the booleans

---

[2] http://www.dcs.st-and.ac.uk/~eb/

size one, to represent the fact that values occupy a single heap cell. We give the size of a natural number as the magnitude of the number it represents.

$$\underline{\text{data}} \quad \dfrac{}{\text{Bool}_\text{S} \ : \ \mathbb{N} \to \star} \quad \underline{\text{where}} \quad \dfrac{}{\text{True}_\text{S} \ : \ \text{Bool}_\text{S} \ 0} \quad \dfrac{}{\text{False}_\text{S} \ : \ \text{Bool}_\text{S} \ 0}$$

$$\underline{\text{data}} \quad \dfrac{}{\text{Nat}_\text{S} \ : \ \mathbb{N} \to \star} \quad \underline{\text{where}} \quad \dfrac{}{\text{O}_\text{S} \ : \ \text{Nat}_\text{S} \ 0} \quad \dfrac{i \ : \ \text{Nat}_\text{S} \ n}{\text{S}_\text{S} \ i \ : \ \text{Nat}_\text{S} \ (\text{s} \ n)}$$

We also take operations such as $\underline{\text{if}}$ ... $\underline{\text{then}}$ ... $\underline{\text{else}}$ and $\le$ as primitive.

For each source function, we identify an output size and its relation to the size of the inputs. Given this, we can construct the type of the TT representation, with the return type as a Size structure. Then the TT function itself is constructed by traversing the syntax tree of the source function, with proof objects inserted where necessary.

4.1 Partitioning a List

The `split` function partitions a list into a pair of lists based on a pivot value (values smaller than or larger than the pivot). The source language definition is:

```
split pivot nil = (nil,nil)
split pivot (cons x xs) = let (l,r) = split pivot xs in
                          if x<=pivot
                            then (cons x l,  r)
                            else (l,  cons x r)
```

With sized types it is difficult to infer an upper bound cost for this function, as the sizes of each element of the pair are considered independently and so inference assumes the worst case for each. However, it should be clear that the operation is size preserving. We use the following (sized) definition of pairs:

$$\underline{\text{data}} \quad \dfrac{A, \ B \ : \ \mathbb{N} \to \star \quad n \ : \ \mathbb{N}}{\text{Pairs} \ A \ B \ : \ \mathbb{N} \to \star} \quad \underline{\text{where}} \quad \dfrac{a \ : \ A \ an \quad b \ : \ B \ bn}{\text{mkPairs} \ a \ b \ : \ \text{Pairs} \ A \ B \ (\text{s} \ (\text{s} \ 0))}$$

As well as the usual projections, **fst** and **snd**, we have **fstS** and **sndS** to project out the size of each component.

We have chosen to represent the size of a pair as 2 (the number of elements). There are other choices we could make here, e.g. the sum of the sizes of the elements. We choose 2 to demonstrate that a function's size predicate can depend on values as well as sizes.

In writing the type of **split**, we need to identify the output size of interest, and its relation to the input size. This is a size preserving relationship — the output size of interest is obtained from the sizes of each element of the pair which is returned, and we express in the type that the sum of the sizes of these elements is equal to the size of the input list:

$$\underline{\text{let}} \quad \dfrac{piv \ : \ \mathbb{N} \quad xs \ : \ \text{List}_\text{S} \ \text{Nat}_\text{S} \ xsn}{\begin{array}{c} \textbf{split} \ piv \ xs \ : \ (S \ (n, v) \ : \ \text{Pairs} \ (\text{List}_\text{S} \ \text{Nat}_\text{S}) \ (\text{List}_\text{S} \ \text{Nat}_\text{S}). \\ xsn \ = \ (\textbf{fstS} \ v) \ + \ (\textbf{sndS} \ v)) \end{array}}$$

The implementation of this follows the structure of the source language implementation, subject to managing the Size structure. We leave the proof obligations as holes to be filled in by the Omega calculator.

$$\textbf{split } piv \quad \textsf{nil}_\textsf{S} \quad \mapsto \textsf{ size } (\textsf{mkPairs nil}_\textsf{S}\textsf{ nil}_\textsf{S}) \; \square_1$$
$$\textbf{split } piv \textsf{ (cons}_\textsf{S}\textsf{ } x\textsf{ } xs) \mapsto \underline{\text{let}} \textsf{ (size (mkPairs } l\textsf{ } r)\textsf{ } p) \; = \; \textbf{split } piv\textsf{ } xs \underline{\text{ in}}$$
$$\underline{\text{if }} (x \le piv)$$
$$\underline{\text{then}} \textsf{ size (mkPairs (cons}_\textsf{S}\textsf{ } x\textsf{ } l)\textsf{ } r) \; \square_2$$
$$\underline{\text{else}} \textsf{ size (mkPairs } l\textsf{ (cons}_\textsf{S}\textsf{ } x\textsf{ } r)) \; \square_3$$

The fact that this definition typechecks (as we have verified in CoQ) gives us a strong static guarantee about the properties that the function satisfies. As the type of **split** specifies the size relationship between the input and the output, a well typed implementation of **split** such as this must satisfy that relationship.

Here, allowing the user to specify size information in advance is beneficial; it is easy to check that the size information is correct although it is difficult to infer. Some methods are proposed to infer a size for **split** — Vasconcelos describes a method based on abstract interpretation in his forthcoming PhD thesis; Hofmann and Jost in [12] are able to infer the appropriate heap space usage using a linear type system, although this method is restricted to functions which admit a linear bound. More recent work (to be described in Jost's forthcoming PhD thesis) allows cost inference for polymorphic and higher order functions.

4.2 Map

Higher order functions present additional complications, in that we need not only the type of the function argument, but also its size information. Consider the map function, defined as follows:

```
map f nil = nil
map f (cons x xs) = cons (f x) (map f xs)
```

Recall that for each function, we identify an output size and its relation to the sizes of the inputs. However, we do not know either of these until we know some more information about f. Therefore the solution we adopt is to associate a size predicate and a size function with the function argument. This allows us to express the size of the higher order function in terms of the size of its arguments. In the case of **map**, this is not such a great problem, given the size metric we have chosen for lists — the length of the resulting list has no relationship to the function argument:

$$\underline{\text{let}} \; \frac{P \; : \; \forall n{:}\mathbb{N}.\; B\; n \to \star \quad fs \; : \; \mathbb{N} \to \mathbb{N} \qquad \qquad \qquad}{\textbf{map } P \; fs \; f \; xs \; : \; \mathcal{S}\,(n,v) \; : \; B.\, n \; = \; xsn} $$

$$ f \; : \; A\; an' \to \mathcal{S}\,(n,v) \; : \; B.\, P\; n\; v\; (fs\; an') \quad xs \; : \; \textsf{List}_\textsf{S}\; A\; xsn $$

Again, the definition of **map** is built by following the syntax tree of the source function, with the addition of the size structures:

$$\text{map } P \text{ } fs \text{ } f \quad \text{nil}_S \quad \mapsto \text{ size nil}_S \text{ } \square_1$$
$$\text{map } P \text{ } fs \text{ } f \text{ (cons}_S \text{ } x \text{ } xs) \mapsto \underline{\text{let}} \text{ (size } val_1 \text{ } p_1) \text{ } = \text{ } f \text{ } x \underline{\text{ in}}$$
$$\underline{\text{let}} \text{ (size } val_2 \text{ } p_2) \text{ } = \text{ map } P \text{ } fs \text{ } f \text{ } xs \underline{\text{ in}}$$
$$\text{size (cons}_S \text{ } val_1 \text{ } val_2) \text{ } \square_2$$

Other higher order functions, such as **zipWith** and **filter** follow a similar pattern, **filter** having a different size metric giving an upper bound on the size of the resulting list, rather than an exact size. In the case of **filter** we can even imagine the framework giving a more precise size where some argument is known — for example, the size of `filter isEven [1,3,...]` is clearly zero; by giving a size expression which depends on the value of the list, this size can be statically determined.

If we were to choose a different size metric for lists, for example total heap usage or maximum stack size, we would be faced with the problem of how to relate the size of f to the size of the resulting list. This is a general problem with the handling of higher order functions, as we shall see in the size of **twice**.

4.3 Twice

The `twice` function simply applies a function to its argument twice; i.e., it is the Church numeral 2. Although conceptually much simpler than `map` it presents a greater difficulty, since the size relationship between input and output is not uniform. It is defined in the source language as follows:

```
twice f x = f (f x)
```

Intuitively, the effect of this function on the size of x should be twice the effect of f on x. However, this is hard to represent in a sized type system; the limitations of the expression language at the type level make it difficult to give a precise cost to many functions, and this is especially the case with higher-order functions. Here, the function is applied twice, with different sizes in each case, but a sized type system cannot represent this.

To represent this in our framework, we again associate a size predicate and function with f. However, this is not quite enough —- we also need to know that the predicate satisfies a transitivity property (intuitively, verifying that the predicate respects repeated application). We therefore associate *three* additional arguments with f, being P, fs and *Ptrans* in the following declaration:

$$\underline{\text{let}} \quad \frac{\begin{array}{l} P \text{ : } \forall n : \mathbb{N}. \text{ } \forall a : A \text{ } n. \text{ } \mathbb{N} \to \star \quad fs \text{ : } \mathbb{N} \to \mathbb{N} \\ Ptrans \text{ : } P \text{ } as \text{ } a \text{ } (fs \text{ } cs) \to P \text{ } bs \text{ } b \text{ } (fs \text{ } as) \to P \text{ } bs \text{ } b \text{ } (fs \text{ } (fs \text{ } cs)) \\ f \text{ : } A \text{ } an' \to (S \text{ } (n, v) \text{ : } A. \text{ } P \text{ } n \text{ } v \text{ } (fs \text{ } an')) \end{array}}{\text{twice } P \text{ } fs \text{ } Ptrans \text{ } f \text{ } a \text{ : } (S \text{ } (n, v) \text{ : } A. \text{ } P \text{ } n \text{ } v \text{ } (fs \text{ } (fs \text{ } an')))}$$

Ptrans is a predicate transformer; it is a predicate level reflection of function composition. We now have enough information in the type to define **twice**:

$$\text{twice } P \text{ } fs \text{ } Ptrans \text{ } f \text{ } x \mapsto \underline{\text{let}} \text{ (size } val_1 \text{ } p_1) \text{ } = \text{ } f \text{ } x \underline{\text{ in}}$$
$$\underline{\text{let}} \text{ (size } val_2 \text{ } p_2) \text{ } = \text{ } f \text{ } val_1 \underline{\text{ in}}$$
$$\text{size } val_2 \text{ } \square_1$$

Again, despite the complicated type, the definition of **twice** follows the same form as the original definition and the proof obligations are straightforward to discharge via the *Ptrans* transformer. In this case, $\square_1$ can be instantiated simply by *Ptrans* p_1 p_2.

This function on its own does not give any direct size information; this should not be surprising since we do not have size information for a specific f. An *application* of **twice** on the other hand will give us this information. For example, given **double**:

$$\underline{\text{let}} \quad \frac{i \ : \ \mathsf{Nat}_\mathsf{S} \ in}{\textbf{double } i \ : \ \mathcal{S}\,(n,p) \ : \ \mathsf{Nat}_\mathsf{S}.\ n = 2 * in}$$

We can apply **twice** to **double**, and get the obvious cost:

$$\underline{\text{let}} \quad \frac{i \ : \ \mathsf{Nat}_\mathsf{S} \ in}{\textbf{twicedouble } i \ : \ \mathcal{S}\,(n,p) \ : \ \mathsf{Nat}_\mathsf{S}.\ n = 4 * in}$$

$$\textbf{twicedouble } i \mapsto \textbf{twice}\,(\lambda a, b : \mathbb{N}.\ a = b)\,(\lambda n : \mathbb{N}.\ 2 * n)\,\square_1 \textbf{ double } i$$

The hole for the transitivity proof is left for the omega tactic to fill in; the proposition to be proven is $\forall a, b, c : \mathbb{N}.\ a = 2 * b \rightarrow b = 2 * c \rightarrow a = 2 * (2 * c)$, which is solved by omega without difficulty, although the proof term itself is non-trivial.

The size predicates and transitivity proof we use are specific to the instance of f. In a more complex case, where f is itself a higher order function, such as (`twice twice`), type correctness requires that the higher order f is applied to a predicate.

4.4   Fold

The `fold` function may be seen as a generalisation of `twice`, applying a function several times across a list. It can be defined in the source language as follows:

```
fold f a nil = a
fold f a (cons x xs) = f x (fold f a xs)
```

Dealing with this in a sized type system presents a difficult problem; we do not know how many times `f` will be applied, nor do we know the content of the list, so an expression language which can only represent size is not strong enough at the type level.

Since TT has a more flexible language at the type level, we can implement `fold`, although it presents more difficulty than **twice**. Firstly, f is now a function of two arguments (and hence so is fs). Secondly, and more importantly, **fold** is recursive and the number of times f is applied depends on the input.

Since we have no partial application, we can write down the types of f and fs as functions of two arguments. The size of the result of the fold depends not only on the size effect of f, but also on the input list itself. Therefore, we create a function **foldSize** to be run at the type level which computes the size of the result of folding a list:

$$\underline{\text{let}} \quad \frac{fs \ : \ \mathbb{N} \rightarrow \mathbb{N} \rightarrow \mathbb{N} \qquad an \ : \ \mathbb{N} \qquad xs \ : \ \mathsf{List}_\mathsf{S}\,B\,xsn}{\textbf{foldSize } fs \ an \ xs \ : \ \mathbb{N}}$$

$$\textbf{foldSize } fs \ an \qquad \mathsf{nil}_\mathsf{S} \qquad \mapsto \ an$$
$$\textbf{foldSize } fs \ an \ (\mathsf{cons}_\mathsf{S} \ x_{xn} \ xs) \mapsto \ fs \ xn \ (\textbf{foldSize } fs \ an \ xs)$$

Note that the implicit size of the x argument to cons_S is used to compute the size; this argument is subscripted. The function follows the structure of the original source language `fold` function, but calculating the size of the result from the size function for f. When we create the TT version of **fold**, we express the result size in terms of **foldSize**:

$$\text{let} \quad \frac{
\begin{array}{l}
P \; : \; \forall n{:}\mathbb{N}.\; A\, n \rightarrow \mathbb{N} \rightarrow \star \quad\; fs \; : \; \mathbb{N} \rightarrow \mathbb{N} \rightarrow \mathbb{N} \\
f \; : \; A\, an' \rightarrow B\, bn' \rightarrow \mathcal{S}\, (n, v) \; : \; A.\, P\, n\, v\, (fs\, an'\, bn') \\
a \; : \; A\, an \quad\; xs \; : \; \text{List}_{\mathsf{S}}\, B\, xsn
\end{array}
}{
\begin{array}{l}
\mathbf{fold}\, P\, fs\, f\, a\, xs \; : \; (\mathcal{S}\, (n, v) \; : \; A. \\
\qquad\qquad\qquad\quad P\, n\, v\, (\mathbf{foldSize}\, fs\, an\, xs)))
\end{array}
}$$

$$
\begin{array}{ll}
\mathbf{fold}\, P\, fs\, f\, a \quad \text{nil}_{\mathsf{S}} & \mapsto\; \text{size}\, a\; \square_1 \\
\mathbf{fold}\, P\, fs\, f\, a\, (\text{cons}_{\mathsf{S}}\, x\, xs) & \mapsto\; \underline{\text{let}}\, (\text{size}\, val_1\, p_1) = \mathbf{fold}\, P\, fs\, f\, a\, xs\, \underline{\text{in}} \\
& \qquad \underline{\text{let}}\, (\text{size}\, val_2\, p_2) = \mathbf{f}\, val_1\, a\, \underline{\text{in}} \\
& \qquad \text{size}\, val_2\; \square_2
\end{array}
$$

However, there is still a problem; how do we provide the required proofs for $\square_1$ and $\square_2$? The solution, as with the *Prefl* predicate transformer used in **twice**, is to require additional predicate transformers as arguments for **fold**. We get the type of these predicate transformers simply by observing which properties we need to prove to complete the definition. The full definition is as follows:

$$\text{let} \quad \frac{
\begin{array}{l}
P \; : \; \forall n{:}\mathbb{N}.\; A\, n \rightarrow \mathbb{N} \rightarrow \star \quad\; fs \; : \; \mathbb{N} \rightarrow \mathbb{N} \rightarrow \mathbb{N} \\
Prefl \; : \; \forall n{:}\mathbb{N}.\, \forall a{:}A\, n.\, P\, n\, a\, n \\
Ptrans \; : \; \forall an{:}\mathbb{N}.\, \forall a{:}A\, an.\, \forall bn{:}\mathbb{N}.\, \forall b{:}A\, bn.\, \forall cn{:}\mathbb{N}.\, \forall dn{:}\mathbb{N}. \\
\qquad\qquad P\, bn\, b\, dn \rightarrow P\, an\, a\, (fs\, bn\, bn) \rightarrow P\, an\, a\, (fs\, cn\, dn) \\
f \; : \; A\, an' \rightarrow B\, bn' \rightarrow \mathcal{S}\, (n, v) \; : \; A.\, P\, n\, v\, (fs\, an'\, bn') \\
a \; : \; A\, an \quad\; xs \; : \; \text{List}_{\mathsf{S}}\, B\, xsn
\end{array}
}{
\begin{array}{l}
\mathbf{fold}\, P\, fs\, Prefl\, Ptrans\, f\, a\, xs \; : \; (\mathcal{S}\, (n, v) \; : \; A. \\
\qquad\qquad\qquad\qquad\qquad\qquad P\, n\, v\, (\mathbf{foldSize}\, fs\, an\, xs)))
\end{array}
}$$

$$
\begin{array}{ll}
\mathbf{fold}\, P\, fs\, Prefl\, Ptrans\, f\, a \quad \text{nil}_{\mathsf{S}} & \mapsto\; \text{size}\, a\, (Prefl\, a) \\
\mathbf{fold}\, P\, fs\, Prefl\, Ptrans\, f\, a\, (\text{cons}_{\mathsf{S}}\, x\, xs) \\
\quad \mapsto\; \underline{\text{let}}\, (\text{size}\, val_1\, p_1) = \mathbf{fold}\, P\, fs\, Prefl\, Ptrans\, f\, a\, xs\, \underline{\text{in}} \\
\qquad \underline{\text{let}}\, (\text{size}\, val_2\, p_2) = \mathbf{f}\, val_1\, a\, \underline{\text{in}} \\
\qquad \text{size}\, val_2\, (Ptrans\, p_1\, p_2)
\end{array}
$$

On applying **fold**, we are required to provide appropriate proof terms to instantiate *Prefl* and *Ptrans*. This is to be expected — it is only when we apply a higher order function that we know enough about its usage to expose concrete proof obligations.

4.5   Sum Types

An important class of function involves construction and case analysis on sum types. One example is the `Either` type, which represents a choice between two values in two separate types:

```
data Either a b = Left a | Right b
```

The `either` function implements a generic elimination of `Either`, and applies the appropriate function depending on which constructor was used to build the instance of `Either a b`:

```
either :: (a->c) -> (b->c) -> Either a b -> c
either f g (Left l) = f l
either f g (Right r) = g r
```

Again, there is a problem in representing this in a sized type system; there are two functions, f and g, only one of which will be applied depending on the value of the Either instance. To represent this with sized types we have to be conservative and assume a worst case, that the function which gives the larger size will be applied.

We can overcome this problem in our framework. To represent Either we take the size to be the size of the value which is stored:

$$\underline{\text{data}} \quad \frac{A, B \;:\; \mathbb{N} \to \star}{\text{Either}_S \; A \; B \;:\; \mathbb{N} \to \star} \quad \underline{\text{where}} \quad \frac{a \;:\; A \; an}{\text{Left}_S \; a \;:\; \text{Either}_S \; A \; B \; an}$$

$$\frac{b \;:\; B \; bn}{\text{Right}_S \; b \;:\; \text{Either}_S \; A \; B \; bn}$$

As with **fold**, we create a type level function **eitherS** which computes the size of the result of **either** given its input. We choose to use the same predicate for l, r and **either**, and define **either** as follows:

$$\underline{\text{let}} \quad \frac{\begin{array}{l} P \;:\; \forall n{:}\mathbb{N}. \; C \; n \to \mathbb{N} \to \star \\ ls \;:\; \mathbb{N} \to \mathbb{N} \quad l \;:\; A \; an \; \to \; \mathcal{S} \, (n, v) \;:\; C. \, P \, n \, v \, (ls \; an) \\ rs \;:\; \mathbb{N} \to \mathbb{N} \quad r \;:\; B \; bn \; \to \; \mathcal{S} \, (n, v) \;:\; C. \, P \, n \, v \, (rs \; bn) \\ x \;:\; \text{Either}_S \; A \; B \; xn \end{array}}{\text{either} \; P \; ls \; l \; rs \; r \; x \;:\; \mathcal{S} \, (n, v) \;:\; C. \, P \, n \, v \, (\text{eitherS} \; ls \; rs \; x)}$$

$$\text{either} \; p \; ls \; l \; rs \; r \; (\text{Left}_S \; a) \;\mapsto\; l \; a$$
$$\text{either} \; p \; ls \; l \; rs \; r \; (\text{Right}_S \; b) \;\mapsto\; r \; b$$

It is possible that we could use different predicates for l and r if **eitherS** also computed an appropriate predicate for the return type. It simplifies the definition to require the same predicates, however, and if at the call site we want to use specific l and r with different predicates, it is possible to combine the predicates — if l's result satisfies predicate P and r's result satisfies predicate Q, then each satisfies predicate $P \vee Q$.

4.6 Summary

We have found that it is straightforward to translate a first order function into the TT framework by hand, simply by identifying an output size and the relationship it has with the input size. In the examples we have looked at, the required equational constraints can be satisfied using COQ's omega tactic.

Higher order functions present more difficulty, as we can not tell anything specific about size from the HOF itself. The examples we have given present a variety of such functions and show how we can overcome this difficulty. The approach we take for higher order functions is to associate the following with each function argument:

– A **size function** which computes the size of the result given the function's input. We can create this for any function by following the syntax tree of the source language function.

- A **size predicate** which specifies the property that the result size (i.e. the result of the size function) must satisfy. We assume that these are provided along with the source function, having been either specified by the user, or given by an external inference system.
- A number of **predicate transformers** which specify the properties the predicate must satisfy; we can generate these mechanically by observing the properties which need to be proved to complete the definition.

4.7 Towards an Automated Transformation

Having shown how to represent these functions in the framework, we need to consider how to automate the translation from the source language into TT; it is important to note that although the definitions of higher order functions look very complex in the TT framework, the programmer will never need to see these definitions.

We believe that the homogeneous framework we have chosen for TT programs will make automated construction straightforward. In most cases, all that is required is the traversal of the structure of the source program, managing Size structures and identifying proof obligations where necessary. In many cases even proof construction is automatable with the omega tactic (or even by simpler proof search methods). In more difficult cases, we envisage a theorem proving interface allowing the user to give hints.

To facilitate the construction of TT terms, we are building a theorem proving library[3] and equipping it with appropriate tactics. In particular, we have implemented tactics for management of the Size structure and identifying the required predicate transformers for higher order functions. Our system keeps track of remaining proof obligations, allowing these to be solved by the user or (in future) by an automated proof search tool such as the Omega calculator. The biggest difficulty we envisage is the presentation of useful diagnostics to the user when the automated tools are unable to solve a proof obligation, whether because the tools are not powerful enough, or because the theorem is unprovable.

5 Related Work

Other than our own work [24], we are aware of three main studies of formally bounded time and space behaviour in a functional setting [5,14,26]. All such approaches are based on restricted language constructs to ensure that bounds can be placed on time/ space usage, and require considerable programmer expertise to exploit effectively. In their proposal for Embedded ML, Hughes and Pareto [14] have combined the earlier *sized type system* [15] with the notion of *region types* [25] to give bounded space and termination for a first-order strict functional language [14]. This language is however restricted in a number of ways: most notably in not supporting higher-order functions, and in requiring the programmer to specify detailed memory usage through type specifications. The practicality of such a system is correspondingly reduced.

There is active research into programming with dependent types — [1] describes the rationale and gives an example of programming in EPIGRAM; [21] gives an example of

---

[3] Available from http://www.dcs.st-and.ac.uk/~eb/TT/

generic programming with dependent types. Augustsson and Carlsson have used dependent types to verify type correctness properties of an interpreter [3]. Xi and Pfenning have also exploited size properties of dependent types in DML for optimising array lookup [29], using dependent types to guarantee the bounds of an array. However, the form of dependent types permitted by DML is limited to a specific constraint domain (e.g. integers, for representing size, with their usual operations) so it is not possible to compute sizes in the type, as in our framework.

Crary and Weirich [7] have developed a dependent type system that provides an explicit upper bound on the number of steps needed to complete a computation. Space is conservatively bounded by the same bound as time. The language does support higher-order functions, although unlike our system their language of cost functions is limited to using a fixed set of operators. Grobauer's work [10] also applies dependent types, extracting time bounds for DML programs, although this is limited to first-order functions.

Hofmann and Jost have shown in [12] how to obtain bounds on heap space consumption of first-order functional programs based on linear types. They are extending these methods to deal with polymorphic and higher order functions, as described in Jost's forthcoming PhD thesis. Vasconcelos also describes methods which extend the basic sized type inference in his forthcoming PhD thesis, using a method based on abstract interpretation. Unlike our framework, these methods have the limitation that they do not allow bounds to depend on input data (as for example we have done with `either`, and may like to do in any case where we know an argument statically). However, these techniques complement our own work — our framework is intended to check externally specified size bounds. Furthermore our framework builds on these systems in that the bounds can be *programmer specified* as well as inferred, allowing resource bounded programs we would not otherwise be able to write (e.g. `either`, or higher order functions which do not admit a linear bound).

6   Conclusions

We have presented a flexible framework for describing and verifying size metrics for functional programs. By using a dependently typed core language, TT, we are able to make explicit the properties which a program must satisfy *in the type* and hence showing that a program satisfies those properties is simply a matter of typechecking. We have implemented these examples in the CoQ theorem prover; by using CoQ's `omega` tactic to construct proofs of the equational constraints required by the Size type automatically, we can see that in principle it should be possible to mechanise the construction of TT code from the source programs.

Within this framework, we have the flexibility to use any appropriate size metric, and to extend the language of constraints in order to be able to express more complex bounds, such as those which arise in higher order functions. The size bounds of a higher order function will often depend on its function arguments, and so having a rich language at the type level allows us to express size in terms of this. Although there are some difficulties here, as demonstrated in particular by the **fold** example, these can be overcome within the framework; the definitions of **fold** and **either** show how we can use type level computation to give a precise cost for higher order functions.

This paper documents the first stage of the design and implementation of a resource-safe intermediate language for multi-stage Hume programs — we have implemented several examples by hand within the framework. By doing so, and in particular by investigating more complex higher order functions such as **fold** and their applications, we hope to be able to derive a method for mechanically constructing TT terms from source language programs. If we wish to use TT as a core language for Hume programs, such a translation method is essential. Nonetheless, we believe that through implementing higher order functions by hand within the framework, we have identified the key features which will need to be considered by an automatic translation — specifically, the separation of a size function and predicate, and the generation of a size function for each source language function.

Acknowledgements

This work is generously supported by EPSRC grants GR/R70545 and EP/C001346/1 and by EU Framework VI IST-510255 (EmBounded).

References

1. T. Altenkirch, C. McBride, and J. McKinna. Why dependent types matter, 2005. Submitted for publication.
2. L. Augustsson. Cayenne — a language with dependent types. In *Proc. ACM SIGPLAN International Conf. on Functional Programming (ICFP '98)*, volume 34(1) of *ACM SIGPLAN Notices*, pages 239–250. ACM, June 1999.
3. L. Augustsson and M. Carlsson. An exercise in dependent types: A well-typed interpreter, 1999.
4. E. Brady. *Practical Implementation of a Dependently Typed Functional Programming Language*. PhD thesis, University of Durham, 2005.
5. R. Burstall. Inductively Defined Functions in Functional Programming Languages. Technical Report ECS-LFCS-87-25, Dept. of Comp. Sci., Univ. of Edinburgh, April 1987.
6. Coq Development Team. The Coq proof assistant — reference manual. http://coq.inria.fr/, 2004.
7. K. Crary and S. Weirich. Resource bound certification. In *the Symposium on Principles of Programming Languages (POPL '00)*, pages 184–198, N.Y., Jan. 19–21 2000. ACM Press.
8. H. B. Curry and R. Feys. *Combinatory Logic, volume 1*. North Holland, 1958.
9. P. Dybjer. Inductive families. *Formal Aspects of Computing*, 6(4):440–465, 1994.
10. B. Grobauer. *Topics in Semantics-based Program Manipluation*. PhD thesis, BRICS, Department of Computer Science, University of Aarhus, August 2001.
11. K. Hammond and G. Michaelson. Hume: a Domain-Specific Language for Real-Time Embedded Systems. In *Proc. Conf. Generative Programming and Component Engineering (GPCE '03)*, Lecture Notes in Computer Science. Springer-Verlag, 2003.
12. M. Hofmann and S. Jost. Static prediction of heap space usage for first-order functional programs. In *Proc. POPL 2003 — 2003 ACM Symp. on Principles of Programming Languages*, pages 185–197. ACM, 2003.

13. W. A. Howard. The formulae-as-types notion of construction. In J. P. Seldin and J. R. Hindley, editors, *To H.B.Curry: Essays on combinatory logic, lambda calculus and formalism.* Academic Press, 1980. A reprint of an unpublished manuscript from 1969.

14. R. Hughes and L. Pareto. Recursion and Dynamic Data Structures in Bounded Space: Towards Embedded ML Programming. In *Proc. 1999 ACM Intl. Conf. on Functional Programming (ICFP '99)*, pages 70–81, 1999.

15. R. Hughes, L. Pareto, and A. Sabry. Proving the correctness of reactive systems using sized types. In *Proc. ACM Symp. on Principles of Prog. Langs. (POPL '96)*. ACM Press, 1996.

16. Z. Luo. *Computation and Reasoning – A Type Theory for Computer Science.* International Series of Monographs on Computer Science. OUP, 1994.

17. Z. Luo and R. Pollack. LEGO proof development system: User's manual. Technical report, Department of Computer Science, University of Edinburgh, 1992.

18. C. McBride. *Dependently Typed Functional Programs and their proofs.* PhD thesis, University of Edinburgh, May 2000.

19. C. McBride. Epigram: Practical programming with dependent types. Lecture Notes, International Summer School on Advanced Functional Programming, 2004.

20. C. McBride and J. McKinna. The view from the left. *Journal of Functional Programming*, 14(1):69–111, 2004.

21. P. Morris, C. McBride, and T. Altenkirch. Exploring the regular tree types. In *Types for Proofs and Programs 2004*, 2005.

22. A. Mycroft and R. Sharp. A statically allocated parallel functional language. In *Automata, Languages and Programming*, pages 37–48, 2000.

23. W. Pugh. The Omega Test: a fast and practical integer programming algorithm for dependence analysis. *Communication of the ACM*, pages 102–114, 1992.

24. A. Rebón Portillo, K. Hammond, H.-W. Loidl, and P. Vasconcelos. A Sized Time System for a Parallel Functional Language (Revised). In *Proc. Implementation of Functional Langs.(IFL '02), Madrid, Spain*, number 2670 in Lecture Notes in Computer Science. Springer-Verlag, 2003.

25. M. Tofte and J.-P. Talpin. Region-based memory management. *Information and Computation*, 132(2):109–176, 1 Feb. 1997.

26. D. Turner. Elementary Strong Functional Programming. In *Proc. 1995 Symp. on Functl. Prog. Langs. in Education — FPLE '95*, LNCS. Springer-Verlag, Dec. 1995.

27. Z. Wan, W. Taha, and P. Hudak. Real-time FRP. In *Proc. Intl. Conf. on Functional Programming (ICFP '01)*, Florence, Italy, September 2001. ACM.

28. Z. Wan, W. Taha, and P. Hudak. Event-driven FRP. In *Proc. 4th. Intl. Sym. on Practical Aspects of Declarative Languages (PADL '02)*. ACM, Jan 2002.

29. H. Xi and F. Pfenning. Eliminating array bound checking through dependent types. In *Proceedings of ACM SIGPLAN Conference on Programming Language Design and Implementation*, pages 249–257, Montreal, June 1998.

Accurate Step Counting

Catherine Hope and Graham Hutton

School of Computer Science and IT
University of Nottingham, UK
{cvh,gmh}@cs.nott.ac.uk

Abstract. Starting with an evaluator for a language, an abstract machine for the same language can be mechanically derived using successive program transformations. This has relevance to studying both the time and space properties of programs because these can be estimated by counting transitions of the abstract machine and measuring the size of the additional data structures needed, such as environments and stacks. In this paper we will use this process to derive a function that accurately counts the number of steps required to evaluate expressions in a simple language, and illustrate this function with a range of examples.

1 Introduction

The problem of reasoning about intensional properties of functional programs, such as the time requirements, is a long-running one. It is complicated by different evaluation strategies and sharing of expressions, meaning that some parts of a program may not be run or only partially so. One of the issues involved in reasoning about the amount of time a program will take to complete is what to count as an atomic unit in evaluation, or an evaluation step.

An evaluator is usually an implementation of the denotational semantics [13] of a language — it evaluates an expression based on the meaning of its sub-expressions. This level of understanding helps us reason about extensional properties of the language, but it doesn't say anything about the underlying way that the evaluation is taking place. By contrast, an operational semantics [10] shows us the method that is being used to evaluate an expression, and the conventional approach is to use this to measure the number of steps that are required. This, however, may not be very accurate because what is usually being measured is β-reductions, each of which may take arbitrarily long. An example of this approach is using the tick monad [15], which counts β-reductions.

It is proposed that a more realistic measure would be to count transitions in an actual machine. The idea is to get more detailed information than by just counting β-reductions, but still have a principled way of obtaining this information. This would not be as accurate as actual time measurements, but would provide a useful half-way house between these two approaches. What is needed is a justification that the machine correctly implements the evaluation semantics and a way to reflect the number of steps required by the machine back to the semantic level.

A. Butterfield, C. Grelck, and F. Huch (Eds.): IFL 2005, LNCS 4015, pp. 91–105, 2006.

Recently Danvy *et al* have explored the basis of abstract machines, and the process of deriving them from evaluators [1, 2, 3, 5]. This process uses, in particular, two program transformation techniques: transformation to continuation passing style, to make order of evaluation explicit; and defunctionalization, to eliminate the consequent use of higher-order functions.

In this paper, we will apply this process to the problem of accurately counting evaluation steps. In brief, this consists of introducing a simple language in which to write expressions, an evaluator for this language, and then deriving a corresponding abstract machine using successive program transformations. Simple step counting is then added to the machine, by threading and incrementing a counter that measures the number of transitions.

The next stage is to apply the same process but in the reverse order, resulting in an evaluator that additionally counts the number of steps, directly corresponding to the number of transitions of the underlying abstract machine. Finally, a direct step counting function will be calculated from this evaluator and will be used to reason about evaluation of some example computations expressed in the language.

A particular aspect of our derivation process is that the program at each stage is *calculated* directly from a specification of its behaviour [8]. All the programs are written in Haskell [9], but no specific features of this language are used, so they may be easily adapted to other functional languages.

2   A Simple Language

To start with we will consider a simple language with expressions consisting of integers and addition, and with integers as values:

> **data** *Expr* = *Add Expr Expr* | *Val Int*
> **type** *Value* = *Int*

Although this language is not powerful enough to be used to analyse the time requirements of any interesting computations, it will be sufficient to show the derivation process without over-complication. An extended language will be presented later to look at some example functions.

2.1   Evaluator

The initial evaluator takes an expression and evaluates it to a value:

> *eval*   :: *Expr* → *Value*
> *eval* (*Val v*)   = *v*
> *eval* (*Add x y*) = *eval x* + *eval y*

That is, evaluating an integer value returns that integer, and evaluating an addition evaluates both sides of the addition to an integer and then adds them together. The order of evaluation is not specified at this level but will be determined by the semantics of the underlying language; in particular, when the expression is an addition, *Add x y*, the evaluation of the *x* or *y* may occur first.

2.2   Tail-Recursive Evaluator

Our aim is to turn the evaluator into an *abstract machine*, a term-rewriting system that makes explicit the step-by-step process by which evaluation can be performed. More precisely, we seek to construct an abstract machine implemented in Haskell as a first-order, tail-recursive function.

The evaluator is already first order, but it is not tail-recursive. It can be made so by transforming it to continuation passing style (CPS) [11]. A continuation is a function that represents the rest of a computation; this makes the evaluation order of the arguments explicit, so intermediate results need to be ordered using the continuation. A program can be transformed in to CPS by redefining it to take an extra argument, a function which is applied to the result of the original one. In our case, the continuation function will take an argument of type *Value* and its result is a *Value*:

type $Con = Value \rightarrow Value$

The new tail-recursive evaluator can be calculated from the old one by using the specification:

$evalTail$ $:: Expr \rightarrow Con \rightarrow Value$
$evalTail\ e\ c = c\ (eval\ e)$

That is, the new evaluator has the same behaviour as simply applying the continuation to the result of the original evaluator. The definition of this function can be calculated by performing induction on the structure of the expression, e.

Case : $e = Val\ v$

$\quad evalTail\ (Val\ v)\ c$
$= \quad$ { specification }
$\quad c\ (eval\ v)$
$= \quad$ { definition of $eval$ }
$\quad c\ v$

Case : $e = Add\ x\ y$

$\quad evalTail\ (Add\ x\ y)\ c$
$= \quad$ { specification }
$\quad c\ (eval\ (Add\ x\ y))$
$= \quad$ { definition of $eval$ }
$\quad c\ (eval\ x + eval\ y)$
$= \quad$ { reverse β-reduction, abstract over $eval\ x$ }
$\quad (\lambda m \rightarrow c\ (m + eval\ y))\ (eval\ x)$
$= \quad$ { inductive assumption for x }
$\quad evalTail\ x\ (\lambda m \rightarrow c\ (m + eval\ y))$
$= \quad$ { reverse β-reduction, abstract over $eval\ y$ }
$\quad evalTail\ x\ (\lambda m \rightarrow (\lambda n \rightarrow c\ (m + n))\ (eval\ y))$
$= \quad$ { inductive assumption for y }
$\quad evalTail\ x\ (\lambda m \rightarrow evalTail\ y\ (\lambda n \rightarrow c\ (m + n)))$

In conclusion, we have calculated the following recursive definition:

$$evalTail \qquad\qquad :: Expr \rightarrow Con \rightarrow Value$$
$$evalTail\ (Val\ v) \quad c = c\ v$$
$$evalTail\ (Add\ x\ y)\ c = evalTail\ x\ (\lambda m \rightarrow$$
$$evalTail\ y\ (\lambda n \rightarrow c\ (m+n)))$$

In the case when the expression is an integer the continuation is simply applied to the integer value. In the addition case, the first argument to the addition is evaluated first, with the result being passed in to a continuation. The second expression argument is then evaluated inside the continuation, with its result being passed in to an inner continuation. Both integer results are added together in the body of this function and the original continuation is applied to the result.

The evaluator is now tail recursive, in that the right hand side is a direct recursive call and there is nothing to be done after the call returns. In making the evaluator tail-recursive we have introduced an explicit evaluation order: the evaluation of the addition now has to occur in left-to-right order.

The semantics of the original evaluation function can be recovered by substituting in the identity function for the continuation:

$$eval\ e = evalTail\ e\ (\lambda v \rightarrow v)$$

2.3   Abstract Machine

The next step is to make the evaluator first order. This is done by defunctionalizing the continuations [11]. At the moment, the continuations are functions of the type $Value \rightarrow Value$, but the whole function space is not required: the continuation functions are only created in three different ways. Defunctionalization is performed by looking at all places where functions are made and replacing them with a new data structure that takes as arguments any free variables required.

The data structure required is as follows,

$$\textbf{data}\ Cont = Top \qquad\qquad \text{for the initial continuation } (\lambda v \rightarrow v)$$
$$\mid AddL\ Cont\ Expr \quad \text{for } (\lambda m \rightarrow evalTail\ y\ (...))$$
$$\mid AddR\ Value\ Cont \quad \text{for } (\lambda n \rightarrow c\ (m+n))$$

The reason for the constructor names is that the data structure is the structure of evaluation contexts for the language [6]. It could alternatively be viewed as a stack, pushing expressions still to be evaluated and values to be saved.

To recover the functionality of the continuation we define an *apply* function which has the same semantics for each instance of the continuation function:

$$apply \qquad\qquad :: Cont \rightarrow Con$$
$$apply\ Top \qquad\quad = \lambda v \rightarrow v$$
$$apply\ (AddR\ m\ c) = \lambda n \rightarrow apply\ c\ (m+n)$$
$$apply\ (AddL\ c\ y)\ \ = \lambda m \rightarrow evalTail\ y\ (apply\ (AddL\ c\ m))$$

We now seek to construct a new evaluator, *evalMach*, that behaves in the same way as *evalTail*, except that it uses representations of continuations, rather than real continuations; that is, we require *evalMach e c = evalTail e (apply c)*. From this specification, the definition of *evalMach* can be calculated by induction on *e*:

Case : *e = Val v*

$$
\begin{array}{ll}
& evalMach~(Val~v)~c \\
= & \{~\text{specification}~\} \\
& evalTail~(Val~v)~(apply~c) \\
= & \{~\text{definition of } evalTail~\} \\
& apply~c~v
\end{array}
$$

Case : *e = Add x y*

$$
\begin{array}{ll}
& evalMach~(Add~x~y)~c \\
= & \{~\text{specification}~\} \\
& evalTail~(Add~x~y)~(apply~c) \\
= & \{~\text{definition of } evalTail~\} \\
& evalTail~x~(\lambda m \rightarrow evalTail~y~(\lambda n \rightarrow apply~c~(m+n))) \\
= & \{~\text{definition of } apply~\} \\
& evalTail~x~(\lambda m \rightarrow evalTail~y~(apply~(AddR~m~c))) \\
= & \{~\text{definition of } apply~\} \\
& evalTail~x~(apply~(AddL~c~y)) \\
= & \{~\text{inductive assumption, for } x~\} \\
& evalMach~x~(AddL~c~y)
\end{array}
$$

We have now calculated the following recursive function:

$$
\begin{array}{ll}
evalMach & :: Expr \rightarrow Cont \rightarrow Value \\
evalMach~(Val~v) & c = apply~c~v \\
evalMach~(Add~x~y)~c & = evalMach~x~(AddL~c~y)
\end{array}
$$

Evaluating an integer calls the *apply* function with the current context and the integer value. Evaluating an addition evaluates the first argument and stores the second with the current context using the *AddL* constructor.

Moving the λ-abstracted terms to the left and applying the specification in the *AddL* case, gives the following revised definition for *apply*:

$$
\begin{array}{ll}
apply & :: Cont \rightarrow Value \rightarrow Value \\
apply~Top & v = v \\
apply~(AddR~m~c)~n & = apply~c~(m+n) \\
apply~(AddL~c~y)~m & = evalMach~y~(AddR~m~c)
\end{array}
$$

The *apply* function takes a context and a value and returns the value if the context is *Top*. When the context is *AddR* this represents the case when both sides of the addition have been evaluated, so the results are added together and the current context is applied to the result. The *AddL* context represents evaluating the second argument to the addition, so the *evalMach* function is called and the result from the first argument and the current context saved using the *AddR* context.

The original semantics can be recovered by passing in the equivalent of the initial continuation, the *Top* constructor:

$eval\ e\ =\ evalMach\ e\ Top$

2.4   Step Counting Machine

The number of time steps required to evaluate an expression is to be measured by counting the number of transitions of the abstract machine. The abstract machine derived can be simply modified by adding a step count that is incremented each time a transition, a function call to *evalMach* or *apply*, is made. The step count is added as an accumulator, rather than just incrementing the count that the recursive call returns, so that it is still an abstract machine.

It is relevant here to note that this is just one possible derivation to produce an abstract machine. Different abstract machines may be generated by applying different program transformations, as demonstrated in [5].

$$
\begin{array}{lll}
\textbf{type } Step & = Int \\
stepMach & :: (Expr, Step) \rightarrow Cont \rightarrow (Value, Step) \\
stepMach\ (Val\ v, s)\quad c & = apply'\ c\ (v, s + 1) \\
stepMach\ (Add\ x\ y, s)\ c & = stepMach\ (x, s + 1)\ (AddL\ c\ y) \\[6pt]
apply' & :: Cont \rightarrow (Value, Step) \rightarrow (Value, Step) \\
apply'\ Top & (v, s) = (v, s + 1) \\
apply'\ (AddL\ c\ y) & (m, s) = stepMach\ (y, s + 1)\ (AddR\ m\ c) \\
apply'\ (AddR\ m\ c) & (n, s) = apply'\ c\ (m + n, s + 1)
\end{array}
$$

In this case we are only counting the machine transitions and the actual addition of the integers is defined to happen instantly, though this could be extended by introducing an additional factor that represents the number of steps to perform an addition.

The evaluation function now returns a pair, where the first part is the evaluated value, and the second is the number of steps taken, which is initialised to zero. Therefore, the semantics of the original evaluator can be recovered by taking the first part of the pair returned:

$eval\ e\ =\ fst\ (stepMach\ e\ 0\ Top)$

2.5   Step Counting Tail-Recursive Evaluator

The aim now is to derive a function that counts the number of steps required to evaluate an expression. The specification for this is the second part of the pair returned by the abstract machine:

$steps\ e\ =\ snd\ (stepMach\ (e, 0)\ Top)$

The first stage in the reverse process is to refunctionalize the representation of the continuation. The original continuation was a function of type $Value \rightarrow Value$, so the type of the new one will be $(Value, Step) \rightarrow (Value, Step)$.

$\textbf{type } Con' = (Value, Step) \rightarrow (Value, Step)$

Again, this can be calculated by induction on e, from the following specification:

$$stepTail\ (e, s)\ (apply'\ c') = evalMach\ (e, s)\ c'$$

The refunctionalized version is:

$$
\begin{aligned}
&stepTail && :: (Expr, Step) \to Con' \to (Value, Step)\\
&stepTail\ (Val\ v) && s\ c = c\ (v, s+1)\\
&stepTail\ (Add\ x\ y)\ s\ c = stepTail\ x\ (s+1)\ (\lambda(m, s') \to\\
&\qquad\qquad\qquad\qquad\qquad\qquad stepTail\ y\ (s'+1)\ (\lambda(n, s'') \to c\ (m+n, s''+1)))
\end{aligned}
$$

The step counting semantics can be redefined as:

$$steps\ e = snd\ (stepTail\ (e, 0)\ ((v, s) \to (v, s+1)))$$

Now, the same program transformations are performed in the reverse order to derive an evaluator that counts steps at the evaluator level, corresponding to the number of transitions of the abstract machine.

2.6 Step Counting Evaluator with Accumulator

The step counting evaluator can be transformed from CPS back to direct style by calculation, using the following specification to remove the continuation:

$$c\ (stepAcc\ (e, s)) = stepTail\ (e, s)\ c$$

The resulting evaluator is:

$$
\begin{aligned}
&stepAcc && :: (Expr, Step) \to (Value, Step)\\
&stepAcc\ (Val\ v) && s = (v, s+1)\\
&stepAcc\ (Add\ x\ y)\ s = \textbf{let }(m, s') = stepAcc\ (x, s+1)\\
&\qquad\qquad\qquad\qquad\qquad\ (n, s'') = stepAcc\ (y, s'+1)\\
&\qquad\qquad\qquad\textbf{in }(m+n, s''+1)
\end{aligned}
$$

The new step counting function becomes:

$$steps\ e = snd\ (stepAcc\ (e, 0)) + 1$$

2.7 Step Counting Evaluator

At the moment the step counting evaluator treats the step count as an accumulator. This can be removed, by calculating a new function without one, using the specification:

$$
\begin{aligned}
stepEval\ e = &\textbf{let }(v, s') = stepAcc\ (e, s)\\
&\textbf{in }(v, s' - s)
\end{aligned}
$$

Again, this can be calculated by induction over the structure of the expression, to give the new step counting evaluator:

$$
\begin{aligned}
&stepEval && :: Expr \to (Value, Step)\\
&stepEval\ (Val\ v) && = (v, 1)\\
&stepEval\ (Add\ x\ y) = \textbf{let }(m, s) = stepEval\ x\\
&\qquad\qquad\qquad\qquad\quad (n, s') = stepEval\ y\\
&\qquad\qquad\qquad\textbf{in }(m+n, s+s'+3)
\end{aligned}
$$

The semantics of the *steps* function can be expressed as:

$$steps\ e = snd\ (stepEval\ e) + 1$$

2.8   Step Counting Function

The final stage is to calculate a standalone steps function. This will take an expression and return the number of steps to evaluate the expression, calling the original evaluator when the result of evaluation is required. The resulting function can be produced by routine calculation:

$$
\begin{aligned}
steps\ e &= steps'\ e + 1\\
steps'\ (Val\ v) &= 1\\
steps'\ (Add\ x\ y) &= steps'\ x + steps'\ y + 3
\end{aligned}
$$

The derived *steps* function shows that that evaluation of an expression is an auxiliary function *steps'* plus a constant one. This increment operation at the end comes from the transition in the abstract machine that evaluates the initial (*Top*) context. In *steps'*, the number of steps to evaluate an integer is a constant one, and the number of steps to evaluate an addition is the number of steps to evaluate each argument plus a constant three. This is more accurate because we now see the overhead of each addition: if we were counting β-reductions then this would only have been a single step of evaluation.

3   Extending the Language

We've now shown the derivation process for a small test language, but this language is not powerful enough to express computations that have interesting time behaviour. We now extend it with the untyped λ-calculus (variables, abstraction and application), lists and recursion over lists in the form of fold-right.

These could have been expressed directly in λ-calculus, for example by using Church encoding instead of integers, but this would introduce an unrealistic overhead in evaluation. Moreover, a more general recursion operator could have been introduced instead of fold-right, but for simplicity one tailored to our data structure, lists, is sufficient. Using fold-right will also simplify the process of reasoning about time properties, just as it has proved useful for reasoning about extensional ones [7].

The language is implemented as the following Haskell data type:

> **data** *Expr* = *Var String* | *Abs String Expr* | *App Expr Expr*
> | *Add Expr Expr* | *Val Value*
> | *Cons Expr Expr* | *Foldr Expr Expr Expr*
>
> **data** *Value* = *Const Int* | *ConsV Value Value* | *Nil* | *Clo String Expr Env*

That is, an expression is either a variable, abstraction, application of two expressions, addition of two expressions, fold-right over an expression (where the function and empty list-case arguments are both expressions), a list containing further expressions or a value. In turn, a value is either an integer, list containing further values or a closure (an abstraction paired with an environment containing bindings for all free variables in the abstraction).

The data type differentiates between expressions and values, in particular lists that contain unevaluated and evaluated expressions, so that there is no need to iterate repeatedly over the list to check if each element is fully evaluated, which would introduce an artificial evaluation overhead.

The primitive functions, such as *Add* and *Foldr*, are implemented as fully saturated, in that they take their arguments all at once. The main reason for this is to make it easier to define what a value is: if they were introduced as constants then, for example, *App Add* 1 would be a value, since it cannot be further evaluated. This doesn't affect what can be expressed in the language; partial application can be expressed by using abstractions, so an equivalent expression would be *Abs* "x" (*Add* 1 (*Var* "x")), which would be evaluated to a closure.

Note that, for simplicity, the language has not been provided with a type system. Rather, in this article we assume that only well-formed expressions are considered.

4   Evaluator

For simplicity, we will consider evaluation using the call-by-value strategy, where arguments to functions are evaluated before the function is applied. Evaluation is performed using an environment, that is used to look up what a variable is bound to. This avoids having to substitute in expressions for variables, which is complicated by the need to deal with avoiding name-capture. Under call-by-value evaluation arguments are evaluated before function application, so variables will be bound to a value. The environment is represented as a list of pairs:

type $Env = [(String, Value)]$

The initial evaluator is given below:

$$
\begin{array}{ll}
eval & :: Expr \to Env \to Value \\
eval \ (Val \ v) & env = v \\
eval \ (Var \ x) & env = fromJust \ (lookup \ x \ env) \\
eval \ (Abs \ x \ e) & env = Clo \ x \ e \ env \\
eval \ (App \ f \ e) & env = \textbf{let} \ Clo \ x \ e' \ env' = eval \ f \ env \\
& \qquad\qquad v = eval \ e \ env \\
& \qquad \textbf{in} \ eval \ e' \ ((x, v) : env') \\
eval \ (Add \ x \ y) & env = \textbf{let} \ Const \ m = eval \ x \ env \\
& \qquad\qquad Const \ n = eval \ y \ env \\
& \qquad \textbf{in} \ Const \ (m + n)
\end{array}
$$

$eval \ (Cons \ x \ xs) \quad env = ConsV \ (eval \ x \ env) \ (eval \ xs \ env)$
$eval \ (Foldr \ f \ v \ xs) \ env = \textbf{case} \ eval \ xs \ env \ \textbf{of}$
$\qquad Nil \to eval \ v \ env$
$\qquad ConsV \ z \ zs \to \textbf{let} \ f' = eval \ f \ env$
$\qquad\qquad\qquad\qquad\qquad x = eval \ (Foldr \ (Val \ f') \ v \ (Val \ zs)) \ env$
$\qquad\qquad\qquad \textbf{in} \ eval \ (App \ (App \ (Val \ f') \ (Val \ z)) \ (Val \ x)) \ []$

That is, values are already evaluated, so they are simply returned. Variables are evaluated by returning the value the variable is bound to in the environment. Under the call-by-value strategy, evaluation is not performed under λ-terms, so abstractions are turned in to values by pairing them with the current environment to make a closure. An application, *App f e*, is evaluated by first evaluating *f* to an abstraction, then evaluating the body of the abstraction, with the environment extended with the variable bound to the value that *e* evaluates to.

Addition is performed by first evaluating both sides to an integer and then adding them together. This will give another integer result and so does not require further evaluation. Evaluating a *Cons* consists of evaluating the first and second arguments (the head and the tail of the list) and then re-assembling them using the *ConsV* constructor to make an evaluated list.

Evaluation of the *Foldr* case proceeds by first evaluating the list argument and doing case analysis. If the list is *Nil* then the result is the evaluation of the second argument, *v*. In the non-empty case, first the function argument is evaluated, then the fold-right applied to the tail of the list, and finally the function is applied to the head of the list and the result of folding the tail of the list. This evaluation is performed with an empty environment, since all the expressions are values at that point.

The evaluation of the fold-right could have been specified in different ways. The completely call-by-value way would be to evaluate the arguments in left to right order, so that the first two arguments are evaluated before the list argument. However, for the *Nil* list argument case, the function argument to *Foldr* is evaluated even though it is not required. The approach in the evaluator is to evaluate the list argument first to allow pattern matching and then evaluate the other arguments depending on what the list evaluated to. So when the list evaluates to *Nil* only the second argument to *Foldr* is evaluated. The justification not to use the purely call-by-value way is that it would introduce some artificial behaviour of the *Foldr* function. When the λ-calculus is extended with a conditional function, for example, it is not implemented to expand both branches under call-by-value evaluation, but more efficiently by evaluating the condition first and then one branch depending on the value of the condition. In practice, this has little effect because the function supplied to the fold is often an abstraction and therefore is already evaluated.

5   Complete Function

Performing the derivation process for this extended language (which, as previously, proceeds by calculation) yields the following *steps* function:

$$
\begin{aligned}
steps\ e &= steps'\ e\ [\,]+1 \\
\quad steps'\ (Val\ v)\quad &env = 1 \\
\quad steps'\ (Var\ x)\quad &env = 1 \\
\quad steps'\ (Abs\ x\ e)\quad &env = 1 \\
\quad steps'\ (App\ f\ e)\quad &env = \textbf{let}\ (Clo\ x\ e'\ env') = eval\ f\ env \\
&\qquad\qquad\quad v = eval\ e\ env
\end{aligned}
$$

$$\mathbf{in}\ steps'\ f\ env + steps'\ e\ env + $$
$$steps'\ e'\ ((x,v):env') + 3$$

$$steps'\ (Add\ x\ y)\qquad env = steps'\ x\ env + steps'\ y\ env + 3$$
$$steps'\ (Cons\ x\ xs)\qquad env = steps'\ x\ env + steps'\ xs\ env + 3$$
$$steps'\ (Foldr\ f\ v\ xs)\ env = steps'\ xs\ env + \mathbf{case}\ eval\ xs\ env\ \mathbf{of}$$
$$\quad Nil \rightarrow steps'\ v\ env + 2$$
$$\quad ConsV\ y\ ys \rightarrow \mathbf{let}\ f' = Val\ (eval\ f\ env)$$
$$\quad\qquad x = Val\ (eval\ (Foldr\ (Val\ f')\ v\ (Val\ ys))\ env)$$
$$\quad\qquad \mathbf{in}\ steps'\ f\ env + steps'\ (Foldr\ (Val\ f')\ v\ (Val\ ys))\ env + $$
$$\quad\qquad\qquad steps'\ (App\ (App\ f'\ (Val\ y))\ x)\ [\,] + 4$$

As mentioned earlier, the derived function has calls to the original evaluator, where the result of evaluation is required. For example, in the *Foldr* case, a case analysis has to be performed on the evaluated third argument, to know if it is empty or not, and so whether to supply the v argument, or to keep folding.

We want to be able to reason about how the time requirements of some example functions depends on the size of the arguments to the function. In the case of functions defined using fold-right, it would be easier to reason about the time usage if it was expressed as a function over the size of the list, rather than as a recursive function — the *steps* function above the *Foldr* case makes a recursive call to fold the tail of the list. This can naturally be expressed as a fold-right over the value list data structure, defined as:

$$foldrVal\qquad\qquad\qquad :: (Value \rightarrow b \rightarrow b) \rightarrow b \rightarrow Value \rightarrow b$$
$$foldrVal\ f\ v\ Nil\qquad\quad = v$$
$$foldrVal\ f\ v\ (ConsV\ x\ xs) = f\ x\ (foldrVal\ f\ v\ xs)$$

Also, if the number of steps to apply the function f to two arguments does not depend on the value of the arguments, such as adding two expressions, then a useful further simplification is to express this as a function over the length of the list argument supplied, defined as:

$$lengthVal = foldrVal\ (\lambda\_\ n \rightarrow n + 1)\ 0$$

6   Example Functions

We can now use the derived *steps* function to look at some examples. Each step counting function produced was simplified by hand and then QuickCheck [4] was used to verify that the result produced was equal to the original function, to check that no errors had been introduced during simplification.

6.1   Summing a List

Summing a list of integers can be expressed using fold-right:

$$sum\ [\,]\qquad\ = 0$$
$$sum\ (x:xs) = x + sum\ xs \qquad \Leftrightarrow \qquad sum\ xs = foldr\ (+)\ 0\ xs$$

The fold-right definition replaces each list constructor (:) with +, and the [] at the end of the list with 0, the unit of addition. First we translate the definition of *sum* into the language syntax and then call the *steps* function on the application of *sum* to an argument. The number of steps required to evaluate applying the *sum* function to a list of integers, *xs*, is given below:

$$steps\ (App\ sum\ (Val\ xs)) = 21 * (length\ Val\ xs) + 10$$

The function can be expressed as a length because the steps required to evaluate the addition of two values is a constant. The step count is a constant multiplied by the length of the list argument plus a constant amount; it is directly proportional to the length of the list argument. Though, of more interest is that we can see the constant factors involved in the evaluation.

6.2   Sum with an Accumulator

An alternative definition of *sum* is to use an accumulator; the fold-right is used to generate a function which is applied to the identity function in the empty list case, and in the non-empty case adds the head of the list to the accumulator.

$$
\begin{array}{ll}
sumAcc\ []\ a & = a \\
sumAcc\ (x:xs)\ a = sumAcc\ xs\ (a+x)
\end{array}
\quad\Leftrightarrow\quad
\begin{array}{l}
sumAcc\ xs = foldr\ f\ id\ xs\ 0 \\
\textbf{where}\ f\ x\ g\ a = g\ (a+x)
\end{array}
$$

Using an accumulator could potentially save on space, because additions could be performed without having to expand the whole list first. It would be useful to know what effect an accumulator has on the number of steps taken.

Translating the accumulator version and applying *steps* gives a result of the same form, linear on the length of the list, but the constant values are larger, because there is an additional overhead in evaluating the extra abstractions:

$$steps\ (App\ sumAcc\ (Val\ xs)) = 26 * (length\ Val\ xs) + 15$$

6.3   Concatenation

Concatenating a list of lists can be defined by folding the *append* function over the list, and *append* can also be expressed as a fold-right:

$$
\begin{array}{ll}
concat\ xs & = foldr\ append\ []\ xs \\
append\ xs\ ys & = foldr\ (:)\ ys\ xs
\end{array}
$$

First we need to analyse the *append* function. The number of steps to evaluate *append* applied to two list arguments is as follows:

$$steps\ (App\ (App\ append\ (Val\ xs))\ (Val\ ys)) = 21 * (length\ Val\ xs) + 15$$

So the number of steps to evaluate an *append* is proportional to the length of the first list argument. The step count of the *concat* function can now be calculated using this function. With the step count from the *append* function inlined, the resulting *steps* function is:

$$steps\ (App\ concat\ (Val\ xss)) = foldr\ Val\ f\ 10\ xss$$
$$\textbf{where}\ f\ ys\ s = 21 * (length\ Val\ ys) + 20 + s$$

The number of steps required in evaluation is the sum of the steps taken to apply the *append* function to each element in the list. If the argument to *concat* is a list where all the list elements are of the same length (so the number of steps taken in applying the *append* function will always be constant), then this can be simplified to:

$$steps \ (App \ concat \ (Val \ xss)) = 20 + \textbf{case} \ xss \ \textbf{of}$$
$$Nil \to 0$$
$$Cons V \ ys \ yss \to (length \ Val \ xss) * (21 * (length \ Val \ ys))$$

The number of steps is now proportional to the length of the input list multiplied by the number of steps to evaluate appending an element of the list, which is proportional to the length of that element.

6.4   Reversing a List

Reversing a list can be expressed directly as a fold-right by appending the reversed tail of the list to the head element made in to a singleton list:

$$\begin{array}{ll} reverse \ [] & = [] \\ reverse \ (x : xs) & = reverse \ xs \ \texttt{++} \ [x] \end{array} \qquad \Leftrightarrow \qquad \begin{array}{l} reverse \ xs = foldr \ f \ [] \ xs \\ \textbf{where} \ f \ x \ xs = xs \ \texttt{++} \ [x] \end{array}$$

Translating the definition of *reverse* in to the language syntax and applying the *steps* function gives the step count function: The steps function for *reverse* is

$$steps \ (App \ reverse \ (Val \ xs)) = fst \ (foldr \ Val \ g \ (10, Nil) \ xs)$$
$$\textbf{where} \ g \ z \ (s, zs) = (s + 21 * (length \ Val \ zs) + 34,$$
$$eval \ (App \ (App \ append \ (Val \ zs)) \ (Val \ (Cons V \ z \ Nil))) \ [])$$

dependent on the steps required to perform the *append* function for each element, which is proportional to length of the first argument to *append*. The size of this argument is increased by one each time, so the function is a sum up to the length of the list:

$$10 + \sum_{x=0}^{length \ xs - 1} 21x + 34$$

Expanding this sum gives the following expression:

$$10 + 34 * (length \ xs) + \frac{21 * (length \ xs - 1) * (length \ xs)}{2} \leqslant c \ (length \ xs)^2$$

This is less than a constant multiplied by the square of the length of the list, for example when $c = 11$ for all lists of length greater than 47. This means that the time requirements are quadratic on the length of the list [14].

6.5   Fast Reverse

The reverse function can also be expressed using an accumulator:

$$\begin{array}{ll} fastrev \ [] \ a & = a \\ fastrev \ (x : xs) \ a & = fastrev \ xs \ (x : a) \end{array} \qquad \Leftrightarrow \qquad \begin{array}{l} fastrev \ xs = foldr \ f \ id \ xs \ 0 \\ \textbf{where} \ f \ x \ g \ a = g \ (x : a) \end{array}$$

This definition should have better time properties because, as shown above, the steps required in evaluating the *append* function is proportional to the length of the first argument, so appending the tail of the list would be inefficient. The *steps* function produced for the accumulator version is directly proportional to the length of the list:

$$steps\ (App\ fastrev\ (Val\ xs)) = 26 * (length\,Val\ xs) + 15$$

7   Conclusion and Further Work

We have presented a process that takes an evaluator for a language, and derives a function that gives an accurate count of the number of steps required to evaluate expressions using an abstract machine for the language. Moreover, all the steps in the derivation process are purely calculational, in that the required function at each stage is calculated directly from a specification of its desired behaviour.

Using an extended λ-calculus under call-by-value evaluation, the examples in the previous section give the expected complexity results, but also show the constants involved. This is useful to know because of the additional overheads that functions of the same complexity may have, for example in summing a list with and without an accumulator. They also show the boundaries at which one function with a lower growth rate but larger constants becomes quicker than another, for example in the two different definitions of the reverse function.

Ultimately, the most accurate information is to do real timing of programs. The approach taken in the profiler [12] that is distributed with the Glasgow Haskell Compiler, is similar to that here, in that abstract machines are used to bridge the gap between a big-step cost semantics and a small-step implementation. A regular clock interrupt is used to collect time information and assign to the costs of functions. However, this is a profiler, and we want to be able to express costs as a function over the arguments supplied, and not just in terms of hard time measurements. The thesis of this paper is that we can obtain this useful information relatively easily.

This work could be extended by considering more complicated evaluation strategies, such as call-by-name or lazy evaluation. It would also be interesting to apply the same technique to look at the space requirements for functions, by measuring the size of the additional data structures produced at the abstract machine level. Finally, a useful addition to this work would be to develop a calculus to automate deriving the step functions.

Acknowledgement

Finally, the authors would like to thank the anonymous referees for their comments and suggestions, which have considerably improved the paper.

References

[1] Mads Sig Ager. From natural semantics to abstract machines. In *Logic Based Program Synthesis and Transformation, 14th International Symposium (LOPSTR 2004), Revised Selected Papers.*

[2] Mads Sig Ager, Dariusz Biernacki, Olivier Danvy, and Jan Midtgaard. A functional correspondence between evaluators and abstract machines. Technical Report RS-03-13, March 2003. 28 pp. Appears in , pages 8–19.

[3] Mads Sig Ager, Olivier Danvy, and Jan Midtgaard. A functional correspondence between call-by-need evaluators and lazy abstract machines. *Information Processing Letters*, 90(5):223–232, 2004. Extended version available as the technical report BRICS-RS-04-3.

[4] Koen Claessen and John Hughes. Quickcheck: a lightweight tool for random testing of haskell programs. In *ICFP*, pages 268–279, 2000.

[5] Olivier Danvy. A rational deconstruction of Landin's SECD machine. Technical Report RS-03-33, October 2003.

[6] Olivier Danvy. On evaluation contexts, continuations, and the rest of the computation. Number CSR-04-1, pages 13–23, Birmingham B15 2TT, United Kingdom, 2004. Invited talk.

[7] Graham Hutton. A Tutorial on the Universality and Expressiveness of Fold. *Journal of Functional Programming*, 9(4):355–372, July 1999.

[8] Graham Hutton and Joel Wright. Calculating an Exceptional Machine. To appear in the Proceedings of the Fifth Symposium on Trends in Functional Programming, 2005.

[9] S. Peyton Jones. Haskell 98 language and libraries: The revised report. Technical report.

[10] G. D. Plotkin. A Structural Approach to Operational Semantics. Technical Report DAIMI FN-19, University of Aarhus, 1981.

[11] John C. Reynolds. Definitional interpreters for higher-order programming languages. *Higher Order Symbol. Comput.*, 11(4):363–397, 1998.

[12] Patrick M. Sansom and Simon L. Peyton Jones. Formally based profiling for higher-order functional languages. *ACM Trans. Program. Lang. Syst.*, 19(2):334–385, 1997.

[13] David A. Schmidt. *Denotational semantics: a methodology for language development*. William C. Brown Publishers, Dubuque, IA, USA, 1986.

[14] Clifford A. Shaffer. *A Practical Introduction to Data Structures and Algorithm Analysis*. Prentice Hall PTR, Upper Saddle River, NJ, USA, 2000.

[15] Philip Wadler. Monads for functional programming. In M. Broy, editor, *Program Design Calculi: Proceedings of the 1992 Marktoberdorf International Summer School*. Springer-Verlag, 1993.

The Implementation of iData
A Case Study in Generic Programming

Rinus Plasmeijer and Peter Achten

Software Technology, Nijmegen Institute for Computing and Information Sciences,
Radboud University Nijmegen
{rinus, P.Achten}@cs.ru.nl

Abstract. The iData Toolkit is a toolkit that allows programmers to create interactive, type-safe, dynamic web applications with state on a high level of abstraction. The key element of this toolkit is the iData element. An iData element is a form that is generated automatically from a type definition and that can be plugged in in the web page of a web application. In this paper we show how this automatic generation of forms has been implemented. The technique relies essentially on *generic programming*. It has resulted in a concise and flexible implementation. The kernel of the implementation can be reused for any graphical package. The iData Toolkit is an excellent demonstration of the expressive power of modern generic (poly-typical) programming techniques.

1   Introduction

In this paper we present the implementation of the iData Toolkit, which is a novel toolkit to program *forms* in dynamic server-side web applications. The low level view, and standard definition, of a form is that of a collection of (primitive) interactive elements, such as text input fields, check boxes, radio buttons, pull down menus, that provide the application user with a means to exchange structured information with the web application. Seen from this point of view, and if programmed that way, creating forms results in a lot of low level HTML coding. A high level view of forms is to think of them as being *editors of structured values* of appropriate type. From the type, the low level realization can be derived automatically. This can be done once by the toolkit developer. Seen from that point of view, and if programmed that way, creating forms is all about creating data types. This results in a lot less code plumbing and no HTML-coding at all.

In the iData Toolkit project, we have adopted the high level view of forms described above. We call these high level forms iData. An iData has two major components: **(i)** a *state*, or *value*, which type is determined by the programmer, and **(ii)** a *form*, or *rendering*, which is derived automatically by the toolkit from the state and its type. The programmer manipulates the iData in terms of the state and its type, whereas the user manipulates the iData in terms of a low-level form. Clearly, the iData Toolkit needs to mediate between these two worlds: every possible type domain must be mapped to forms, and every user action on

A. Butterfield, C. Grelck, and F. Huch (Eds.): IFL 2005, LNCS 4015, pp. 106–123, 2006.

these forms must be mapped back to the original type domain, with a possibly different value. This is the challenge that is addressed in this paper.

An approach as sketched above can be implemented in any programming language with good support for data types and type-driven programming. Modern functional programming languages such as Clean [22,2] and Haskell [19] come with highly expressive type systems. One example of type-driven programming is *generic programming*[12,13,1], which has been incorporated in Clean and GenericH∀skell [16]. In this paper we use Clean. We assume the reader is familiar with functional and generic programming.

Generic programming has proven productive in the iData Toolkit by providing us with concise and flexible solutions for many of the chores of web programming. In this paper we focus on its crucial contribution to solving the main challenge in the context of the iData Toolkit: the automatic creation of forms from arbitrary data types, and the automatic creation of the correct data type and value from a user-manipulated form. The key idea is that each iData is fully responsible for keeping track of its rendering, its state recovery, and correctly handling user-edit operations. They, and only they, can do this because they have all type information that is necessary for these operations.

It should be observed that although we give a few examples, this paper is about the implementation of the iData Toolkit. Due to limitations of space, we cannot explain the programming method. This is presented elsewhere [20,21]. We have used the iData Toolkit to create realistic real world applications, such as a web shop. These demonstrate that this technique can be used in practice.

This paper is structured as follows. We first introduce the concept and implementation challenges of iData (Sect. 2). Then we present the concrete implementation of iData (Sect. 3). After this, we discuss the achieved results (Sect. 4). We present related work (Sect. 5) and conclude (Sect. 6).

2   The Concept of iData

In this section we explain the main concepts of the iData Toolkit by means of a few key toy examples (Sect. 2.2–2.6). They illustrate the implementation challenges that need to be solved. These are summarized in Sect. 2.7. Please notice that although the code of these examples has a static flavor, each of these examples are complete interactive web applications. We first present the major design decisions in Sect. 2.1.

2.1   Major Design Decisions

The key idea of an iData Toolkit program is that it is a function that computes an HTML page that contains a set of interconnected iData elements. An iData element is a self contained interactive element that is in charge of its state. The state can be any programmer defined data type. The iData Toolkit is constructed in such a way that the state of an iData element is always a valid instance of the type. Type constraints on the input are not always sufficient: individual iData elements can impose additional constraints on the values of their state that can not be expressed with types, or they are interconnected and need to modify their state as a consequence of the modification of another iData change. For this reason, every *complete*[1] user manipulation of an iData element requires a response of that element and the iData elements that are connected with it. Currently, this has been implemented by enforcing a round trip between browser and server.

The code of an iData Toolkit application is a single function that is evaluated every time a client web browser requires a web page from this application. Initially, no previous states are available to the application, and the iData elements are activated with their initial values. During subsequent requests, the web browser provides the states of all iData elements and detailed information about which iData element has been modified by the user. The implementation of the toolkit uses this information to recover previous unaltered states, and create a valid altered new state. This is hidden completely from the programmer. He can reason about the program as a collection of interconnected iData elements, one of which has a modified state value.

Generic programming has been crucial to implement the core functionality of the iData Toolkit: rendering state in terms of low-level forms, recovering previous states, and incorporating arbitrary user modifications in states. Generic programming has also been used for tasks that could have been done with more traditional means: (de-)serialization of states, and printing HTML. A key advantage of generic programming is that one has a default application for free for any type. If this generic solution is not appropriate, the programmer (or toolkit developer) can use *specialization* to replace the default solution with a more suitable solution. Specialization can be done for individual iData elements, but also for complete types. With specialization, the iData Toolkit can be extended with elements that have more logic at the client side, for instance for specialized text input parsers.

The number and types of iData elements in an HTML page that is generated by an iData Toolkit application depends on the values of the states of its iData elements. During evaluation of the application, these iData elements are activated and need to recover their previous, or altered, state from this collection of states. This requires an identification mechanism that is able to associate typed iData elements with serialized states. Exceptional cases are the absence of such a state (initial occurrence of an iData element), or that the serialized state is of incorrect type (page originated from a different application). The problem is reminiscent of manipulating typed content that comes from files. Currently, this has been implemented pragmatically: iData elements are identified with text labels. The state of an iData element can be recovered successfully if it is present in the set of previous states and can be converted successfully to a value of its type. In every other case, the iData element obtains the initialization value with which it is associated in the program code. This makes the approach robust. We are

---

[1] In a text box this is the completion of the input, either by changing the input focus or - for single line edit boxes - pressing the enter key.

well aware that this is a deficient solution, particularly considering the strongly typed discipline that we advocate with the iData Toolkit.

The code below shows the standard overhead of every iData Toolkit program:

```
module IFL2005Examples
import StdEnv, StdHtml                                              1.

Start :: *World → *World                                           2.
Start world = doHtml example world                                3.
```

The proper library modules need to be imported (line 1). Lines 2–3 declare the main function of every Clean program. The *uniqueness attribute* * just in front of World guarantees that values of this type are always used in a *single threaded manner*. Clean uses *uniqueness typing* [5,6] to allow destructive updates and side-effects. The opaque type World represents the entire external environment of the program. The iData program is given by the function example :: *HSt → (Html,*HSt). The wrapper function doHtml turns this function into a common Clean program. It initializes the HSt value with all serialized values that can be found in the HTML page, and includes the World as well. This implies that every iData Toolkit application has full access to the external world, and can, for instance, connect to databases and so on. Below, we only show the example functions, and skip the standard overhead.

2.2   iData Have Form

The first example demonstrates the fact that iData elements are type driven. It creates a simple Int editor (Fig. 1(a)).

```
example :: *HSt → (Html,*HSt)                                      1.
example hst                                                        2.
    ♯ (nrF,hst) = mkEdit (nIDataId "nr") 1 hst                     3.
    = mkHtml "Int editor" [ H1 [] "Int editor", BodyTag nrF.form ] hst   4.
```

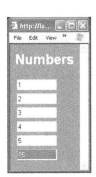

Fig. 1. Key toy examples: **(a)** a simple integer iData, **(b)** summing the value of iData, **(c)** sharing iData, and **(d)** model-view separation of iData

Passing multiple environments around explicitly is supported syntactically in Clean by means of ♯-definitions. These are non-recursive *let*-definitions, which scope extends to the bottom, but not the right-hand side. This is the standard approach in Clean. Even though the examples in this paper do not exploit the flexibility of multiple environment passing (by for instance connnecting to a database system), we present them in this style.

Key features of the iData Toolkit that are illustrated in this small example are the activation of an iData element, nrF, from an initial value and its type, 1::Int. It is identified throughout the program with the value (nDataId "nr") :: IDataId. This is done with the function mkEdit (line 3). This iData element has a rendering in terms of a form, nrF.form ($r.f$ denotes the selection of field f from record r). The rendering is a text edit box in which only integer denotations can be entered. In general, a user can only enter input that is type-safe.

The definition of the web page, given by the function mkHtml :: String [BodyTag] *HSt → (Html,*HSt), is cleanly separated from the definition of the iData elements. The [BodyTag] argument represents the page content. The algebraic type BodyTag is discussed in more detail in Sect. 3.5. In these examples, we use its data constructor H1 which represents the <h1></h1> HTML tag, and its data constructor BodyTag which turns a list of BodyTags into a single BodyTag.

2.3   iData **Have Value**

In this example we show that iData not only have a form rendering, but also a value in terms of the type that generated them.

```
example hst                                                            1.
    ♯ (nrFs,hst) = seqList [mkEdit (sumId nr) nr \\ nr ← [1..5]] hst   2.
    = mkHtml "Numbers" [ H1 [] "Numbers", sumtable nrFs ] hst          3.

sumtable nrFs = STable [] ([nrF.form \\ nrF ← nrFs]                    4.
                            ++                                         5.
                          [[toHtml (sum [nrF.value \\ nrF ← nrFs])]])  6.
sumId i      = nDataId ("sum"<$i)                                      7.
```

Fig. 1(**b**) shows the result of the above code. Five iData elements are activated: nrFs :: [IData Int] (line 2). The function sumtable (lines 4-6) places their *forms* in a column, underneath of which the sum of their *values* is displayed. Whenever the user alters one of the iData elements, the new sum is calculated and displayed at the bottom of the iData elements. The reason that this statically looking program has interactive behaviour, is that the behaviour is delegated to each of the iData elements that are activated. This is why we prefer to speak of activation of iData.

The value of an iData is given by the .value field of that iData. The library function toHtml uses the generic form rendering function to render values of arbitrary type into HTML. The overloaded operator <$ appends a String version of its second argument to its first argument.

2.4 iData **Have Sharing**

iData elements with the same identification value refer to the same iData element. A first advantage of this scheme is that iData serve as storages of arbitrary types. Hence, we do not need to introduce a separate concept for storing data. A second advantage is that both the value and rendering of iData can be used arbitrarily many times in a HTML page without causing ambiguity problems. We illustrate the latter by replicating the column of integer iData and their sum in the example below (see Fig. 1(**c**)):

```
example hst
  ♯ (nrFs,hst) = seqList [mkEdit (sumId nr) nr \\ nr ← [1..5]] hst
  = mkHtml "Numbers"
      [ H1 [] "Numbers", STable [] [[sumtable nrFs],[sumtable nrFs]] ] hst
```

Editing any of the iData elements also automatically affects the other iData in the same row. The sum is displayed twice, at the bottom of both columns.

2.5 iData **Have Model-View Separation**

In this example we demonstrate that the type of an iData can be uncoupled from its rendering. The rendering can be derived instead from a different data type, provided that the programmer defines the mapping between these two data types. In this way, the type of the iData serves as its *model*, whereas the rendered data type serves as its *view*. In Sect. 3.1, we explain the mapping and its implementation in detail. Here, we assume the existence of a function, counterIData, that has an Int model type, but a (Counter Int) view type, where Counter is defined as a synonym type :: Counter a :== (a,Button,Button).

```
counterIData :: IDataId Int *HSt → (IData Int,*HSt)
```

If we replace mkEdit in example 2.3, line 2, with counterIData then we obtain a program that displays five counters instead of five integer editors (see Fig. 1(**d**)). The counters are *self contained*. The counter iData ensures that its integer value is incremented/decremented at every corresponding button press. Still, it has an integer interface to the programmer, so the remainder of the program does not change. Self contained iData are fully compositional.

2.6 iData **Have Specialization**

In this example we show that iData can be specialized, just as generic functions can. Suppose we like the counters in Sect. 2.5 much better than the default integer editors that were used in Sect. 2.2 and 2.3. We need to specialize the generic HTML rendering function gForm for the Int type. This is done by:

```
gForm{|Int|} iDataId i hst  = specialize asCounter iDataId i hst      1.
where asCounter :: IDataId Int *HSt → (IData Int,*HSt)                 2.
        asCounter iDataId i hst                                        3.
            ♯ (counterF,hst) = counterIData iDataId i hst             4.
```

```
            = ( { changed    = counterF.changed                    5.
              , value        = fst3 counterF.value                 6.
              , form         = counterF.form }, hst )              7.
fst3 (x,_,_) = x   // Clean standard library function
```

Function `asCounter` (lines 2-7) defines the specialization using `counterIData` (this function is also defined via the specialization mechanism). Also, `asCounter` is a good example of showing the flexibility of iData programming.

The library function

```
specialize :: (IDataId a *HSt → (IData a,*HSt))
              IDataId a *HSt → (IData a,*HSt) | gUpd{|*|} a
```

is able to 'plug in' the specialization function into any arbitrary other iData structure. Given this specialization of `Int` values, in any place where an iData of an `Integer` value is needed, a counter iData will be made. In such a setting, the programs 2.2, 2.3, and 2.4 now display self contained counters that behave as expected instead of plain integer editors, without any change in the code of these examples.

2.7 Implementation Challenges

The examples given in this section show that an implementation of the iData Toolkit has to be able to perform the following tasks in a strongly typed programming language context: (i) map values of arbitrary types to forms, (ii) map edit operations in forms to new values of the given types, (iii) handle iData elements as elements with shared value and shared rendering, (iv) handle model-view separation correctly, and (v) handle specialization correctly. The key idea to solve these challenges is by delegating this functionality to each iData element. The implementation is discussed in the next section.

3 The Implementation of iData

In this section we present the implementation of iData. This is based on a single, pivotal function, `mkIData` which applies a number of generic functions to handle the challenges (i) upto (v) that were mentioned in Sect. 2.7. Because of its complexity, we split up its discussion. In Sect. 3.1 we focus on `mkIData`, its arguments and results, and the way that it incorporates the model-view separation (iv). In Sect. 3.2 we explain the architecture of the `HSt` environment, in which all iData values are stored (iii). In Sect. 3.3 we discuss all rendering issues of iData. Rendering must be done in such a way that forms are generated from types (i), and that user edit operations are correctly mapped back to values of the source type (ii). In Sect. 3.4 we show how specialization (v) uses the framework to nest arbitrarily many iData elements inside each other. Finally, we briefly touch on the issue of emitting proper HTML code in the toolkit in Sect. 3.5.

3.1   The Pivotal mkIData Function

The iData Toolkit revolves around a single concept, that of an iData. The toolkit has exactly one function to create iData, mkIData with type signature:

```
mkIData :: IDataId m (IBimap m v) *HSt → (IData m,*HSt)
         | gForm{|*|}, gUpd{|*|}, gPrint{|*|}, gParse{|*|} v
```

This function is applied to *four* arguments.

The *first* argument is of type IDataId. Values of this type unambiguously identify an iData element. The programmer (carefully) chooses String identifiers, which is a typical way of identifying forms in web applications. It is the task of the programmer to use unambiguous names in such a way that every use of (mkIData id) refers to the same iData element of some type m. IDataId values are created with one of the functions {n,s,p}[d]IDataId :: String → IDataId. The programmer also controls the *life span* and *edit mode* of iData elements with IDataId values.

```
:: IDataId = { id::String, lifespan::LifeSpan, mode::Mode }
:: LifeSpan = Page | Session | Persistent
:: Mode     = Edit | Display
```

The life span of an iData element is determined by {n,s,p}: its value is remembered as long as its page is being viewed (n), is stored persistently during a session (s), or independently of sessions (p). By default, values can be edited in the browser. If they should be displayed only, then any of the {n,s,p}dIDataId functions can be used.

The *second* argument of mkIData is the initial value of the iData element. It is used only when no iData element with given IDataId exists. This happens for instance when the page is viewed for the first time.

The *third* argument of mkIData defines the model-view abstraction that has been presented in example 2.5. This allows the application to work with iData that have state values of type m, but that are *visualized* by means of values of type v. This is a variant of the well-known model(-controller)-view paradigm [15]. What is special about it in this context, is that views are also defined by means of a data type, and hence can be handled generically in exactly the same way! This is clearly expressed in the type signature of mkIData, which states that the generic machinery must be available for the view model v.

The relation between a model m and its view v is given by the following collection of functions of type IBimap m v:

```
:: IBimap m v = { toView    :: m → Maybe v → v
                , updView   :: Bool → v → v
                , fromView  :: Bool → v → m
                , resetView :: Maybe (v → v) }
```

Model values are transformed to views with toView. It can use the previous view value if available. The self contained behavior of an iData element is given by updView. Its first argument records if it has been changed by the user. The same argument is passed to the function fromView which transforms view values back to model values. Finally, `resetView` is an optional separate normalization *after* the local behavior function `updView` has been applied.

The function `nextModelView` computes a new model-view pair with these functions in the following way:

```
nextModelView :: (IBimap m v) m (Maybe v) Bool → (m,v)
nextModelView ibm init_m maybe_v changed
    ♯ v = ibm.toView    init_m  maybe_v
    ♯ v = ibm.updView   changed v
    ♯ m = ibm.fromView  changed v
    ♯ v = case ibm.resetView of Nothing    = v
                                Just reset = reset v
    = (m,v)
```

This explains how the self contained counters in example 2.5 can be constructed. They use the `updView` function to correctly set their integer value.

The *fourth*, and final, argument of `mkIData` is the `HSt` environment that is used to store all iData values in. This environment is discussed thoroughly in Sect. 3.2. Here, we assume that we have the following access functions available on `HSt` environment values:

```
findIDataValue:: IDataId   *HSt → (Bool,Maybe a,*HSt)  |gParse{|*|}, gUpd{|*|} a
replaceState  :: IDataId a *HSt → *HSt                 |gPrint{|*|} a
resetCount    ::           *HSt → *HSt
```

The function `findIDataValue` locates the stored state of the identified iData element. The boolean result indicates whether this value has been edited by the application user. It uses the generic functions `gParse` and `gUpd` for deserialization purposes and updating values that may have been altered by the user. New iData values are stored in the `HSt` environment with the function `replaceState`. Because these values are serialized, they require the generic function `gPrint`. Finally, `resetCount` makes sure that the internal counting mechanism of the `HSt` environment is reset to zero. The reason for this is also explained in Sect. 3.2.

When applied to the arguments described above, `mkIData` activates the indicated iData element. As a result, it returns a modified `HSt` environment, and an (`IData m`) record value. This record holds the *form* rendering of the iData element, its *value*, as has been discussed in examples 2.2 and 2.3, and the boolean that states iff the iData element has been altered.

```
:: IData m = { form::[BodyTag], value::m, changed::Bool }
```

We can now explain what `mkIData` does with model values of type `m` and view values of type `v`. We walk through its implementation:

```
mkIData :: IDataId m (IBimap m v) *HSt → (IData m,*HSt)
        | gForm{|*|}, gUpd{|*|}, gPrint{|*|}, gParse{|*|} v
mkIData iDataId init_m ibm hst = nextIData (findIDataValue iDataId hst)   1.
where nextIData (changed,maybe_v,hst)
            ♯ (m,v)          = nextModelView ibm init_m maybe_v changed   2.
            ♯ (iData_v,hst) = gForm{|*|} iDataId v (resetCount hst)        3.
            | iData_v.changed && not changed                               4.
```

$$= \texttt{nextIData} \ (\texttt{True}, \texttt{Just} \ \texttt{iData\_v.value}, \texttt{hst})$$ 5.

```
  | otherwise
      # hst       = replaceState iDataId iData_v.value hst          6.
      # iData_m    = {changed=changed,value=m,form=iData_v.form}    7.
      = (iData_m,resetCount hSt)
```

First the possibly modified value of the given iData element is retrieved (line 1), using the HSt access function `findIDataValue` that was introduced above. This is a view value, and hence has type v. From this value, new model and view values need to be computed (line 2). Next, the view value is rendered (line 3), using the generic rendering function gForm (Sect. 3.3). As we have seen in example 2.6, gForm can be specialized. With specialization, the programmer *nests* iData inside each other. It may be the case that one of these nested iData has been altered by the user. Due to recursion, its altered value shows up at this level. If this occurs (condition on line 4 holds), then `mkIData` should proceed with the altered value (line 5). In the end, the value of the resulting view iData is stored in the HSt environment (line 6). The final iData has as value the new model value that was computed by `nextModelView`, but as rendering the view rendering (line 7).

The function `mkIData` is a powerful tool to create model-view abstractions with. Frequently occurring patterns of this function have been captured with wrapper functions. Consider the `mkEdit` function that we have used in examples 2.2 and 2.3. It can be used as a 'store' in Display mode, or as a straight editor in Edit mode.

```
mkEdit :: IDataId m *HSt → (IData m, *HSt)
       | gForm{|*|}, gUpd{|*|}, gPrint{|*|}, gParse{|*|} m
mkEdit iDataId=:{mode} m hst
  = mkIData iDataId m
          { toView    = λnew old → case old of (Just v) → v; _ → new
          , updView   = case mode of Edit → λ_ v → v; Display → λ_ _ → m
          , fromView  = λ_ v → v
          , resetView = Nothing } hst
```

3.2   The Implementation of HSt

The HSt environment keeps track of the serialized states of active iData elements in an iData Toolkit application. These states are either stored locally in the HTML page of the web application (in case of {n,s}[d]IDataId values) or reside on disk on the server side (in case of p[d]IDataId values). In addition, it holds a global counter to generate position values in the generic representation of state values.

```
:: *HSt     = { cntr::InputId, states::*IDataStates, world::*World }
:: InputId  :== Int
```

IDataStates stores the serialized states of iData elements, together with their IDataId value, and if they have been changed by the user. IDataStates is basically an association list with a look-up function `lookupState` and update function `replaceState` (`replaceState` was also encountered in Sect. 3.1).

```
lookupState   :: IDataId    *HSt → (Bool,Maybe a,*HSt) | gParse{|*|} a
replaceState :: IDataId a *HSt → *HSt                   | gPrint{|*|} a
```

These require the World environment in case of persistent forms. The generic functions gParse and gPrint are used for (de)serialization purposes.

In addition to the serialized states of iData, the *HSt environment also keeps track of the user modifications by storing *what* has been changed into which *new value*. This information can be retrieved by the function

```
getUserEdit :: *HSt → ((Maybe a,Maybe b),*HSt) | gParse{|*|} a & gParse{|*|} b
```

The type of getUserEdit reveals that we are dealing with serialized values. The first result is *what* has been changed, and the second result is its *new value*. For the identification purpose an *identification triplet* is used. Its first element is the identification string of the iData element. For convenience, it can be retrieved separately as well with

```
getIDataName :: *HSt → (String,*HSt)
```

The second element of the triplet is the value that has been changed. Generically speaking, this can only be a basic value (alternatives UpdI upto UpdS) or a data constructor (the name of which is stored in the UpdC alternative).

```
:: UpdValue = UpdI Int | UpdR Real | UpdB Bool | UpdS String | UpdC String
```

Of course, also the new value can be encoded in this way. The third element is the position of the generic element in the generic representation. Because the generic representation is a tree structure, this position can be obtained with a straightforward numbering scheme. This information is sufficient to determine for *any* iData element *whether* it has been changed, and, if so, *which* generic component has been changed into *what* new value. This case analysis is performed by decodeInput:

```
:: FormUpdate :== (InputId,UpdValue)
```

```
decodeInput :: IDataId *HSt → (Maybe FormUpdate,(Bool,Maybe a,*HSt))
               | gParse{|*|} a
decodeInput iDataId hst
   ♯ (name,hst) = getIDataName hst
   | name == iDataId.id
     = case getUserEdit hst of
          ((Just (sid,pos,UpdI i),newi),hst) // case distinction on Int
             = let ni = case newi of (Just ni) → ni; _ → i
               in (Just (pos,UpdI ni),lookupState {iDataId & id=sid} hst)
          (_,hst) = ... // case distinction on other basic types
   | otherwise
     = (Nothing, lookupState iDataId hst)
```

This function checks whether the iData element that is identified by IDataId has been edited. If so, its exact location in the generic representation is returned (of type FormUpdate), as well as its current value (the result of using lookupState). It should be noted that lookupState may fail to parse the input (e.g. the user entered 42.0 instead of 42 for an integer form). In that case, parsing fails, and the previous (correct) value is restored. This makes the system *type safe*.

In the previous section the pivotal function mkIData used the function

```
findIDataValue:: IDataId *HSt → (Bool,Maybe m,*HSt) | gParse{|*|} , gUpd{|*|} m
```

that was able to retrieve the possibly modified value of an iData identified by the IDataId argument. Before we can explain its definition, we need to delve into the generic function gUpd that is able to repair any value of type a to a new modified value of the same type a. It must be a generic function because it needs to traverse the generic data representation of the old value in order to locate the generic element that has been changed. This location is passed to the application in the identification value.

generic gUpd a :: UpdMode a → (UpdMode,a)

:: UpdMode = UpdSearch UpdValue InputId | UpdCreate [ConsPos] | UpdDone

The UpdMode type represents the two passes gUpd goes through: (UpdSearch newv cnt) represents the search for the generic element at location cnt with new value newv, and (UpdCreate path) represents the creation of new values for a selected data constructor that can be found at path (:: ConsPos = ConsLeft | ConsRight).

We illustrate the working of gUpd for basic types with the case for integers (the other cases for basic types are analogous):

```
gUpd{|Int|} (UpdSearch (UpdI new) 0) _ = (UpdDone,new)              1.
gUpd{|Int|} (UpdSearch val cnt)      i = (UpdSearch val (cnt-1),i)  2.
gUpd{|Int|} (UpdCreate 1)            _ = (UpdCreate 1,0)            3.
gUpd{|Int|} mode                     i = (mode,i)                   4.
```

An existing value is replaced with new somewhere in a generic value at position cnt if cnt = 0, otherwise it is not changed and the position is decreased (lines 1 and 2). The default value for new integers is 0 (line 3).

The remaining code of gUpd proceeds polytypically except for OBJECTs. The generic constructor OBJECT marks the occurrence of a type constructor. It has access to all data constructors of that type. In this case its new value is determined by the name of the selected data constructor (cname). At that point, gUpd switches from searching mode into creation mode, in order to create arguments of the data constructor. The route to the desired data constructor is returned by getConsPath :: GenericConsDescriptor → [ConsPos].

```
gUpd{|OBJECT of desc|} gUpd_obj (UpdSearch (UpdC cname) 0) (OBJECT obj)
   ♯ (mode,obj) = gUpd_obj (UpdCreate path) obj
   = (UpdDone,OBJECT obj)
where path = getConsPath (hd [cons \\ cons ← desc.gtd_conses
                              | cons.gcd_name == cname ]
```

We now have gathered all the building blocks to explain the behavior of findIDataValue. As we have stated in the introduction, the key idea to the iData Toolkit is to delegate state handling to every individual iData element. Every manipulation in a web page that changes the current value of a form triggers the execution of the Clean application on the server side. The application, and hence every iData element, has to figure out why it has been launched. There can be only three reasons: **1.** *The* iData *has no previous state.* This is the case for instance for all iData when a page is created for the first time. The iData should be initialized. **2.** *The* iData *has a previous state, but it was not edited.* This is the case when another iData has been edited. The iData should recover its previous state. **3.** *The* iData *was edited.* The application user has altered the iData. The iData should calculate its new state, given the update information and the recovered previous state. This case analysis is performed by findIDataValue (the numbers to the right coincide with the above cases):

```
findIDataValue :: IDataId *HSt → (Bool,Maybe m,*HSt) | gUpd{|*|}, gParse{|*|} m
findIDataValue iDataId hst
  = case decodeInput iDataId hst of
      (Just (cnt,newv),(changed,Just m,hst))                        3.
         ♯ m = if changed (snd (gUpd{|*|} (UpdSearch newv cnt) m)) m
         = (True, Just m,  hst)
      (_,(_,Just m,hst))                                            2.
         = (False, Just m,  hst)
      (_,(_,_,hst))                                                 1.
         = (False, Nothing,hst)
```

It uses decodeInput to deserialize the input data that has been passed to the web application and look for the iData element with the given identification. The reason of activating the iData element can then be determined straightforwardly.

3.3   Rendering iData

The final part of the implementation of the iData Toolkit is the rendering of iData elements into forms in such a way that forms are generated for any type, and that user manipulations can be traced back to a modified value of the same type. The key idea to realize this relationship is by associating the identification triplet (Sect. 3.2) with each element along the generic representation, and make it send the new value in case of a user action. The generic function gForm creates this form rendering of an iData element with a model value of type m:

```
generic gForm m :: IDataId m *HSt → (IData m,*HSt)
```

The basic types are handled in the same way, using the function mkInput and the union type Value:

```
gForm{|Int|} iDataId i hst
  ♯ (form,hst) = mkInput iDataId (IV i) (UpdI i) hst
  = ({changed=False,value=i,form=[form]},hst)
```

```
:: Value = IV Int | RV Real | BV Bool | SV String | NQV String
```

The code of mkInput is given below. As mentioned earlier, we have used a types-as-grammar approach to specify HTML. Readers that are familiar with HTML, may be able to deduce the HTML output that is printed systematically from these algebraic data types (Sect. 3.5). We discuss the interesting parts.

```
mkInput :: IDataId Value UpdValue *HSt → (BodyTag,*HSt)
mkInput iDataId val updval hst=:{cntr}                                    1.
= ( Input [ Inp_Type Inp_Text, Inp_Value val, Inp_Size defsize           2.
          : case mode of                                                 3.
                 Edit    = [ Inp_Name      identification_triplet         4.
                           , 'Inp_Std      [EditBoxStyle]                 5.
                           , 'Inp_Events   [OnChange callClean]]          6.
                 Display = [ Inp_ReadOnly ReadOnly                        7.
                           , 'Inp_Std      [DisplayBoxStyle] ]] ""        8.
  , {hst & cntr=cntr+1} )                                                 9.
where identification_triplet = encodeInfo (iDataId.id,cntr,updval)       10.
```

Basic forms in `Display` mode are read-only, and show this to the user (lines 7-8).
When `Edited`, the web application on the server side needs to resurrected, and
provided with the proper information. A script is called that sends all serialized
states, the identification triplet (line 4 and 10), and the new value of the edited
element back to the server, causing the application to be started with the new
data (Sect. 3.2).

For the generic constructors (`UNIT`, `PAIR`, `EITHER`, `OBJECT`, and `CONS`) gForm proceeds polytypically. `UNIT` values are displayed as `EmptyBody`. (`PAIR a b`) values are
placed below each other. (`EITHER a b`) values proceed recursively and display either their left or right value. (`OBJECT o`) values proceed recursively. The form
that corresponds with (`CONS c`) values requires more HTML programming because it deals with the selection of data constructors. It generates a pull down
menu which entries correspond with all data constructors. In `Edit` mode, the
user can select one of these data constructors. Changes are handled in the same
way as with basic types, except that the selected constructor name is passed as
argument. All in all, gForm's implementation requires 150 *loc*.

Finally, gForm has been specialized for several standard form elements. We do
not discuss their implementation. They are similar to the above `Int` instance.

3.4   Handling Specialization

In example 2.6, we have shown that programmers can specialize the iData Toolkit
in the same way as generic functions using the function `specialize`.

```
specialize :: (IDataId a *HSt → (IData a,*HSt))
               IDataId a *HSt → (IData a,*HSt) | gUpd{|*|} a
specialize f iDataId v hst=:{cntr}
  # newIDataId     = {iDataId & id = iDataId.id<@"_"<@cntr}              1.
  # (vF,hst)       = f newIDataId v (resetCount hst)                     2.
  # (UpdSearch _ c) = fst (gUpd{|*|} (UpdSearch (UpdI 0) -1) v)          3.
  = (vF,setCount (cntr - (c+1)) hst)                                     4.
```

It is the task of this function to embed the iData result of its argument function
inside the generic representation of an arbitrary data structure. What it does is
to create a new iData element that has a new `IDataId` identification value (line
1), and in which position counting starts afresh at zero (line 2). The proper
new count can be derived by creatively using the functionality of gUpd: having

it search for an integer value at position -1 always fails, but it does return the size of the generic representation of the newly created iData (line 3). This size c is used to calculate the next legal position value (line 4).

3.5   Handling HTML

We have used a *types-as-grammar* approach to capture the official HTML grammar with a family of algebraic data types. We have encountered them in the above sections. The algebraic type BodyTag represents the collection of HTML tags from anchors (A) to variables (Var), and includes a few data constructors that allow flexible HTML generation:

```
:: BodyTag = A      [A_Attr]      [BodyTag]   | ... | Var [Std_Attr] String
           | STable [Table_Attr] [[BodyTag]]  | BodyTag [BodyTag] | EmptyBody
```

One generic function, gHpr, has been written that generates proper HTML code from values of these types. Generic programming is not strictly necessary for this purpose. It does provide us with a concise generic function that can display any HTML code. Its core definition is only 27 *loc*. Printing of 73 types can be derived. Specialization is required for a few types, which adds 170 *loc*.

4   Discussion

In the previous section we have presented the implementation of the iData Toolkit. The implementation relies essentially on generic programming: the functions gForm and gUpd are able to manipulate values of arbitrary types in a type-safe way. The generic descriptions of these functions are small: 150 *loc* for gForm, and 80 *loc* for gUpd. We can provide specializations of these functions without changing the core definition. This greatly enhances their flexibility.

For serialization and deserialization we have used folklore generic printing and parsing functions that come with the standard generic Clean distribution. These generic functions are not essential for the iData Toolkit. Currently we are investigating whether we can use Clean dynamics for this purpose. They have as advantage that they can handle higher-order data types as well. However, their use and implementation is very delicate when compared with the robustness of their string based generic counterparts. The types-as-grammar approach of handling HTML is also very suited for generic programming. Again, it is not essential, but it has proven to provide us with concise code that is easily maintainable.

Finally, the architecture of the iData Toolkit allows us to target any arbitrary GUI library without much code modification. This is due to the fact that only state information and the change information, both in serialized form, is required by an iData Toolkit application in order to resurrect its next state and rendering.

5   Related Work

iData components are form abstractions. A pioneer project to experiment with form-based services is Mawl [4]. The <bigwig> project [8] uses Powerforms [7].

Both projects provide *templates* which, roughly speaking, are HTML pages with *holes* in which scalar data as well as lists can be plugged in (Mawl), but also other *templates* (<bigwig>). Powerforms reside on the client-side of a web application. The type system is used to filter out illegal user input. They advocate compile-time systems, just as we do, because this allows one to use type systems and other static analysis. The main differences are that in our approach *all first order user types* are admissible in iData, that iData are automatically derived from these types, and that we can use the expressiveness of the host language to obtain higher-order forms/pages.

Continuations are a natural means to structure interactive web applications. This has been done by Hughes [14], using his Arrow framework; Queinnec [23], who takes the position that continuations are at the essence of web browsers; Graunke *et al* [10], who have explored continuations as (one of three) functional compilation technique(s) to transform sequential interactive programs to CGI programs. Our approach is simpler because for every page we have a complete (set of) model value(s) that can be stored and retrieved generically in a page. An application is resurrected by recovering its previous state, merging the user modification, if any, and computing the proper next state that is re-rendered.

Many authors have worked on creating and manipulating HTML (XML) pages in a strongly typed setting. Early work is by Wallace and Runciman [26] on XML transformers in Haskell. The Haskell CGI library by Meijer [17] frees the programmer from dealing with CGI printing and parsing. Hanus uses similar types [11] in Curry. Thiemann constructs typed encodings of HTML in extended Haskell in an increasing level of precision for *valid* documents [24,25]. XML transforming programs with GenericH∀skell has been investigated in UUXML [3]. Elsman and Larsen [9] have worked on typed representations of XML in ML [18]. Our *types-as-grammar* approach eliminates all syntactically incorrect programs, but we have not put effort in eradicating all semantically incorrect programs. Our research interest is in the automatic creation of forms from type specifications, and less in the definition of the HTML pages in which they reside.

6   Conclusions

This paper focusses on the implementation of the iData Toolkit. We have not been able to show how realistic, interconnected, real world applications are constructed with the toolkit. We have made a number of large applications, one of which is a web shop that uses many interconnected iData elements in a dynamic way, using server side data storage. Even these kind of applications can be made in the same declarative style as shown by the key toy examples in this paper.

Creating the iData Toolkit is truly a challenge because it boils down to implementing a multi-purpose unit, the iData, that automatically takes care of initialization, state recovery and update, abstraction, and rendering. Generic programming brings down the complexity significantly. It also provides us with an open-ended implementation: without modifications to the core implementation, program developers can specialize the toolkit to their own preferences and needs per application. Although the iData Toolkit was designed for web applications, its architecture can be targeted at any graphical user interface platform without significant changes. This is a major improvement to our previous work on desktop applications. The implementation is concise, elegant, and efficient. In all, the results of this project show that the iData Toolkit is an excellent case study in the appropriateness of generic programming.

Acknowledgements

Jan Kuper coined the name iData for our editor components. Pieter Koopman provided input for the gUpd function. Paul de Mast kindly provided us with a web server application written in Clean which has allowed us to readily test the iData Toolkit. Javier Pomer Tendillo, as an Erasmus guest, has been helpful in setting up the toolkit, and find out the nitty-gritty details of HTML programming. Finally, we thank the anonymous referees.

References

1. A. Alimarine. *Generic Functional Programming - Conceptual Design, Implementation and Applications.* PhD thesis, University of Nijmegen, The Netherlands, 2005. ISBN 3-540-67658-9.
2. A. Alimarine and R. Plasmeijer. A Generic Programming Extension for Clean. In T. Arts and M. Mohnen, editors, *The 13th International workshop on the Implementation of Functional Languages, IFL'01, Selected Papers*, volume 2312 of *LNCS*, pages 168–186. Älvsjö, Sweden, Springer, Sept. 2002.
3. F. Atanassow, D. Clarke, and J. Jeuring. UUXML: A Type-Preserving XML Schema-Haskell Data Binding. In *International Symposium on Practical Aspects of Declarative Languages (PADL'04)*, volume 3057 of *LNCS*, pages 71–85. Springer-Verlag, June 2004.
4. D. Atkins, T. Ball, M. Benedikt, G. Bruns, K. Cox, P. Mataga, and K. Rehor. Experience with a Domain Specific Language for Form-based Services. In *Usenix Conference on Domain Specific Languages*, Oct. 1997.
5. E. Barendsen and S. Smetsers. Uniqueness typing for functional languages with graph rewriting semantics. In *Mathematical Structures in Computer Science*, volume 6, pages 579–612, 1996.
6. E. Barendsen and S. Smetsers. *Graph Rewriting Aspects of Functional Programming*, chapter 2, pages 63–102. World scientific, 1999.
7. C. Brabrand, A. Møller, M. Ricky, and M. Schwartzbach. Powerforms: Declarative client-side form field validation. *World Wide Web Journal*, 3(4):205–314, 2000.
8. C. Brabrand, A. Møller, and M. Schwartzbach. The <bigwig> Project. In *ACM Transactions on Internet Technology (TOIT)*, 2002.
9. M. Elsman and K. F. Larsen. Typing XHTML Web applications in ML. In *International Symposium on Practical Aspects of Declarative Languages (PADL'04)*, volume 3057 of *LNCS*, pages 224–238. Springer-Verlag, June 2004.
10. P. Graunke, S. Krishnamurthi, R. Bruce Findler, and M. Felleisen. Automatically Restructuring Programs for the Web. In M. Feather and M. Goedicke, editors, *Proceedings 16th IEEE International Conference on Automated Software Engineering (ASE'01)*. IEEE CS Press, Sept. 2001.

11. M. Hanus. High-Level Server Side Web Scripting in Curry. In *Proc. of the Third International Symposium on Practical Aspects of Declarative Languages (PADL'01)*, pages 76–92. Springer LNCS 1990, 2001.

12. R. Hinze. A new approach to generic functional programming. In *The 27th Annual ACM SIGPLAN-SIGACT Symposium on Principles of Programming Languages*, pages 119–132. Boston, Massachusetts, January 2000.

13. R. Hinze and S. Peyton Jones. Derivable Type Classes. In G. Hutton, editor, *2000 ACM SIGPLAN Haskell Workshop*, volume 41(1) of *ENTCS*. Montreal, Canada, Elsevier Science, 2001.

14. J. Hughes. Generalising Monads to Arrows. *Science of Computer Programming*, 37:67–111, May 2000.

15. G. Krasner and S. Pope. A cookbook for using the Model-View-Controller user interface paradigm in Smalltalk-80. *Journal of Object-Oriented Programming*, 1(3):26–49, August 1988.

16. A. Löh, D. Clarke, and J. Jeuring. Dependency-style Generic Haskell. In *Proceedings of the eighth ACM SIGPLAN International Conference on Functional Programming (ICFP'03)*, pages 141–152. ACM Press, 2003.

17. E. Meijer. Server Side Web Scripting in Haskell. *Journal of Functional Programming*, 10(1):1–18, 2000.

18. R. Milner, M. Tofte, R. Harper, and D. MacQueen. *The Definition of Standard ML (Revised)*. MIT Press, 1997.

19. S. Peyton Jones and Hughes J. et al. *Report on the programming language Haskell 98*. University of Yale, 1999. http://www.haskell.org/definition/.

20. R. Plasmeijer and P. Achten. Generic Editors for the World Wide Web. In *Central-European Functional Programming School*, Eötvös Loránd University, Budapest, Hungary, Jul 4-16 2005.

21. R. Plasmeijer and P. Achten. iData For The World Wide Web - Programming Interconnected Web Forms. In *Proceedings Eighth International Symposium on Functional and Logic Programming (FLOPS 2006)*, volume 3945 of *LNCS*, Fuji Susono, Japan, Apr 24-26 2006. Springer Verlag.

22. R. Plasmeijer and M. van Eekelen. *Concurrent CLEAN Language Report (version 2.0)*, December 2001. http://www.cs.ru.nl/~clean/.

23. C. Queinnec. The influence of browsers on evaluators or, continuations to program web servers. In *Proceedings Fifth International Conference on Functional Programming (ICFP'00)*, Sept. 2000.

24. P. Thiemann. WASH/CGI: Server-side Web Scripting with Sessions and Typed, Compositional Forms. In S. Krishnamurthi and C. Ramakrishnan, editors, *Practical Aspects of Declarative Languages: 4th International Symposium, PADL 2002*, volume 2257 of *LNCS*, pages 192–208, Portland, OR, USA, January 19-20 2002. Springer-Verlag.

25. P. Thiemann. A Typed Representation for HTML and XML Documents in Haskell. *Journal of Functional Programming*, 2005. Under consideration for publication.

26. M. Wallace and C. Runciman. Haskell and XML: Generic combinators or type-based translation? In *Proc. of the Fourth ACM SIGPLAN Intnl. Conference on Functional Programming (ICFP'99)*, volume 34–9, pages 148–159, N.Y., 1999. ACM.

A High-Level Implementation of Composable Memory Transactions in Concurrent Haskell

Frank Huch and Frank Kupke

University of Kiel, Institute of Computer Science
Olshausenstr. 40, 24098 Kiel, Germany
{fhu,frk}@informatik.uni-kiel.de

Abstract. Composable memory transactions are a new communication abstraction for Concurrent Haskell which provides the programmer with a composable communication concept. Unfortunately, composable memory transactions are implemented as external functions for ghc version 6.4 and not available for other implementations of Concurrent Haskell. We present an implementation of memory transactions within Concurrent Haskell. The presented library can be executed within older ghc versions as well as with the popular Hugs system. Benchmarks show that our library performes well. Furthermore, our (high-level) implementation can be extended and maintained more easily than the low-level implementation provided by ghc 6.4.

1 Introduction

Harris, Marlow, Peyton Jones and Herlihy proposed a new communication abstraction for Concurrent Haskell [12,11], called *software transactional memory* (STM) [8]. The approach is based on the transaction concept known from databases and allows programmers to specify transaction sequences which are executed atomically. In comparison to lock-based approaches, this concept provides:

- freedom from deadlock and priority inversion
- automatic roll-back on exceptions or timeouts
- freedom from the tension between lock granularity and concurrency

The approach is efficiently implemented as external C primitives in the newest release (6.4) of the Glasgow Haskell Compiler (*ghc*) [6]. The implementation relies on the fair implementation of Concurrent Haskell within ghc and is not portable to other implementations of Concurrent Haskell, as in Hugs [10].

We present an implementation of STMs within Concurrent Haskell which is executable on every platform providing Concurrent Haskell, including Hugs (which also implements Concurrent Haskell within Haskell [2]). Although our (final) implementation is slower than the external implementation provided in ghc, it will be sufficiently fast in many applications (which usually do not perform transactions all the time as our benchmark programs do) and appears to be a good platform for experiments with possible extensions of STMs. A high-level

A. Butterfield, C. Grelck, and F. Huch (Eds.): IFL 2005, LNCS 4015, pp. 124–141, 2006.

implementation has also the opportunity of being more maintainable. Finally, our completely different implementation could also inspire the developers of the external implementation for more elegant or even more efficient code.

The paper is organized as follows: Section 2 introduces STMs and Section 3 defines our basic STM monad definition. Our first implementation is defined in Section 4 which is then redefined to our second approach in Section 5. More implementation details are presented in Section 6, before we discuss benchmarks in Section 7 and conclude in Section 8.

2 Software Transactional Memory

Transactions provided by ghc 6.4 and described in [8] provide a monad STM as an abstract data type for transactions. The execution of a transaction is guaranteed to be "atomic" with respect to other concurrently executed threads. STMs provide *optimistic synchronization*, which means transactions are interleaved with other transactions. A transaction is committed only if no other transaction has modified the memory its execution depended on. Otherwise, the transaction is restarted.

For communication inside the STM monad it provides transactional variables, in terms of the abstract data type TVar. The interface is defined as follows:

```
data STM a   -- abstract
instance Monad STM

-- Exceptions
throw :: Exception -> STM a
catchSTM :: STM a -> (Exception->STM a) -> STM a

-- Running STM computations
atomically :: STM a -> IO a
retry :: STM a
orElse :: STM a -> STM a -> STM a

-- Transactional variables
data TVar a   -- abstract
newTVar   :: a -> STM (TVar a)
readTVar  :: TVar a -> STM a
writeTVar :: TVar a -> a -> STM ()
```

Transactions are started within the IO monad by means of atomically[1]. When a transaction is finished, it is validated that the transaction was executed on a consistent system state, i.e. no other finished transaction may have modified relevant parts of the system state in the meantime. In this case, the modifications of the transaction are committed. Otherwise, they are discarded and the transaction is re-executed. Accordingly, inconsistent program states i.e. shared resources that are blocked by concurrent tasks can be detected by programmers and aborted

---

[1] In [8] this function was called atomic.

manually by calling **retry**. The provided implementation of **retry** avoids busy waiting and suspends the thread performing **retry** until a re-execution again makes sense. On top of **retry**, as a kind of alternative composition, it is possible to combine transaction as: stm_1 `orElse` stm_2. If stm_1 performs a **retry** action, then this is caught and stm_2 is executed. If stm_1 succeeds, then stm_2 is not executed at all.

Data modifiable by transactions is stored in **TVars** which can only be manipulated within the **STM** monad. Beside modifications of **TVars**, no other side effects like input/output are allowed within the **STM** monad which makes it possible to re-execute transactions.

Finally, the **STM** monad provides exception handling, similar to the exception handling ghc provides for the **IO** monad. For details see [8].

As a simple example, we present an implementation of the well-known dining philosophers using STMs. The sticks are represented by boolean **TVars**. **True** means the stick is laying on the table, i.e. it is available.

```
import STM
type Stick = TVar ()

takeStick :: Stick -> STM ()
takeStick s = do b <- readTVar s
                 if b then writeTVar s False
                      else retry

putStick :: Stick -> STM ()
putStick s =  writeTVar s True

phil :: Int -> Stick -> Stick -> IO ()
phil n l r = do atomically $ do takeStick l
                                takeStick r
                putStrLn (show n++". Phil is eating.")
                atomically $ do putStick l
                                putStick r
                phil n l r

startPhils :: Int -> IO ()
startPhils n = do sync <- newEmptyMVar
                  ioSticks <- atomically $ do
                    sticks <- mapM (const (newTVar True)) [1..n]
                    return sticks
                  mapM_ (\(l,r,i)->forkIO (phil eatings sync i l r))
                    (zip3 ioSticks (tail ioSticks) [1..n-1])
                  phil n (last ioSticks) (head ioSticks)
```

When trying to take a non-available stick, **takeStick** performs **retry**. The philosopher suspends until its neighbor puts the stick back onto the table. In the definition of **putStick** we do not perform a similar check since the behavior of each philosopher thread guarantees that the stick is not laying on the table (the **TVar** contains **False**) when performing **putStick**. However, this would be possible, too, and we used such a version for benchmarking as well. By combining the two actions for taking the sticks as one atomic STM transaction, the program is deadlock free. Putting the sticks back on the table in one atomic action is not necessary, but is shorter than writing atomically twice.

The code for starting n philosophers is just presented for completeness and not discussed any further.

3 Implementing STMs in Concurrent Haskell

We present two different implementations of STMs within Concurrent Haskell. Both can be used in any Concurrent Haskell implementation, like older ghc versions and Hugs. In comparison to the STM implementation available in ghc 6.4, our implementations have a (worst-case) slow down between 3 to 40.

In both approaches we define the STM monad as an extension of the IO monad with a state used for collecting information about the execution of a transaction. The STM monad is defined similarly to other IO monad extensions, e.g. the GUI monad defined in TclHaskell [4] or other libraries for graphical user interfaces:

```
data STM a = STM (STMState -> IO (STMResult a))

instance Monad STM where
  (STM tr1) >>= k = STM (\state -> do
                           stmRes <- tr1 state
                           case stmRes of
                             Success newState a ->
                               let (STM tr2) = k a in
                                 tr2 newState
                             Retry newState -> return (Retry newState)
                             Invalid -> return Invalid
                         )
  return x = STM (\state -> return (Success state x))

data STMResult a = Retry STMState
                 | Invalid
                 | Success STMState a
```

The data type STMResult covers the relevant results of an STM action. The type STMState is the state carried through the STM monad. Its concrete realization will be discussed further in each implementation.

4 Collecting Modifications in TVars

Our first approach for implementing STMs is closely related to the implementation presented in [8] where a thread-local transaction log is used to collect and share all TVar accesses within a thread. The transaction log holds references to all used TVars and is responsible for the necessary verify and commit actions.

The original STM implementation [8] uses thread-local TLogs referencing the global TVars. Therefore, each TLog is a list pointing to each TVar used in its thread. Unfortunately, in general, TVars have different types. This prohibits using the same data structure in our implementation because of Haskell's strict type system. We use the opposite referencing structure instead: each TVar contains a log which simply stores a list of its new local values of all threads/atomic blocks it was modified by. This list maps transaction identifiers (IDs, discussed in more detail in Section 6.2) to locally modified values.

The TVar value itself is stored in an IORef (IORef a). As a consequence, TVar values can later be compared by pointer comparison of the inner IORefs. Whenever a value is written to a TVar in a thread, we create a new IORef which means the comparison with the old value IORef will indicate the modification. Finally, the TVar contains a wait queue for retries (discussed in Section 4.1):

```
data TVar a = TVar (IORef (IORef a))    -- the TVar content
                   (MVar [(ID,IORef a)] -- thread local TVar copies
                   (IORef [MVar ()])    -- wait queue on retry
```

If a readTVar or writeTVar action is performed, the corresponding thread updates its local version of the TVar value. To guarantee atomic modifications of the TVar copies, these are embedded into an MVar. The local TVar value is accessed by a transaction identifier. Here we first used ThreadIds to emulate the thread-local TLog structure used in [8]. ThreadIDs can be used to identify each transaction as each thread can execute only one atomic transaction at a time. Since ThreadIds are not available in Hugs each STM action obtains a fresh stmId when started instead. Details how we provided identifiers are discussed in Section 6.2. The stmId is part of the STMState record (defined later in this section) passed through our STM monad. Writing a TVar can now easily be defined as follows:

```
writeTVar (TVar _ tLog _) v = STM $ \stmState -> do
  tLogs <- takeMVar tLog
  putMVar tLog ((stmId stmState,v):tLogs)

readTVar (TVar tVarRef tLog _) = STM $ \stmState -> do
  tLogs <- takeMVar tLog
  case lookup (stmId stmState) tLogs of
    Just v ->  do return v
                  putMVar tLog tLogs
    Nothing -> do tVarVal <- (readIORef tVarRef)
                  putMVar tLog tLogs
                  readIORef tVarVal
```

This implementation simply masks old values within the log list. In the real implementation these values are replaced, to keep log lists short[2].

Now, we have to find an implementation for checking the validity of a transaction and committing all modifications performed within a transaction. Again,

---

[2] There are more efficient ways, e.g., balanced search trees, to represent the TVar log which are not discussed here as we will present a more efficient solution without such a log in Section 5.

the type system does not allow holding a list of all read (for checking validity) and written (for committing) TVars. As a solution, we collect respective IO functions and eventually execute them at the end of the atomic block. For validating, this is an action of type IO Bool and for committing of type IO (). Furthermore, we need a function for discarding the logs within the TVars.

Now, we have introduced most of the information to be kept in the STMState which is defined as the following record:

```
data STMState = STMState {isValid   :: IO Bool,
                          commit    :: IO (),
                          discard   :: IO (),
                          wait      :: IO (),
                          retryMVar :: MVar (),
                          stmId     :: ID}
```

The components wait and retryMVar are needed for suspending in retry and discussed in Section 4.1. Validation, commit and discard actions within the state are extended in each readTVar or writeTVar action. The function readTVar extends the already stored validation by a comparison of its own value with the new value stored in its log:

```
readTVar (TVar tVarRef tLog _) = STM $ \stmState -> do
  ... -- read the value of the TVar bound in variable val
  oldVal <- readIORef tVarRef
  let newState = stmState{isValid   = do
                              b <- isValid stmState
                              if b then do
                                   tVarVal <- readIORef tVarRef
                                   return (tVarVal == oldVal)
                                   else return False}
  return (Success newState val)
```

In a writeTVar action the commit function is built up to copy the local TVar value into the real TVar thus committing a successful atomic action.

```
writeTVar tVar@(TVar tVarRef tLog waitQ) = STM $ \stmState -> do
  ...
  let newState = stmState{
      commit  = do commit stmState
                   commitAct (stmId stmState) tVar
                   notify waitQ,
      discard = do tLogs <- takeMVar tLog
                   let (pres, _:posts) = filter ((stmId/=) . fst)
                                                tLogs
                   putMVar tLog (pres ++ posts)
                   discard stmState}
  return (Success newState ())
```

with commitAct defined as

```
commitAct :: ID -> TVar a -> IO ()
commitAct stmId (TVar tVarRef tLog _) = do
  tLogs <- readMVar tLog
  let Just newRef = lookup stmId tLogs
  v <- readIORef newRef
  newTVarVal <- newIORef v
  writeIORef tVarRef newTVarVal
```

The action `commit` does not only copy new values within the `TVars`. It also notifies other transactions suspended within a `retry` action. This and the implementation of `notify` are discussed in more detail in Section 4.1.

The function `atomically` starts and validates transactions. Non-valid transactions are discarded (the corresponding `TVar` copies are deleted) and restarted. Valid transactions are committed, i.e. the original `TVar` value is overwritten by the value stored for the actual `stmId`. The `IO` functions for discarding and committing values are constructed in `readTVar` and `writeTVar` and stored in the `STMState` as shown above. The whole process of validating, committing and discarding may not be interupted by any other concurrent thread which is guaranteed by calling the functions `takeGlobalLock` and `freeGlobalLock`. Possible implementations are discussed in Section 6.1.

```
atomically :: STM a -> IO a
atomically stmAction = do
  stmResult <- startSTM stmAction
  case stmResult of
    Invalid -> atomically stmAction
    Success newSTMState res -> do takeGlobalLock
                                  valid <- isValid newSTMState
                                  if valid
                                    then do
                                      commit newSTMState
                                      discard newSTMState
                                      freeGlobalLock
                                      return res
                                    else do
                                      discard newSTMState
                                      freeGlobalLock
                                      atomically stmAction
```

So far, a distinction between `Invalid` and `Retry` actions is not necessary and we only consider the `STMResult Invalid`. The discussion of `orElse` in Section 6.3 will distinguish these two cases.

4.1   Retry

In STMs it is also possible that the programmer marks a branch of the execution as invalid, by executing the `retry` action. For instance, a dining philosopher calls `retry` when trying to take a non-available stick. Of course, if he already sucessfully took his first stick, then he should put back his first stick, again. Naturally, this is implemented within an atomic action as shown before.

When implementing `retry` it does not make sense to directly restart the transaction, because the computation would execute exactly the same transaction again and deterministically reach the same `retry` action. Its branching behavior only depends on the values of the `TVar`s it read during its execution. Hence, `retry` should suspend until any of the `TVar`s read during its execution is modified by another thread.

In Concurrent Haskell a thread can only suspend on exactly one `MVar`. Hence, we introduce a `retryMVar :: MVar ()` in the `STMState`, on which it suspends in `retry`. Again, we guarantee the atomic execution of validation, commit and restore by a global lock:

```
retry :: STM a
retry = STM (\stmState -> do
            takeGlobalLock
            valid <- isValid stmState
            discard stmState
            if valid then do wait stmState
                             freeGlobalLock
                             takeMVar (retryMVar stmState)
                             return Invalid
                      else do
                             freeGlobalLock
                             return Invalid)
```

After validating a transaction all stored modifications are discarded. Then, in case of a valid transaction the thread should suspend. However, beforehand, it has to register itself for being awoken again in each read `TVar`. This is implemented by means of an accumulated `wait` action extending wait queues in all read `TVar`s in a similar way as presented for `isValid`, `commit`, and `discard`:

```
readTVar (TVar tVarRef tLog waitQ) = STM $ \stmState -> do
   ... -- val is bound here
   let newState = stmState{...
                           wait = do
                             wait stmState
                             queue <- readIORef waitQ
                             putMVar waitQ (retryMVar stmState:queue)}
   return (Success newState val)
```

After executing all `wait` actions `retry` suspends on its `retryMVar` and after being awoken returns `Invalid` which initiates restarting the transaction in the enclosing `atomically`.

For awaking suspended transactions, each committed `writeTVar` action sets all registered `retryMVars`. The call to this notification was already integrated in the definition of the `commit` action in `writeTVar`. For completeness, we present the missing definition of `notify`:

```
notify :: IORef [MVar ()] -> IO ()
notify waitQ = do
  queue <- readIORef waitQ
  writeIORef waitQ []
  mapM_ tryPutMVar queue
```

Note, that race conditions between different `notifys` in different `commit` actions are already avoided by locking the execution before committing. Hence, there is no need to store the wait queue of a `TVar` within an `MVar`, an `IORef` is sufficient.

Benchmarks for this implementation show that the approach could be used in practice. However, our implementation is (for programs only performing transactions) up to 40 times slower than ghc's internal implementation.

5   The Collecting Approach

Profiling programs using the presented `STM` implementation shows that

- much time is spent for modifying `TVars` and
- validation, commit and notification are very fast.

Since collecting actions performs very well, it would be nice to extend this idea for the modifications while reading and writing as well. Inspecting transactions from a more abstract point of view we observe that

- reading is in most cases performed on original `TVars` and
- writing is delayed to copying in commit.

Hence, why don't we collect the `writeTVar` actions themselves in the `commit` actions instead of an action which copies a value within the `TVar`? Then, the only problematic case would be reading a `TVar` written beforehand. A modification of a `TVar` is only available after performing the commit.

In practice, programmers will try to avoid reading an already written `TVar` since the value written to the `TVar` is already known within the transaction. On the other hand, composing transactions may create such cases in which two composed transactions modify and read the same `TVar` more than once. We assume that this case may occur in practice (and has to be handled correctly by our implementation), but that it is not the regular case for every `TVar` in every transaction. Furthermore, the programmer can avoid this case and optimize programs by hand if necessary. Hopefully, the loss of efficiency for this special case will not matter compared to the gained speedup of using collected actions instead of modifying data structures within the `TVar` representations.

But how can we correctly access the value of an already modified `TVar`? The problem is that we may not modify `TVars` to obtain the actual value, but the only place where this value is stored is the accumulated commit action. A solution is motivated by the search for deadlocks in Concurrent Haskell programs in [1]. Modifications of communication abstractions can be reversed. Hence, in parallel to accumulating the commit action, we accumulate a restore action. With these two actions we can solve the problem of reading already written TVars. After setting a global lock and checking validity of the actual transaction we can commit all TVar modifications, read the actual value, and revert the modified TVars. Fortunately, the overhead for this expensive operation will in some cases be balanced by the fact that the earlier validation restarts the transaction earlier.

To identify the situation in which an already written TVar is read we have to collect all modified TVars within the STMState. Again, Haskell's type system does not allow such a data structure. As before, this problem can be solved by using unique identifiers which in this case identify the different TVars:

```
data TVar a = TVar (IORef (IORef a))  -- the TVar content
                 ID                    -- TVar identifier
                 (IORef [MVar ()])     -- wait queue on retry
```

In this implementation, all components of the TVar can be stored in IORefs, in contrast to the thread local copies which had to be stored in an MVar to avoid race conditions for concurrent modifications. The exclusive access to the TVar content and the wait queue will be guaranteed by locking before their modifications.

The identifiers of all modified TVars within a transaction are stored in the STMState. The modified STMState is defined as follows:

```
data STMState = STMState {stmId        :: ID,
                          modifiedTVars :: [ID],
                          isValid      :: IO Bool,
                          commit       :: IO (),
                          notify       :: IO (),
                          restore      :: IO (),
                          wait         :: IO (),
                          retryMVar    :: MVar ()}
```

If such an already modified TVar is read, then we have to consider the "actual" value of this TVar within our STM Monad. Otherwise, readTVar behaves as before.

```
readTVar (TVar tVarRef tId waitQ) = STM $ \stmState ->
  if elem tId (modifiedTVars stmState) then do
    takeGlobalLock
    valid <- fIsValid
    if valid then do commit stmState
                     tVarVal <- readIORef tVarRef
                     val <- readIORef tVarVal
                     restore stmState
                     freeGlobalLock
                     return (Success stmState val)
             else do freeGlobalLock
                     return Invalid
  else ...
```

Note, that the commit and restore actions have to be protected by a validation check to ensure consistency. For completeness, we also present the new writeTVar code. The modifications of commit and notify stay unchanged.

```
writeTVar (TVar tVarRef tId waitQ) v = STM $ \stmState -> do
  tVarVal <- readIORef tVarRef
  let newState =
      stmState{modifiedTVars = n:modifiedTVars threadState,
               commit = ...
               notify = ...
               restore = do writeIORef tVarRef tVarVal
                            restore stmState}
  return (Success newState ())
```

Within the implementation details of [8] a potential problem arising from inconsistency has been highlighted with the following example:

```
f :: Integer -> Bool
f x = if x==0 then True else f (x-1)
foo v = atomically $ do
          x <- readTVar v
          y <- readTVar v
          if f (x-y) then ... else ...
```

An inconsistent view of v can lead to nontermination. The solution proposed in [8] is to check for consistency whenever the scheduler is about to switch a thread engaged in a transaction. Of course, with our high-level approach access to the scheduler is not easily feasable. Fortunately, this problem is similar to the problem of reading an already written TVar. The solution is easy. We extend the modifiedTVars of a transaction to a list of touchedTVars which is also extended when reading a TVar. Then, an additional validity check can be started when reading a TVar for the second time. For long transactions taking many schedule switches this may perform even better than the approach taken in [8].

The nice idea behind the collecting approach is accumulating the whole transaction within IO actions which may then be performed when reaching the end of the transaction. Benchmarks show that this implementation performs very well, as we will discuss in Section 7.

6   More Implementation Details

So far, we presented the whole implementation of STMs in Concurrent Haskell. However, some aspects of the implementation are not discussed yet.

6.1   Global Locks

In the presented implementations, we had to ensure that in some cases threads do not interfere, e.g., for validating and committing transactions. In the presented code, we called functions takeGlobalLock and freeGlobalLock in the corresponding cases. The simplest implementation of a global lock can be implemented as a global MVar () constant by means of unsafePerformIO:

```
globalLock :: MVar ()
globalLock = unsafePerformIO (newMVar ())

takeGlobalLock :: IO ()
takeGlobalLock = takeMVar globalLock

freeGlobalLock :: IO ()
freeGlobalLock = putMVar globalLock ()
```

However, it is also possible to avoid this `unsafePerformIO` call. We extend TVars with a lock MVar ():

```
data TVar a = TVar (IORef (IORef a))   -- global TVar itself
                 ID                    -- TVar identifier
                 (MVar ())             -- TVar lock
                 (IORef [MVar ()])     -- wait queue on retry
```

and extend the `touchedTVars` in the STMState with such lock MVars as well:

```
data STMState = STMState{...
                         touchedTVars :: [(ID,MVar ())]
                         ...}
```

During the computation of a transaction the lock MVars of all touched TVars are collected, like in the definition of `readTVar`:

```
readTVar (TVar tVarRef tId tVarLock waitQ) = STM $ \stmState -> do
  if isJust lookup tId (touchedTVars stmState)
    then ...
    else do
      ...
      let newState = stmState{wait = ...
                              touchedTVars =
                                (tId,tVarLock):touchedTVars stmState}
      return (Success newState val)
```

Instead of setting a global lock before validating and committing it is now possible to only lock the touched TVars by performing `takeMVar` on these collected lock MVars. To avoid race conditions, it is important to sort these collected lock MVars with respect to their IDs before taking the lock MVars. Unlocking the touched TVars of a transaction is done by again putting () into these lock MVars.

Measurements show that this implementation is up to 20% slower than using a global lock. Usually, the time for which a global lock is set is very short. Hence, we use a global lock in our implementation. However, for the execution on multi-processor machines [7] and [3] show that implementations without using global locks perform better in many cases. Hence, it is important to have such an implementation as well. Further interesting investigations would be how our implementation scales for the examples in [3] on multi-processor machines.

6.2   Unique Identifiers

In both approaches we needed unique identifiers: for identifying different STMs in the first approach and different TVars in the second approach.

Again, a simple implementation uses a global state of Integer values (defined by unsafePerformIO) which can only be increased when getting a new ID.

```
type ID = Integer

globalCount :: MVar ID
globalCount = unsafePerformIO (newMVar [0..])

getGlobalId :: IO ID
getGlobalId = do
  num <- takeMVar globalCount
  putMVar globalCount (num+1)
  return num
```

Again, it would be nice to have an implementation without unsafePerformIO. The idea is to use IORefs instead of numbers, since it is possible to compare them.

```
type ID = IORef ()

getGlobalId :: IO ID
getGlobalId = newIORef ()
```

The garbage collector takes care of unused IORefs. There is no need for explicit releasing of identifiers at the end of an atomic block. However, the convenience of these runtime system provided identifiers has to be paid by a slight slow down. An alternative unsafePerformIO free implementation of unique identifiers can be obtained by using stable pointers of Haskell's Foreign Function Interface [5,13]. Being able to avoid using unsafePerformIO is nice and shows the elegance of the presented implementation.

6.3   OrElse

So far, we have not considered the implementation of orElse. The semantics of combining two transaction as stm_1 `orElse` stm_2 is that if stm_1 performs a retry action, then all modifications within stm_1 are discarded and stm_2 is performed. Hence, validating the whole transaction means validating that stm_1 is still valid (reaching retry) and stm_2 is valid. However, accumulated commit/restore actions within stm_1 have to be discarded. We implement this behavior by extending commit, restore, and notify to lists (stacks) of IO actions, the other parts of the STMState stay unchanged:

```
data STMState = STMState{...
                    commits  :: [IO ()],
                    notifys  :: [IO ()],
                    restores :: [IO ()],
                    ...}
```

When accumulating these actions in `readTVar` and `writeTvar` we only extend the actions stored in the head position of these lists (the top-level stack frame).

At this point the distinction of the `STMResults` `Invalid` and `Retry` becomes relevant. Only for `Retry` our `orElse` implementation may execute the second transaction. In our second implementation `Invalid` is a possible intermediate `STMResult`, since reading an already modified `TVar` performs an intermediate validation.

```
orElse :: STM a -> STM a -> STM a
orElse (STM stm1) (STM stm2) =
  STM (\stmState -> do
        stm1Res <- stm1 stmState{commits  = return ():commits stmState,
                                 notifys  = return ():notifys stmState,
                                 restores = return ():restores stmState}
        case stm1Res of
          Retry newState ->
              stm2 newState{commits = tail (commits newState),
                            notifys = tail (notifys newState),
                            restores = tail (restores newState)}
          _ -> return stm1Res)
```

Note, that `orElse` extends the list of commit/notify/restore actions when executing `stm1` and pops them again when (in case of `retry`) `stm2` is executed. As a matter of course, executing these actions in the definition of `atomically` (and `readTVar` as well) must consider the list structure. For instance, instead of `commit stmState` we have to perform:

```
sequence_ (reverse (commits stmState))
```

Reverting the list is necessary, because earlier modifications are located deeper in the list. And the chronological order is important if the same `TVar` is written twice within a transaction.

6.4   Exceptions

Exception handling as proposed for STMs can also be integrated into the presented implementations. Unfortunately, the semantics of STM exceptions has a strange behavior as the following example shows:

```
main = do
  t <- atomically (newTVar 42)
  r <- atomically (do
      writeTVar t 43
      catchSTM (do
          writeTVar t 44
          seq undefine (return True))
        (\e -> return False))
  print r
  v <- atomically (readTVar t)
  print v
```

Executing this program, the following output is produced:

```
False
44
```

Although an exception occurs and is caught both modifications of t are committed. To us, it is not clear how a programmer is supposed to identify which parts of a transaction are committed if an exception occurs. We would prefer that only the transactions before catchSTM are committed when catching an exception. This can also be implemented more easily and more efficiently. However, we want to cover exactly the semantics proposed in [8].

To track STM actions until an exception occurs, we extend the STMState with an additional case for exceptions

```
data STMState = ...
             | Exception StmState Exception
```

Furthermore, we extend the Monad instance for STM with these cases and catch exceptions which may occur during the execution of tr2 newState, by means of ghc's catch function:

```
instance Monad STM where
  (STM tr1) >>= k =
    STM (\state -> do
            stmRes <- tr1 state
            case stmRes of
              Success newState a ->
                let (STM tr2) = k a in
                  catch (tr2 newState)
                        (\e -> return (Exception newState e))
              Retry newState -> return (Retry newState)
              Invalid -> return Invalid
              Exception newState e -> return (Exception newState e)
        )
```

It is not necessary to catch exceptions in tr1. These can be caught when starting the STM monad in atomically.

By means of these explicit exceptions within the STM monad, we can easily define catchSTM:

```
catchSTM (STM stm) stmHandler = STM (\stmState -> do
  res <- stm stmState
  case res of
    Exception newState e ->
      case stmHandler e of
        STM ioHandler -> ioHandler newState
    Success newState r -> return (Success newState r)
    Retry newState     -> return (Retry newState)
    InValid            -> return InValid)
```

Performing catch for each (>>=) operator is expensive. Hence, we improved our code such that catch is only executed inside catchSTM by means of a boolean flag in the STMState. This flag is set and reset by catchSTM and exceptions are only caught if the flag is set.

7 Benchmarks

It is quite challenging to generate a reliable benchmark analysis for concurrent programs using STMs. Execution times depend on the actual scheduling thus sometimes differing significantly from each other. This is also true for ghc 6.4's STM implementation itself. In addition benchmark results depend on the test programs used and their frequency of TVar accesses. Finally, our benchmarks perform mostly transactions. Therefore, small modifications (e.g., using a global state or IORefs for implementing IDs) can yield a significant impact. Real applications will usually behave much more homogenious relative to the different libraries used as real programs should also compute something. Hence, the execution time of transactions will be less relevant and most applications will work fine with any correct implementation.

However, we want to present some results and conclusions of our benchmark tests. We present benchmark test results of three different Haskell applications using the STM library generated out of the final implementation mentioned in this paper (*collect*) and the standard ghc 6.4 library as reference (*ghcLib*). The applications shown are: A standard dining philosopher implementation based on the one shown in Section 2 (*DinPhil*), a modified dining philosopher implementation with the philosophers atomically taking and putting their sticks three times in a row before finally taking them (*DinPhil3*) and an STM stress test called *conc049* presented in [14].

Each of the executables has been run and timed repeatedly on different machine configurations. Figure 1 presents median execution times in seconds, standard deviation of the runs and the slow down factor in comparison to ghc of both approaches. All programs are compiled using ghc's optimization option.

As expected our library is slower than the built in C implementation provided by ghc. However, for common usage of transaction like in *DinPhil* and *conc049* our implementation is only three times slower. For strange application modifying

benchmark	library	median execution time	standard deviation	slow down factor
DinPhil	*ghcLib*	0.77	0.002	1
	collect	2.53	0.173	3.3
DinPhil3	*ghcLib*	1.39	0.003	1
	collect	18.43	0.736	13.2
conc049	*ghcLib*	0.16	0.075	1
	collect	0.43	0.342	2.7

Fig. 1. Benchmark results

and reading the same TVar within one transaction like *DinPhil3* our implementation is 13.2 times slower than ghc's STMs. With this test we expose the weak point of our implementation. However, such cases should be uncommon in real applications and they can be easily optimized by the application programmer in most cases. Furthermore, real applications will not only perform transactions, but also perform other computations. In many real applications there should be no noticeable slow down using our library.

A further analysis of the benchmark figures shows that the statistical deviation between different runs is significantly higher using our library than ghc's. We suspect that the "synchronization" of verify and commit actions with the scheduler in the ghc library implementation ([8]) is one reason for a more consistent behavior between different runs. Further research has to be made to analyze these effects.

8   Conclusion

We have presented two re-implementations of software transactional memory within Concurrent Haskell. The first implementation is closer related to the implementation in ghc 6.4. Analyzing the run-time behavior of this implementation yields to a more high-level implementation accumulating commit and validation actions within the state inside the STM monad. Benchmarks show that this implementation is between three to in the worst case 13 times slower than the implementation in ghc 6.4. However, in real applications this will usually not be a problem, since these programs will also perform other computations.

On the other hand, our implementation also has some advantages: it can be executed in any Concurrent Haskell implementation, including Hugs and older ghc versions. It works independently of the underlying scheduling model. It is an implementation in a high-level language which can be maintained and extended more easily. Hence, it should be a good platform for further research on transaction based communication in Concurrent Haskell. The library is available from the first author's web page.

For future work, we want to investigate how software transactions could be extended and how they could be used for distributed programming. A good basis should be the implementation of Distributed Haskell [9] which extends Concurrent Haskell to a distributed setting.

Acknowledgment

We thank the anonymous reviewers for their very detailed comments on the first version of our paper and for uncovering a bug hidden in our first implementation.

References

1. Jan Christiansen and Frank Huch. Searching for deadlocks while debugging concurrent haskell programs. In *ICFP '04: Proceedings of the ninth ACM SIGPLAN international conference on Functional programming*, pages 28–39, New York, NY, USA, 2004. ACM Press.

2. Koen Claessen. A poor man's concurrency monad. *Journal of Functional Programming*, 9(3):313–323, 1999.
3. Anthony Discolo, Tim Harris, Simon Marlow, Simon Peyton Jones, and Satnam Singh. Lock free data structures using STMs in Haskell. In *FLOPS 2006: Eighth International Symposium on Functional and Logic Programming*, April 2006.
4. Chris Dornan. Tcl + Haskell = TclHaskell. In *Glasgow FP Group Workshop, Pitlochry, Scotland*, September 1998. More information at http://www.dcs.gla.ac.uk/~nww/TkHaskell/TkHaskell.html.
5. Manuel Chakravarty (ed.). The Haskell 98 foreign function interface 1.0: An addendum to the Haskell 98 report. http://www.cse.unsw.edu.au/chak/haskell/ffi/.
6. The Glasgow Haskell compiler. http://www.haskell.org/ghc/.
7. Tim Harris, Simon Marlow, and Simon Peyton Jones. Haskell on a shared-memory multiprocessor. In *Haskell '05: Proceedings of the 2005 ACM SIGPLAN workshop on Haskell*, pages 49–61. ACM Press, September 2005.
8. Tim Harris, Simon Marlow, Simon Peyton-Jones, and Maurice Herlihy. Composable memory transactions. In *PPoPP '05: Proceedings of the tenth ACM SIGPLAN symposium on Principles and practice of parallel programming*, pages 48–60, New York, NY, USA, 2005. ACM Press.
9. Frank Huch and Ulrich Norbisrath. Distributed programming in Haskell with ports. In *Proceedings of the 12th International Workshop on the Implementation of Functional Languages*, volume 2011 of *Lecture Notes in Computer Science*, pages 107–121, 2000.
10. The Haskell interpreter Hugs. http://www.haskell.org/hugs/.
11. Simon Peyton Jones. Tackling the awkward squad: monadic input/output, concurrency, exceptions, and foreign-language calls in Haskell. In *Engineering theories of software construction, Marktoberdorf Summer School 2000, NATO ASI Series*. IOS Press, 2001.
12. Simon Peyton Jones, Andrew Gordon, and Sigbjorn Finne. Concurrent Haskell. In *Conference Record of POPL '96: The 23rd ACM SIGPLAN-SIGACT Symposium on Principles of Programming Languages*, pages 295–308, St. Petersburg Beach, Florida, 21–24 1996.
13. Simon Marlow, Simon Peyton Jones, and Wolfgang Thaller. Extending the Haskell foreign function interface with concurrency. In *Proceedings of the ACM SIGPLAN workshop on Haskell*, pages 57–68, Snowbird, Utah, USA, September 2004.
14. A Concurrent Haskell Testsuite. http://cvs.haskell.org/cgi-bin/cvsweb.cgi/fptools/testsuite/tests/ghc-regress/concurrent/should_run/.

Polytypic Syntax Tree Operations

Arjen van Weelden, Sjaak Smetsers, and Rinus Plasmeijer

Institute for Computing and Information Sciences
Radboud University Nijmegen
The Netherlands
{A.vanWeelden, S.Smetsers, R.Plasmeijer}@cs.ru.nl

Abstract. Polytypic functional programming has the advantage that it can derive code for generic functions automatically. However, it is not clear whether it is useful for anything other than the textbook examples, and the generated polytypic code is usually too slow for real-life programs. As a real-life test, we derive a polytypic parser for the Haskell 98 syntax and look into other front-end compiler syntax tree operations.

We present a types–as–grammar approach, which uses polytypic programming (in both Generic Haskell and Clean) to automatically derive the code for a parser based on the syntax tree type, without using external tools. Moreover, we show that using polytypic programming can even be useful for data–specific syntax tree operations in a (functional) compiler, such as scope checking and type inference.

Simple speed tests show that the performance of polytypic parsers can be abominable for real-life inputs. However, we show that much performance can be recovered by applying (extended) fusion optimization on the generated code. We actually have a derived parser whose speed is close to one generated by a specialized Haskell parser generator.

1 Introduction

The construction of complex software often starts by designing suitable data types to which functionality is added. Some functionality is data type specific, other functionality only depends on the structure of the data type. Polytypic programming is considered an important technique to specify such generic functionality. It enables the specification of functions on the structure of data types, and therefore, it is characterized as type dependent (type indexed) programming. The requested overall functionality is obtained by designing your data types such that they reflect the separation of specific and generic functionality. By overruling the polytypic instantiation mechanism for those parts of the data type that correspond to specific functionality, one obtains the desired overall behavior. In essence, a programmer only has to *program the exception* and a small polytypic scheme, since polytypic functions automatically work for the major part of the data types. Examples of such generic operations are equality, traversals, pretty-printing, and serialization.

The number of such generic operations in a specific program can be quite small, and hence the applicability of polytypic programming seems limited. Polytypic functions that are data specific only make sense if the involved data types

A. Butterfield, C. Grelck, and F. Huch (Eds.): IFL 2005, LNCS 4015, pp. 142–159, 2006.

themselves are complex or very big. Otherwise, the definition of the polytypic version of an operation requires more effort than defining this operation directly. Moreover, the data-dependent functionality should be restricted to only a small portion of the data type, while the rest can be treated generically.

This paper investigates the suitability of polytypic programming as a general programming tool, by applying it to (a part of) compiler construction. Compilers involve both rich data structures and many, more or less complex, operations on those data structures. We focus on the front-end of compilers: parsing, post-parsing, and type inference operations on the syntax tree. There exist many special tools, e.g., parser generators and compiler compilers, that can be used for constructing such a front-end. We show that polytypic programming techniques can also be used to elegantly specify parsers. This has the advantage that the polytypic functional compiler can generate most of the code. Another advantage it that one can specify everything in the functional language itself, without synchronization issues, e.g., between the syntax tree type and the grammar definition, with external tools.

We have implemented polytypic parsers in both Generic Haskell [1] (a preprocessor for Haskell [2]) and Clean [3]. We use (Generic) Haskell to present our implementation in this paper, the Clean code is very similar. The polytypic parser we use in this paper differs from those commonly described in papers on polytypic programming [4,5]. Our parser is based on the *types–as–grammars* approach: the context-free syntax of the language to parse is specified via appropriate data type definitions. The types–as–grammar approach was previously used to construct a new version of the Esther shell originally described in Weelden and Plasmeijer [6]. The shell uses polytypic programming to specify the parser and post-parsing operations on expressions the size of a single command-line. This paper tackles larger inputs and grammars, including the Haskell syntax.

Apart from its expressiveness, a programming technique is not very useful if the performance of the generated code is inadequate. The basic code generation schema that is used in the current implementations of polytypic systems produces inefficient code. We asses the efficiency of both the Generic Haskell and the Clean implementations and compare them with the code generated by an optimization tool by Alimarine and Smetsers [7]. This tool takes a polytypic Clean program as input and produces a Haskell/Clean-like output without the polytypic overhead.

To summarize, the main contributions of this paper are:

- We show that polytypic programming, introduced in Sect. 2, is not only suited for defining more or less inherently generic operations, but also for specifying data specific functionality.
- We describe a technique that allows us to derive a parser for context-free languages automatically from the definition of a syntax tree in Sect. 3. The technique is based on the idea to interpret types as grammar specifications.

- We show that the same technique applies to several related syntax tree operations in Sect. 4. As operations become more data specific, we gain less from using polytypic programming. However, we show that it is not totally unsuitable for non-generic algorithms.
- As most polytypic programmers know, polytypic programs (including our parsers) have serious performance problems. Fortunately, we show in Sect. 5 that an appropriate optimization tool recovers a lot of efficiency, and that our parsers can approach the speed of parsers generated by external tools.

Related work is discussed in Sect. 6, and we conclude in Sect. 7.

2   Polytypic Programming

Specifying polytypic functions is a lot like defining a type class and its instances. The main difference is that a polytypic compiler can derive most of the instances automatically, given a minimal fixed set of instances for three or four (generic) types. The programmer can always overrule the derived instance for a certain type by specifying the instance manually. This powerful derivation scheme even extends to kinds (the types of types), which we will neither use nor explain in this paper.

The fact that polytypic functions can be derived for most types is based on the observation that any (user defined) algebraic data type can be expressed in terms of eithers, pairs, and units. This generic representation, developed by Hinze [8], is used by Generic Haskell and is encoded there by the following Haskell types:

```
data Sum a b = Inl a | Inr b — either/choice between (In)left and (In)right
data Prod a b = a :*: b       — pair/product of two types, left associative
data Unit = Unit              — the unit type
```

A data type and its generic representation are isomorphic. The corresponding isomorphism can be specified as a pair of conversion functions. E.g., for lists the generic representation and automatically generated associated conversion functions are as follows.

```
type GenericList a = Sum (Prod a [a]) Unit
```

```
fromList :: [a] → GenericList a          toList :: GenericList a → [a]
fromList (x:xs) = Inl (x :*: xs)         toList (Inl (x :*: xs)) = x:xs
fromList []     = Inr Unit               toList (Inr Unit)       = []
```

Note that the generic representation type GenericList is not recursive and still contains the original list type. A polytypic function instance for the list type can be constructed by the polytypic system using the generic representation. The derived instance for the list type uses the given instances for Sum, Prod, Unit, and once again the currently deriving instance for lists. This provides the recursive call, which one would expect for a recursive type such as lists.

To define a polytypic function, the programmer has to specify its function type, similar to a type class, and only the instances for the generic types (Prod, Sum, and Unit) and non-algebraic types (like Int and Double). The polytypic instances for other types that are actually used inside a program are automatically derived. Polytypic functions are, therefore, most useful if a large collection of (large) data types is involved, or if the types change a lot during development.

To illustrate polytypic programming we use the following syntax tree excerpt:

```
data Expr = Apply Expr Expr          | Lambda Pattern Expr
          | Case Expr [(Pattern, Expr)] | Variable String
          | If Expr Expr Expr        | ···

data Pattern = Var String | Constructor String [Pattern] | ···

data ···
```

We define a Generic Haskell function print of type a → String that is polytypic in the type variable a, similar to Haskell's show of type Show a ⇒ a → String that is overloaded in a. Instead of instances for the Show class, we define type instances for print using the special parentheses ⦃ ⦄ .

```
print ⦃ a ⦄  :: a → String

print ⦃ Int ⦄     i        = show i           — basic type instance

print ⦃ Unit ⦄    Unit     = ""               — unit instance

print ⦃ Sum a b ⦄ (Inl l)  = print ⦃ a ⦄ l    — left either instance
print ⦃ Sum a b ⦄ (Inr r)  = print ⦃ b ⦄ r    — right either instance

print ⦃ Prod a b ⦄ (l :*: r)                  — pair instance
      = print ⦃ a ⦄ l ++ " " ++ print ⦃ b ⦄ r

print ⦃ Con d a ⦄ (Con x)                     — instance for constructors
      = "(" ++ conName d ++ " " print ⦃ a ⦄ x ++ ")"
```

To print the parameterized type Sum, and also Prod, print requires printing functions for the parameter types a and b. These are automatically passed under the hood by Generic Haskell, similar to dictionaries in the case of overloading. print ⦃ Sum a b ⦄ can refer to these hidden dictionary functions using print ⦃ a ⦄ and print ⦃ b ⦄. Furthermore, the type Con, used in this example, was added to the set of generic types in Generic Haskell as well as in Clean. Run-time access to some information about the original data constructors is especially convenient when writing trace functions, such as print, for debugging purposes.

```
data Con a = Con a;        data ConDescr = { conName :: String, ··· }
```

When used in Generic Haskell, Con *appears* to get an additional argument d. This is not a type argument but a denotation that allows the programmer to access information about the constructor, which is of type ConDescr. In the example print {| Con d a |} applies conName to d to retrieve the name of the constructor.

Observe that this polytypic print function does not depend on the structure of the syntax tree type. If this type definition changes during development, the underlying system will automatically generate a proper version of print. This implementation of print is quite minimal, with superfluous parentheses and spaces. It is easy to adjust the definition to handle these situations correctly, see for example Jansson and Jeuring [4].

It is not difficult to specify the polytypic inverse of the print function. Using a monadic parser library, with some utility functions such as symbol(s) and parseInt that take care for low-level token recognition, one could specify a polytypic parse function (similar to Haskell's read) as follows:

```
type Parser a = ···  — some monadic parser type

parse {| a |}  :: Parser a

parse {| Unit |}      = return Unit

parse {| Sum a b |}  = mplus  (parse {| a |} >>= return . Inl)
                              (parse {| b |} >>= return . Inr)

parse {| Prod a b |} = do    l ← parse {| a |}
                             r ← parse {| b |}
                             return (l :*: r)

parse {| Con d a |}  = do    symbol '('
                             symbols (conName d)
                             symbol ' '
                             x ← parse {| a |}
                             symbol ')'
                             return (Con x)
parse {| Int |}       = parseInt
```

Such a simple parser follows the print definition very closely and is easy to understand. parse is obviously print's inverse, and it can only parse input generated by the print function, including redundant spaces and parentheses.

3   Polytypic Parsing of Programming Languages

This section introduces the types–as–grammar approach to polytypically derive a parser. This parser builds on a small layer of monadic parser combinators, to abstract from the lower level token recognition machinery. We use very naive parser combinators (shown below) because they are easy to use and explain.

To abstract from the parsing issues at the lexical level, we assume a separated scanner/lexer and that the parser will work on a list of tokens. Later in Sect. 5, we will test the efficiency of the polytypic parser using also a set of continuation parser combinators that improve the error messages. The naive monadic parser, using the Maybe monad, is implemented as follows.

```
newtype Parser a = Parser { parser :: [Token] → Maybe (a, [Token]) }

data Token = IdentToken String | LambdaToken | ArrowToken
           | IfToken | ThenToken | ElseToken | ···          — all tokens

token :: Token → Parser Token
token tok = Parser (λts → case ts of
                          (t:ts') | t = tok → Just (t, ts')
                               _            → Nothing

instance Monad Parser where
    return x = Parser (λts → Just (x, ts))              — success parser
    l >>= r  = Parser (λts → case parser l ts of        — sequence parser
                         Just (x, ts') → parser (r x) ts'
                         Nothing       → Nothing              )

instance MonadPlus Parser where
    mzero    = Parser (λts → Nothing)                    — fail parser
    mplus l r = Parser (λts → case parser l ts of        — choice parser
                         Just (x, ts') → Just (x, ts')
                         Nothing       → parser r ts   )
```

The mplus instance above defines a deterministic (exclusive) choice parser: if the left argument of mplus parses successfully, the right argument is never tried. This is done out of speed considerations and, if the parsers are written in the right way, it does not matter for deterministic grammars. Algebraic data constructors have unique names, which makes the grammar deterministic. This is also reflected in the Parser type, i.e., the parser returns a Maybe result, which shows that it returns at most one result.

To parse real programming languages we should not parse the constructor names that occur in the syntax tree type. Instead, we should parse all kinds of tokens such as **if**, λ, and → This requires writing most of the instances for the polytypic function **parse** by hand. Another option is adding these tokens to the abstract syntax tree, which becomes a non-abstract, or rich, syntax tree. Since we instruct the polytypic parser using types, we cannot reuse the (constructors of the) Token data type. Instead, we specify each token as a separate data type. This gives us the ability to parse our own tokens, without the constructors getting in the way. We can now define, for example, a nicer parser for lists that uses the [] and _:_ notation.

```
data List a = Cons a ColonToken (List a) | Nil EmptyListToken

data ColonToken     = ColonToken
data EmptyListToken = EmptyListToken

parse {| ColonToken |}     = symbol ':'   ≫  return ColonToken
parse {| EmptyListToken |} = symbols "[]" ≫  return EmptyListToken

parse {| Con d a |}        = parser {| a |}  ≫= return . Con
```

intListParser = parse {| List Int |}   — automatically derived by the system

We partly reuse the **parse** definition from Sect. 2. We do not want to parse the constructor names, therefore, we replace the **Parse** {| Con d a |} alternative from Sect. 2 with the one shown above. Not parsing constructor names means that the order of alternatives is important. Since **parse** {| Sum a b |} uses the exclusive **mplus**, it gives priority to the Inl(eft) alternative over the Inr(ight) alternative. Therefore, the textual order of the constructors of an algebraic data type determines the order of parsing, which is similar to function definitions with multiple alternatives in Haskell and Clean.

One can parse any context-free syntax by specifying the grammar using algebraic data types. The grammar below is an excerpt of a small functional programming language. It uses the convention that N*type* represents the non-terminal *type* and T*type* represents a terminal symbol *type*.

```
data Nexpression = Apply Nexpression Nexpression
                 | Lambda Tlambda Nvariable Tarrow Nexpression
                 | If Tif Nexpression Tthen Nexpression
                                           Telse Nexpression
                 | Variable Nvariable
                 | Value Nvalue

data Nvariable = Variable String

data Nvalue = Integer Int | Boolean Bool

data Tlambda = Tlambda;   data Tarrow = Tarrow
data Tif     = Tif;       data Tthen  = Tthen;    data Telse = Telse

parse {| Con d a |} = parse {| a |}      ≫= return . Con
parse {| String |}  = identifierToken ≫= λ(IdentToken s) → return s

parse {| Tlambda |} = token LambdaToken ≫ return Tlambda
parse {| Tarrow |}  = token ArrowToken  ≫ return Tarrow
parse {| Tif |}     = token IfToken     ≫ return Tif
parse {| Tthen |}   = token ThenToken   ≫ return Tthen
parse {| Telse |}   = token ElseToken   ≫ return Telse
```

If we remove all constructors from the type definitions above, we end up with something that looks very similar to the following grammar description in BNF notation:

```
<expression> ::= <expression> <expression>
             |  "λ" <variable> "→" <expression>
             |  "if" <expression> "then" <expression>
                                  "else" <expression>
             |  <variable>
             |  <value>

<variable>   ::= String

<value>      ::= Int | Bool
```

It is also easy to support extended BNF (EBNF) notation by introducing some auxiliary data types: `Plus` to mimic $(\cdots)^+$, `Option` to mimic $[\cdots]$, and `Star` to mimic $(\cdots)^\star$. The parsers for all of them can be derived automatically.

```
data Plus a    = Plus a (Plus a) | One a
type Star a     = Option (Plus a)
type Option a   = Maybe a

data Nexpression = ···
                | Lambda Tlambda (Plus Nvariable) Tarrow Nexpression
                | ···
```

The use of parameterized data types, such as `Plus`, can make the definition of the syntax tree type very concise. It is similar to two-level or van Wijngaarden grammars [9]. We can now specify a lambda expression with multiple arguments using `Plus` as shown above. Clearly, this corresponds to the following EBNF grammar:

```
<expression> ::= ···
             |  "λ" <variable>⁺ "→" <expression>
             |  ···
```

An issue with this *types–as–grammar* approach is left-recursive type definitions. Most parser combinator libraries do not support left-recursive parser definitions and run out of heap or stack space. Recently, Baars and Swierstra developed parser combinators [10] that detect and remove left-recursion automatically . Our current solution is manually removing the (few occurrences of) left-recursion by splitting the left-recursive type, as shown below. Only `Nexpression` is (mutually) left-recursive because it has no argument of type T*token* before the `Nexpression` arguments. We write a small parser for the left-recursive part, making sure that most of the parser is still derived automatically.

```
data Nexpression = Apply Nexpression Nexpression
                | Term Nterm                  — separate non-recursive part
```

```
data Nterm        = Lambda Tlambda (Plus Nvariable) Tarrow Nexpression
                  | ...

parse {| Nexpression |} = parse {| Plus Nterm |} >>= return . app
  where
    app (One t)        = Term t
    app (Plus t ts)  = app' (Term t) ts
    app' acc (One t)     = Apply acc t
    app' acc (Plus t ts) = app' (Apply acc t) ts
```

We extended this example to a basic functional language grammar, to test our generated parser. Moreover, as a larger test, we converted Haskell's grammar to types and derived a parser for it. The results of those tests appear in Sect. 5.

4   Other Polytypic Syntax Tree Operations

Polytypic parsing and several other polytypic syntax tree operations are used in the current version of the Esther shell [6], which is written using Clean's generics. The Esther shell offers a basic lazy functional language as shell syntax. Its grammar is specified as a type, using the approach of Sect. 3. This section uses excerpts from the Esther shell to give an impression about how data specific syntax tree operations, written using polytypic programming techniques, improve conciseness, modularity, and allow easy changes to the syntax by adding and rearranging types.

4.1   Restructuring Infix Expressions

A common syntax tree operation is re-parsing expressions that contain user defined infix operators. Because they are user defined, they cannot be correctly parsed during the first parse. The usual solution is to restructure the syntax tree after parsing, once the precedence and associativity information is available.

data FixityInfo = ··· — precedence and associativity information

```
fixInfix {| a | m |}  :: (Functor m, Monad m) ⇒ a → FixityInfo → m a

fixInfix {| Int |}       i        ops = return i
fixInfix {| Unit |}      Unit     ops = return Unit
fixInfix {| Sum a b |}   (Inl l)  ops = do    l' ← fixInfix {| a |} l ops
                                              return (Inl l')
fixInfix {| Sum a b |}   (Inr r)  ops = do    r' ← fixInfix {| b |} r ops
                                              return (Inr r')
fixInfix {| Prod a b |}  (l :*: r) ops = do   l' ← fixInfix {| a |} l ops
                                              r' ← fixInfix {| b |} r ops
                                              return (l' :*: r')
```

```
fixInfix {| Nexpression |}  (Term t) ops = do
                                  t' ← fixInfix {| Nterm |}  t ops
                                  return (Nterm t)
fixInfix {| Nexpression |}  (Apply e1 e2) ops = ···— rebuild expression tree
```

We overloaded fixInfix with the Monad class because this operation can fail due to conflicting priorities. Generic Haskell requires mentioning this type variable m at the left side of the function type definition. The polytypic restructuring fixInfix function can be derived for all types except Nexpression, which is where we intervene to restructure the syntax tree. Note that manually removing the left-recursion and splitting the Nexpression type allows us to override the polytypic function derivation at exactly the right spot. We lack the space to show exactly how to restructure the expression tree. This can be found in the current version of the Esther shell [6].

The traversal code in the instances for the generic representation types is a common occurring pattern. This shows that we can elegantly and concisely specify a syntax tree operation that operates on a very specific part of the tree. There is no need to specify traversal code for any other type in the syntax tree, these are all automatically derived.

4.2   Adding Local Variable Scopes

Another common operation is checking variable declarations in the context of local scope. Scope can easily be added into the syntax tree using polytypic programming. We simply define the Scope data type below and inject it into the syntax tree where appropriate.

```
data Scope a  = Scope a

data Nterm     = LambdaWithScope (Scope Nlambda)
               | ···
data Nlambda   = Lambda Tlambda (Plus Npattern) Tarrow Nexpression
data Ncase     = Case Tcase Nexpression Tof
                                  (Plus (Scope Nalt, Tsemicolon))
data Nalt      = Alternative (Plus Npattern) Tarrow Nexpression
data Npattern = ···
               | VariablePattern Nvariable
```

We overrule the derived polytypic code for chkVars at the following positions in the syntax tree types: Nvariable is an applied occurrence, except for occurrences after a VariablePattern constructor (part of the Npattern type), where it is a defining occurrence. Furthermore, we override the polytypic instance for Scope, which ends a variable scope after lambda expressions and case alternatives.

```
chkVars {| a | m |}  :: (Functor m, Monad m) ⇒ a → [String] → m [String]

chkVars {| Unit |}      _       vs = return vs
chkVars {| Int |}       _       vs = return vs
```

```
chkVars {| Prod a b |}   (l :*: r)  vs = chkVars {| a |}  l  vs >>= chkVars {| b |}  r
chkVars {| Sum a b |}    (Inl l)    vs = chkVars {| a |}  l  vs
chkVars {| Sum a b |}    (Inr r)    vs = chkVars {| b |}  r  vs

chkVars {| Nvariable |}  (Variable v) vs
          | v 'elem' vs = return vs
          | otherwise   = fail ("unbound variable: " ++ v)

chkVars {| case VariablePattern |}  (VariablePattern (Variable v)) vs
          = return (v:vs)          — polytypic instance for a single constructor

chkVars {| Scope a |}  (Scope x) vs = chkVars {| a |}  x vs >> return vs
```

We make use of a Generic Haskell feature in the chkVars example above, which is not found in Clean: overriding the generic scheme at the constructor level. Instead of writing code for all constructors of the Npattern type, we only specify the semantics for the VariablePattern (hence the use of the **case** keyword) and let Generic Haskell derive the code for the other alternatives of the type.

4.3   Type Inference

As the compilation process proceeds, syntax tree operations tend to be less generic and more data specific. Program transformations and code generation, but also type checking, usually require writing polymorphic instances for almost all types, since each type must be treated differently. At first sight, it seems as if polytypic programming is no longer useful to implement such operations. In this section, we will show that even for more data specific functions a polytypic definition improves modularity because it splits the specification per type, even if there is little profit from the automatic derivation mechanism. As an example, we specify a type inference algorithm in a polytypic way. Type inference is much more data specific than any other example in this paper, nevertheless, it illustrates the way to polytypically specify syntax operations that occur later in the compilation process.

The algorithm is based on the idea of strictly separating type inference into the generation of constraints (in the form of type equations), and solving these constraints by standard unification. We restrict ourselves to the generation part, which is usually done by traversing the syntax tree and collecting constraints corresponding to each syntactical construct. Such an algorithm not only takes the syntax tree as input but also an environment containing type declarations for functions, constructors, and variables. Moreover, during the generation process we sometimes need fresh type variables, e.g., to instantiate a function's type scheme or to create local type variables used to express dependencies between derivations. Therefore, we supply the generation function with a heap data structure and we use an accumulator to collect type equations. This leads to the following polytypic function type and auxiliary type definitions.

```
data Type = TVar String         | TTVar VHeap   | TBasic TBasic
          | TApp String [Type] | TArr Type Type | TAll [String] Type

data TBasic = TBool | TInt
data Equ    = Equ Type Type

type TypeState a = State (VHeap, [Equ]) a     — a state monad

gtype {| t |} :: t → Envs → TypeState Type
```

The VHeap is used to allocate fresh type variables. Mostly it suffices to generate unique integers to distinguish different type variables. These fresh variables are represented by the TTVar-alternative in the definition of Type. The other alternatives are used to represent type variables, basic types, type constructor applications, arrow types, and type schemes, respectively.

The type equations are represented as a list of Equ elements. Together with the VHeap, they form the state of the polytypic function. For convenience, the implementation of the polytypic gtype function is based on the standard State monad. For creating fresh variables, and for extending the list of type equations we introduce the following functions.

```
freshVar :: TypeState VHeap
freshVar = State {runState = λ(vh, eqs) → (vh, (vh+1, eqs))}

newEqu :: Type → Type → TypeState ()
newEqu dt ot = State
                  {runState = λ(vh, eqs) → ((), (vh, Equ dt ot:eqs))}
```

The polytypic instance declarations are straightforward. We chose to interpret a Prod of two terms as an application of the first to the second. The advantage is that we can derive the instance for the type Nexpression automatically.

```
gtype {| Sum a b |}   (Inl l)   env = gtype {| a |} l env
gtype {| Sum a b |}   (Inr r)   env = gtype {| b |} r env
gtype {| Prod a b |}  (x :*: y) env = do   tx ← gtype {| a |} x env
                                           ty ← gtype {| b |} y env
                                           fv ← freshVar
                                           newEqu (TArr ty (TTVar fv)) tx
                                           return (TTVar fv)
```

Clearly, there are not many other types for which we use the polytypic version; most of the instances have to be given explicitly. E.g., for TfunctionId we can use the following definition:

```
gtype {| TfunctionId |} (FunctionId name) env
      = freshType name (fun_env env)
```

The overall environment has three separate environments: for functions, for constructors, and for type variables.

```
type Env  = String → Type
data Envs = Envs { fun_env :: Env, cons_env :: Env, var_env :: Env }
```

The function `freshType` takes care of the instantiation of the environment type. It can be defined easily, using the `freshVar` function, for type variables introduced by a `TAll` type. Another example is the alternative for `Nif`. Again, its definition is straightforward.

```
gtype {| Nif |}  (If Tif c Tthen t Telse e) env = do
        tc ← gtype {| Nterm |} c env
        newEqu tc (TBasic TBool)
        tt ← gtype {| Nterm |} t env
        te ← gtype {| Nterm |} e env
        newEqu tt te
        return tt
```

Although we have to specify many instances explicitly, it is not inconvenient to use a polytypic specification: it splits the implementation into compact polytypic instances, which are easy to write while the resulting structure of the algorithm remains clear.

Concluding this section, we want to remark that polytypic programming allowed easy changes to the syntax by adding and rearranging types. Usually, this was done by *adding* types and instances to polytypic functions, instead of *rewriting* existing instances.

5   Performance of Polytypic Parsers

In this section we investigate the efficiency of the generated parsers for two different grammars/languages. Our elegant types–as–grammar technique is of little practical use if the resulting programs perform poorly because of the automatically derived code by the polytypic system. Who cares about the advantage of not having to use an external tool, when the polytypic parsers performs an order of magnitude worse than parser generator based parsers.

5.1   A Basic Functional Language Parser

The first example is the derived parser for the basic functional language from Sect. 3. Since we are not interested in lexical analysis, we have tokenized the test input for the parser manually resulting in a list of 663 tokens representing 45 small functions in this language. The programs under test copy the input list of tokens 100 times and parse the resulting list 100 times. The results are shown in Table 1. For Haskell we used Generic Haskell (GH) 1.42, which requires the GHC 6.2.2 compiler. For Clean we used the Clean 2.1.1 distribution.

All programs were run with a heap size of 256MB. It's remarkable to see that the Haskell version used only a quarter of the heap allocated by the Clean version. At first glance, it might not be clear that the generated executables are very slow and consume huge amounts of memory. Both Generic Haskell

Table 1. Performance figures for the derived basic functional language parser, using Maybe parsers

	Execution time (s)	Garbage collection (s)	Total time (s)	Total heap allocation (MB)
GH+GHC	27.2	1.4	28.6	3,500
Clean	45.0	6.7	51.8	11,600

and Clean have some built-in specific optimization techniques to improve the performance of the derived functions. Moreover, these derived functions also benefit from standard optimizations, such as dictionary elimination, higher-order removal, etc. However, it appears that this is insufficient to obtain any acceptable performance.

5.2 Improving the Automatically Derived Code

In [7] Alimarine and Smetsers present an optimization technique, called *fusion*, of which they claim that it removes all the overhead introduced by the compilation scheme for polytypic functions (developed by Hinze [8]) that is used both in Generic Haskell and in Clean. Like *deforestation*, fusion aims at removing intermediate data used for passing information between function calls. This is done by combining nested pairs of *consumer* and *producer* calls into a single function application, making the construction of intermediate data structures from the producer to the consumer superfluous.

Fusion is not implemented in the Clean compiler, but incorporated in a separate source–to–source translator. The input language for this translator is a basic functional language extended with syntactical constructs for specifying polytypic functions. The translator first converts polytypic definitions into ordinary function definitions and optimizes these generated functions, by eliminating data conversions that are necessary to convert each object from and to its generic representation. The optimized output is both Clean and Haskell syntax compatible, so it was easy to include performance figures using both compilers as a back–end. These figures are shown in Table 2.

The programs ran under the same circumstances as those shown in Table 1. Each test yields a syntax tree consisting of approximately 300,000 constructors per iteration. In the optimized Haskell version this leads to an allocation of 12

Table 2. Execution times for the optimized basic functional language parser, using Maybe parsers

	Execution time (s)	Garbage collection (s)	Total time (s)	Total heap allocation (MB)
Fusion+GHC	4.3	0.03	4.5	340
Fusion+Clean	6.3	0.4	6.7	1,500

bytes per node. Representing a similar syntax tree in an imperative language would require approximately the same number of bytes per node.

5.3 Using Continuation Based Parser Combinators

A nice aspect of our approach, is that the polytypic specification of the parser in Sect. 3 and the underlying parser combinator library are independent: we are free to choose different combinators, e.g., combinators that produce better error messages, without having to adjust the polytypic definitions. To illustrate this, we replaced the simple Maybe-combinators, by a set of continuation based parser combinators, which collect erroneous parsings. These are similar to the combinators by, e.g., Koopman [11] or Leijen and Meijer [12]. Although the error reporting technique itself is simple, it appears that the results are already quite accurate. Of course, one can fine-tune these underlying combinators or even switch to an existing set of advanced combinators, e.g., Parsec [12], without having to change the polytypic parser definition itself.

Table 3. Execution times for the derived and optimized basic functional language parser, using continuation based parsers

	Execution time (s)	Garbage collection (s)	Total time (s)
GH+GHC	137.9	10.2	148.2
Clean	77.3	20.0	97.3
Fusion+GHC	18.6	0.41	19.0
Fusion+Clean	55.5	8.74	64.2

We have tested the unoptimized as well as the optimized version of the continuation based parser, see Table 3. This time, the figures are more difficult to explain, in particular if you compare them with the execution times from the previous tables. In the literature, continuation passing parsers are often presented as an efficient alternative for the naive combinators. However, our measurements do not confirm this. The polytypic, as well as the optimized versions, are much slower than the corresponding parser from the first test set, up to a factor of ten. One might believe that the additional error information causes this overhead. However, the loss in efficiency is almost the same when this information is not included. Apparently, the gain that is obtained by avoiding explicit constructors and pattern matching is completely undone by the use of continuations and, therefore, higher-order applications.

5.4 A Haskell 98 Parser

As a second test we have implemented a (nearly) complete Haskell parser, simply by deriving polytypic parser instances for the Haskell syntax specified as a collection of algebraic data types. These data types were obtained by a direct conversion of the Haskell syntax specification as given in section 9.5 of the

Haskell 98 Report [2]. Again, we have compared the results for Generic Haskell and Clean for both the `Maybe` and the continuation passing combinators. We also optimized the generic code and compared the performance of all different versions. The results are shown in Table 4. The parsers were run on an example input consisting of approximately 500 again manually tokenized lines of Haskell code, 2637 tokens

An optimization that replaces update-frames with indirections was added to the Clean run-time system, reducing both heap and stack usage enough too complete the tests on a 1.5Ghz 512MB Windows PC.

Table 4. Performance figures for the derived and optimized Haskell 98 parser, using both `Maybe` and continuation bases parsers

	GH+GHC (s)	Clean (s)	Fusion+GHC (s)	Fusion+Clean (s)
Maybe	20.6	17.6	0.03	2.30
CPS	182	15.2	1.12	5.40

These execution times are quite revealing. We can conclude that Generic Haskell as well as Clean generate extremely inefficient polytypic code. It is doubtful whether these polytypic language extensions are really useful for building serious applications. However, the optimization tool changes this completely, at least for Haskell. The performance gain for the `Maybe`-parsers is even a factor of 700. This test indicates once more that the continuation passing parsers are less efficient. It is strange to see that for Haskell the difference is much bigger than for Clean: a factor of 35 and 2, respectively. We do not have an explanation for the factor of 75 between GHC and Clean for the optimized `Maybe`-parsers.

We have also compared the efficiency of the optimized parsers with a Haskell parser generated with the *Happy* tool [13]. This parser is included in the libraries of the GHC Haskell compiler we used. The result is surprising: its execution time is exactly the same as our Fusion+GHC `Maybe`-parser! To get more significant results we ran both with 100 times the input (50,000 lines of Haskell code, using a 4MB heap). Our parser is five percent faster, but does not have a lexer or decent error messages. Nonetheless, we believe that this shows that fusion is really needed and that fusion works for polytypic parsers.

6   Related Work

Parsers are standard examples for polytypic programming (see Jansson and Jeuring [4], Hinze [14]). However, the common definition gives a parser that can only recognize expressions that can be defined in the corresponding programming language itself. This is very natural because the type definitions in a programming language can be regarded as a kind of grammar defining legal expressions in the corresponding programming language. We have shown that this also works for any context-free grammar.

It has also been shown how a parser for another language can be constructed from a grammar description. Atanassow, Clarke, and Jeuring [15] construct parsers for XML from the corresponding DTD description. To the best of our knowledge this paper is the first that describes the use of algebraic data type definitions as a grammar for deriving polytypic parsers for arbitrary languages.

There exist other (lazy, functional) parser generator tools and combinator libraries [13, 16, 10–12], which may generate better parsers than our approach, due to grammar analysis or handwritten optimizations. What makes our approach appealing, is that the tool used to generate the parser is part of the language. This removes the need to keep your syntax tree data structures synchronized with an external tool: one can do it within the polytypic functional language, and efficiently too, using extended fusion.

7   Conclusions

With this paper we have illustrated that polytypic programming techniques, as offered by the Generic Haskell preprocessor and the Clean compiler, can effectively be used for compiler construction. Additionally, we hope to have illustrated that the technique is interesting for programming in general.

Polytypic functions are type driven, it is therefore important to know what can be expressed in a type. In this paper we have shown that context-free grammars can be encoded in a straightforward way using algebraic data types. We have defined a polytypic parser using a types–as–grammar approach. Using such a polytypic definition, a parser for an arbitrary context-free language can be derived automatically. The polytypic function is defined in terms of parser combinators, and one can easily switch from one library to another.

Moreover, we have shown how other convenient polytypic post-parsing operations on the resulting rich syntax tree can be defined, even if not all syntax tree operations gain much from the polytypic programming style. It gives you the flexibility of moving data types within larger type structures, mostly by adding polytypic instances without having to change (much of) the existing code.

Finally, we have shown that optimizations that remove the polytypic overhead are really necessary to make polytypic programs usable. Currently, polytypic programming, in either Generic Haskell or Clean, may be suitable for toy examples and rapid prototyping but the derived code is definitely not efficient enough for larger programs. Using the extended fusion optimization technique, the parser's efficiency came close to a parser generated by Happy. We believe that fusion makes polytypic programming for real-world applications possible.

References

1. Löh, A., Clarke, D., Jeuring, J.: Dependency-style Generic Haskell. In: Proceedings of the eighth ACM SIGPLAN International Conference on Functional Programming ICFP'03, ACM Press (2003) 141–152
2. Peyton Jones, S.: Haskell 98 language and libraries: the Revised Report. Cambridge University Press (2003) http://www.haskell.org/definition/.

3. Alimarine, A., Plasmeijer, R.: A Generic Programming Extension for Clean. In Arts, T., Mohnen, M., eds.: The 13th International workshop on the Implementation of Functional Languages, IFL'01, Selected Papers. Volume 2312 of LNCS., Älvsjö, Sweden, Springer (2002) 168–186

4. Jansson, P., Jeuring, J.: Polytypic compact printing and parsing. In Swierstra, S.D., ed.: Proceedings 8th European Symposium on Programming, ESOP'99, Amsterdam, The Netherlands, 22–28 March 1999. Volume 1576., Berlin, Springer-Verlag (1999) 273–287

5. Jansson, P., Jeuring, J.: Polytypic data conversion programs. Science of Computer Programming **43**(1) (2002) 35–75

6. van Weelden, A., Plasmeijer, R.: A functional shell that dynamically combines compiled code. In Trinder, P., Michaelson, G., eds.: Selected Papers Proceedings of the 15th International Workshop on Implementation of Functional Languages, IFL'03. Volume 3145 of LNCS., Springer (2003) 36–52

7. Alimarine, A., Smetsers, S.: Improved fusion for optimizing generics. In Hermenegildo, M., Cabeza, D., eds.: Proceedings of Seventh International Symposium on Practical Aspects of Declarative Languages. Number 3350 in LNCS, Long Beach, CA, USA, Springer (2005) 203–218

8. Hinze, R.: Generic Programs and proofs (2000) Habilitationsschrift, Universität Bonn.

9. van Wijngaarden, A.: Orthogonal design and description of a formal language. Technical Report MR 76, Mathematisch Centrum, Amsterdam (1965)

10. Baars, A.I., Swierstra, S.D.: Type-safe, self inspecting code. In: Proceedings of the ACM SIGPLAN workshop on Haskell, ACM Press (2004) 69–79

11. Koopman, P., Plasmeijer, R.: Layered Combinator Parsers with a Unique State. In Arts, T., Mohnen, M., eds.: Proceedings of the 13th International workshop on the Implementation of Functional Languages, IFL'01, Ericsson Computer Science Laboratory (2001) 157–172

12. Leijen, D., Meijer, E.: Parsec: Direct style monadic parser combinators for the real world. Technical Report UU-CS-2001-35, Departement of Computer Science, Universiteit Utrecht (2001) http://www.cs.uu.nl/~daan/parsec.html.

13. Gill, A., Marlow, S.: Happy: The parser generator for Haskell (2001) http://www.haskell.org/happy/.

14. Hinze, R., Peyton Jones, S.: Derivable Type Classes. In Hutton, G., ed.: 2000 ACM SIGPLAN Haskell Workshop. Volume 41(1) of ENTCS., Montreal, Canada, Elsevier Science (2001)

15. Atanassow, F., Clarke, D., Jeuring, J.: Scripting XML with Generic Haskell. Technical report uu-cs-2003, University of Utrecht (2003)

16. Hutton, G.: Higher-order Functions for Parsing. Journal of Functional Programming **2**(3) (1992) 323–343

Implementing a Numerical Solution of the KPI Equation Using Single Assignment C: Lessons and Experiences

Alex Shafarenko[1], Sven-Bodo Scholz[1], Stephan Herhut[1],
Clemens Grelck[2], and Kai Trojahner[2]

[1] Department of Computer Science, University of Hertfordshire, AL10 9AB, U.K.
[2] Institute of Software Technology and Programming Languages, University of
Lübeck, Germany

Abstract. We report our experiences of programming in the functional
language SAC[1] a numerical method for the KPI (Kadomtsev-Petiviashvili
I) equation. KPI describes the propagation of nonlinear waves in a dispersive
medium. It is an integro-differential, nonlinear equation with third-order
derivatives, and so it presents a noticeable challenge in numerical solution,
as well as being an important model for a range of topics in computational
physics. The latter include: long internal waves in a density-stratified ocean,
ion-acoustic waves in a plasma, acoustic waves on a crystal lattice, and
more. Thus our solution of KPI in SAC represents an experience of solving
a "real" problem using a single-assignment language and as such provides
an insight into the kind of challenges and benefits that arise in using the
functional paradigm in computational applications. The paper describes
the structure and functionality of the program, discusses the features of
functional programming that make it useful for the task in hand, and
touches upon performance issues.

1 Introduction

It is common knowledge that the uptake of the functional programming technology is impeded by the lack of convincing evidence of the functional paradigm
efficacy and suitability of expression. There is a considerable interest in seeing
so-called 'real-life' applications programmed in a functional language, especially
where these implementations show acceptable run-time performance and design
advantages of the functional programming method.

In functional programming, component algorithms, rather than whole problems, tend to be used as benchmarks. We ourselves evaluated the performance
of the Fast Fourier Transform component in the past [2] and so did the authors
of [3]; paper [4] uses the conjugate gradient method as a benchmark, and the
authors of [5] study the intricacies of matrix multiplication.

There is a significant advantage in using a whole application rather than a
component algorithm as a benchmark. Firstly, it provides a balance of design
patterns that may reflect more adequately the mix of methods, access patterns

A. Butterfield, C. Grelck, and F. Huch (Eds.): IFL 2005, LNCS 4015, pp. 160–177, 2006.

and programming techniques characteristic of a real-life programming project. Secondly, one stands a better chance of discovering situations in which the quality of expression or indeed the quality of generated code is properly challenged, so that one may learn some important lessons.

This paper has precisely such intent. We have selected a problem in computational mathematics which is complex enough to be interesting, yet not too complex, so that we are able to present the results and explain the design decisions in a short conference paper. The rest of the paper is organised as follows. The next Section introduces the equation and the solution method, Section 3 discusses the SAC implementation issues, Section 4 presents the conclusions we have drawn from implementing the solution method in SAC, next Section briefly discusses our equivalent FORTRAN code, Section 6 presents the results of performance studies involving several platforms and commercial compilers as a basis for comparison, and finally there are some conclusions.

2   The Equation

For this study we chose a problem that one of the authors had been familiar with from the time some 20 years back when he was doing his PhD in computational physics at University of Novosibirsk[6]: a Kadomtsev-Petviashvili equation. The KPI (Kadomtsev Petviashvili I) has the following canonic form:

$$\frac{\partial}{\partial x}\left(\frac{\partial u}{\partial t} + 6u\frac{\partial u}{\partial x} + \frac{\partial^3 u}{\partial x^3}\right) - 3\frac{\partial^2 u}{\partial y^2} = 0 \,.$$

For computational reasons, it is more convenient to use the equivalent form of KPI:

$$\frac{\partial u}{\partial t} + 6u\frac{\partial u}{\partial x} + \frac{\partial^3 u}{\partial x^3} - 3\int_{-\infty}^{x}\frac{\partial^2 u}{\partial y^2} = 0$$

which can be written as

$$\frac{\partial u}{\partial t} = N(u) + L(u) \,,$$

where

$$N(u) = -6u\frac{\partial u}{\partial x} + 3\int_{-\infty}^{x}\frac{\partial^2 u}{\partial y^2} \qquad L(u) = \frac{\partial^3 u}{\partial x^3} \,,$$

are the nonlinear, diffractive part and the dispersion term, respectively.

The KPI model is very general indeed. It describes any physical system in which waves propagate mostly in one direction, but suffer from diffraction, i.e. the divergence of a wave packet across the propagation direction; dispersion, i.e. the widening of the wave along the propagation direction due to different parts of it propagating at different velocities; and hydrodynamic non-linearity, i.e. the fact that the wave tends towards steeper and steeper shapes until it either breaks or the steepening is arrested by the dispersion effects.

To give an idea of where the KPI model may apply, we quote its original application to water surface waves[7], its use as a model of ion-acoustic waves in plasma[8] and the application to string theory in high-energy physics[9], but also such a down-to-earth area as computing wave-resistance of a ship that travels at high speed along a waterway [10].

The numerical method for this paper has been borrowed from [11], except the boundary conditions whose discretisation was not defined there, so we used one of our own, bearing in mind that its effect on performance is insignificant.

The spatial derivatives in L and N were discretised thus:

$$-\frac{\partial^3 u}{\partial x^3} \rightarrow -\frac{u_{i+2,j} - 2u_{i+1,j} + 2u_{i-1,j} - u_{i-2,j}}{2\Delta x^3},$$

$$\frac{\partial u}{\partial x} \rightarrow \frac{u_{i+1,j} - u_{i-1,j}}{2\Delta x}$$

and

$$\frac{\partial^2 u}{\partial y^2} \rightarrow \frac{u_{i,j+1} - 2u_{i,j} + u_{i,j-1}}{2\Delta y}.$$

The integration along x was discretised by Simpson method and modified to take account of the boundary conditions.

The resulting scheme can be summarized as follows:

$$u^{n+1/3} = u^n + \gamma_1 \Delta t N(u^n) + \alpha_1 \Delta t \frac{L(u^{n+1/3}) + L(u^n)}{2},$$

$$u^{n+2/3} = u^{n+1/3} + \gamma_2 \Delta t N(u^{n+1/3}) + \rho_1 \Delta t N(u^n) + \alpha_2 \Delta t \frac{L(u^{n+2/3}) + L(u^{n+1/3})}{2},$$

$$u^{n+1} = u^{n+2/3} + \gamma_3 \Delta t N(u^{n+2/3}) + \rho_2 \Delta t N(u^n) + \alpha_3 \Delta t \frac{L(u^{n+1}) + L(u^{n+2/3})}{2},$$

which accounts for the Crank-Nicholson representation of the diffractive term and the conventional Runge-Kutta time-integration to the third order of accuracy. Here all α, γ and ρ are scalar constants chosen to achieve the required approximation accuracy. The boundary conditions are periodic in y and absorbing $\frac{\partial^2 u}{\partial x^2} = 0$ in x at both ends of the interval. The upper indices $n+1/3$, $n+2/3$, and $n + 1$ refer to the 3 substeps of time-integration that make up a full step.

3   Implementation

With the above equations as a starting point, we identify the following tasks. First of all, since the above scheme is implicit in x, and a 5-point stencil is used for L, a pentdiagonal solver is required for all three substeps. The solver (which is a re-write of [12]) is a particular case of the LU-decomposition solver, taking advantage of the fact that the matrix only has five nonzero diagonals to reduce the solution complexity from $O(n^3)$ down to $O(n)$ by recurrent substitution. While this algorithm is recurrent in x, it is fully data-parallel in y. Hence we decided to produce a one-dimensional implementation of the solver (the recurrences in question) which will take as many additional axes as required by the environment. The number of additional axes in our case would be one, since we are focusing on the two-dimensional KPI; however the equation itself is defined for three dimensions as well, hence the aforementioned additional flexibility is quite important for developing a future-proof program. Next, the pentdiagonal solver has, naturally, an elimination and a back-substitution phase, of which the former can be pre-computed (save for the right-hand side), thanks to the linearity of the scheme in the third derivative. Hence we need two functions, one for the eliminator and one for the rest of the solver. The eliminator is displayed in Fig. 1. Notice that the code is rank-monomorphic, in that it expects a fixed rank of its arguments a, b, c, d, e, which are the contents of five nonzero diagonals of the equation matrix, and in that it produces four fixed-rank arrays. Contrast that with the main solver, presented in Fig. 2. Here the result has undeclared rank, which can be 1,2, or more, which is decided on the basis of the shape of the similarly undeclared right-hand side f. The function *pent* will ensure that the shape of the result agrees with the shape of the argument; in any case, only the first dimension of both f and the result is explicitly referred to in the code. The very significant advantage of that has been that we could fully test this function on short one-dimensional data and then use it in the program for 2d arguments without any uncertainty as to its correctness in that case. Such rank invariance is not available with conventional array programming using, e.g., FORTRAN-90.

Similarly we designed a little function for Simpson integration, Fig. 3, which is rank-invariant, so it could be fully tested in a single dimension and then applied in two dimensions as the scheme demands.

Figure 14 displays the main program. It defines several constants and creates the first copy of u, which is the field array, by setting its shape and filling it in with the known soliton distribution (for which the SAC code is not shown). Next, it prepares the 5 diagonals a-e for the solver taking into account the boundary conditions. This results in a code pattern whereby first an array is initialised with the regular value, and then the boundaries are set by specific definitions. Notice that the five arrays are in fact two-dimensional, which has nothing to do with the two dimensions of the KPI equation, but merely reflects the fact that the numerical scheme has three substeps, so it is convenient to initialize the diagonals for all three substeps at once (by grouping them into a dimension) and then use the correct vector at each substep. This is achieved by using a 3-element vector *eps* in defining the default value for each of the diagonals. Finally the eliminator *prepent* is run for all substeps simultaneously, using the second dimension of the diagonal arrays.

The actual time stepping is performed by a for-loop at the end of the main function. During the step the array u is redefined three times, each time with the corresponding scheme formula. With little difficulty, one can see the original mathematics by looking at the program. The main discrepancy is the choice of indices for the constants α, γ and ρ which have to start from 0 since that is the C

```
 1 inline
     double [.] ,              /* p */
 3   double [.] ,              /* q */
     double [.] ,              /* bet */
 5   double [.]                /* den */
   prepent ( double [.] a,
 7            double [.] b,
            double [.] c,
 9            double [.] d,
            double [.] e)
11 {
     n = shape ( a ) [0];
13   buf = genarray ( [n] , undef );
     p = buf; q = buf; bet = buf; den = buf;
15
     bet [0] = 1.0 / c [0];
17   p [0] = -d [0] * bet [0];
     q [0] = -e [0] * bet [0];
19
     bet [1] = -1.0 / ( c [1] + b [1] * p [0]);
21   p [1] = ( d [1] + b [1] * q [0]) * bet [1];
     q [1] = e [1] * bet [1];
23   den [1] = b [1];
25   for ( i=2; i<n; i++) {
       bet [i] = b [i] + a [i] * p [i-2];
27     den [i] = -1.0 / ( c [i] + a [i] * q [i-2] +
                         bet [i] * p [i-1]);
29     p [i] = ( d [i] + bet [i] * q [i-1]) * den [i];
       q [i] = e [i] * den [i];
31   }
33   return ( p, q, bet, den );
   }
```

Fig. 1. SAC code of the eliminator of the pentdiagonal solver

convention, while they start from 1 in the algorithm. Other than that, we have managed to represent the numerical scheme well near ditto.

4   Lessons and Conclusions

First of all, we must report that the programmer on this project is the first author of the present paper, and that he had no prior experience in SAC programming, was not associated with the SAC development team (while the other authors belong to it) and therefore was a good model of a brave 'computational scientist', willing to learn a new language. This was helped further by the fact that the author in question *is* a computational scientist by training (up to and including

```
   inline
 2    double [*]
   pent ( double [.] p,
 4           double [.] q,
             double [.] bet,
 6           double [.] den,
             double [.] a,
 8           double [.] f)
   {
10    n = shape ( a ) [0];
      u = genarray ( shape ( f), undef);
12    u [0] = f [0] * bet [0];
      u [1] = ( den [1] * u [0] - f [1]) * bet [1];

14
      for ( i=2; i<n; i++) {
16       u [i] = ( a [i] * u [i-2] + bet [i] * u [i-1] - f [i]) *
                  den [i];
18    }
      u [n-2] = u [n-2] + p [n-2] * u [n-1];

20
      for ( i=n-3; i>=0; i--) {
22       u [i] = u [i] + p [i] * u [i+1] + q [i] * u [i+2];
      }

24
      return ( u);
26 }
```

Fig. 2. The main part of the pentdiagonal solver written in SAC

the doctoral level), with an established research record in this area. Hence the experiment in SAC coding should be considered relevant, if only small-scale. There is, of course, a slight inadequacy in that the author in question, while not being familiar with SAC at the start of the experiment, had taught various undergraduate subjects pertaining to functional programming, and so cannot be considered totally unfamiliar, even though a conscious effort was made to approach the task with a completely open, pragmatically driven mind.

Nevertheless, the first experience to be reported is that

Programming in SAC does not require any re-tuning of the application programmer's mental skills.

Indeed, as the code displayed so far suggests, the programmer only uses very familiar language features:

– *definitions*, perceived as assignments;
– *data-parallel definitions*, encoded as so-called *with-loops*, but which feel almost like normal elementwise assignment found in FORTRAN. The difference, while profound on the conceptual level, is superficial for an applications programmer.

```
   inline
2    double[*]
   simps( double[*] f,
4          double h)
   {
6    r = genarray( shape( f), undef);
     n = shape( f)[0];
8    r = with (i)
          ([0]<=[i]<=[0])  :   (11.0*f[0]+14.0*f[1]-f[2])/24.0;
10        ([1]<=[i]<=[n-2]) : (f[i-1]+4.0*f[i]+f[i+1])/3.0;
        genarray( [n], 0.0);
12
     rs = r[2]; r[2] = r[1]; r[1] = r[0]; r[0] = 0.0;
14
     for ( i=3; i<=n-1; i++) {
16      x = r[i];
        r[i] = r[i-2] + rs;
18      rs = x;
     }
20
     return( r * h);
22 }
```

Fig. 3. The integrator

- *functions* which, due to the availability of multiple results, feel more like FORTRAN procedures with the input and output parameters neatly separated out.

The conclusion is that SAC does not frighten off a computational scientist to the extent that fully-fledged functional languages would. There are plenty of familiar features in SAC, presented in a very slight guise, making the whole concept of SAC totally nonthreatening. More importantly, the following features of functional languages do *not* play any role in SAC, namely

- recursive functions and recursive data structures. Indeed, while the underlying mechanisms might be recursive, the appearance of the code is data-parallel (with-loops) and iterative/recurrent (for-loops). We did not use any of the generally recursive mechanisms of the functional paradigm.
- higher-order functions. These would be the main kind of "glue" in mainstream functional programming, and would normally present a considerable difficulty to a computational scientist, especially where cost intuitions are essential. A SAC applications programmer does not make any use of these at all.

To summarise, the reason why a computational scientist would find SAC usable are the absence of fundamentally unfamiliar concepts and the presence of familiar ones albeit in a somewhat unusual form.

The lack of control flow does not preclude "update mentality", thanks to the single-assignment rather than non-assignment semantics and terminology, but requires the programmer to be aware of the two major programming modes: data-parallel, via with-loops, and recurrent, via for-loops.

The programmer in this experiment felt acutely aware of recurrences. Indeed, the code shows the importance of recurrent definitions (and their explicit representations) quite convincingly. The integration function, the pentdiagonal solver and even the main computational scheme are all recurrent as well as being data-parallel. The programmer was assured by the other authors that the for-loop is translated efficiently by the SAC compiler, so recurrences need not be avoided. Equally, the programmer was continually aware of the data-parallelism of SAC constructs. In approaching those, the most important feature turned out to be rank subtyping, which allowed arrays to be represented in lower dimensions and consistently used in higher dimensions, as mentioned in the previous Section. This simplified testing as well as making the code unusually flexible.

Substitutional nature of SAC definitions positively encourages the programmer to introduce as much notation as may be required to achieve readability and expressiveness.

Under normal circumstances, the programmer is wary of extra variables in a program, as these normally cause additional memory allocation and, more importantly, additional memory cycles, synchronisation (if multithreading is used), cache conflicts, etc. So one's instinct would be to only use scalar "work" variables when formulae start to get too large. This applies even more to the use of functions, since the machinery of local variables and parameter-passing inflicts additional costs.

SAC, on the other hand, allows the programmer to forget such concerns completely. Indeed, the programmer in this experiment was assured by the SAC team that any variables defined in a function will be completely transparent: data will be "pulled through" them with no additional memory allocation or synchronisation being at all necessary. The same applies to inlined functions. They are completely transparent to the code generator of SAC, so it can be safely assumed that such functions act merely as substitutions at the source level, both semantically and efficiency-wise. The programmer has found that to be very useful.

It should be mentioned that the substitutional nature of variable definitions in SAC liberates the programmer from the duty to assiduously declare every variable that he may for any reason wish to introduce. Having to declare every variable is seen as a virtue in the imperative world: a modern FORTRAN programmer writes a proud "IMPLICIT NONE" in each module to prevent the compiler from using default types. However if the whole point of a variable is to denote a chunk of unwieldy expression which happens to have an application meaning, then there is no reason why that denotation must be fully attributed and potentially hold memory. It was a refreshing experience to use SAC variables as pure notation, not memory address synonyms, for which the functional style ought to be credited.

5   FORTRAN Blues

For our performance studies, we have re-implemented the numerical method in FORTRAN 90/95 as a basis for comparison. One must note that writing the same code in FORTRAN was neither easy nor convenient. The main problem was that the whole rank structure of the algorithm had to be reconsidered. While, theoretically, rank polymorphism is available to the user of FORTRAN 95, in practice this is severely impeded by the total lack of rank subtyping. It turned out to be impossible to define a function that takes an argument of a higher rank and treats it as a uniform collection of lower-rank array components to be processed componentwise. The only exception is so-called elementwise functions

```
   function simps(f,h)
2     implicit none
      DOUBLE PRECISION ,intent(in),dimension(0:XM-1,0:YM-1)::f
4     DOUBLE PRECISION , intent(in) :: h
      DOUBLE PRECISION , dimension(0:XM-1,0:YM-1) :: simps
6     DOUBLE PRECISION :: rs, w

8     integer :: i,j

10    do j=0, YM-1
        simps(0,j) = (11*f(0,j)+14*f(1,j)-f(2,j))/24*h
12      do i=1,XM-1
          simps(i,j) = (f(i-1,j)+4.0*f(i,j)+f(i+1,j))/3*h
14      end do
      end do
16
      do j=0, YM-1
18      rs=simps(2,j)
        simps(2,j)=simps(1,j)
20      simps(1,j)=simps(0,j)
        simps(0,j)=0
22
        do i=3,XM-1
24        w=simps(i,j);
          simps(i,j)=simps(i-2,j)+rs
26        rs=w
        end do
28    end do

30 end function
```

Fig. 4. The FORTRAN version of the Simpson integrator

```
    subroutine prepent(a,b,c,d,e,P,Q,BET,DEN)
2     implicit none
      DOUBLE PRECISION,intent(in),dimension(0:XM-1)::a,b,c,d,e
4     DOUBLE PRECISION,intent(out),dimension(0:XM-1)::P,Q
      DOUBLE PRECISION,intent(out),dimension(0:XM-1)::BET,DEN
6
      BET(0) = 1/c(0)
8     P(0)   = -d(0)*BET(0)
      Q(0)   = -e(0)*BET(0)
10
      BET(1) = -1/(c(1)+b(1)*P(0))
12    P(1)    = (d(1)+b(1)*Q(0))*BET(1)
      Q(1)    = e(1)*BET(1)
14    den(1) = b(1)
16    do i=2, XM-1
       BET(i)=b(i)+a(i)*P(i-2);
18     DEN(i)= -1.0/(c(i)+a(i)*Q(i-2)+BET(i)*P(i-1));
       P(i)=(d(i)+BET(i)*Q(i-1))*DEN(i);
20     Q(i)=e(i)*DEN(i);
      end do
22  end subroutine
```

Fig. 5. Elimination in FORTRAN

that can apply themselves to scalar components. The design ploy referred to earlier, when a function was defined on 1d arrays and applied to 2d arrays implicitly along the lower dimension, is not possible in FORTRAN.

We consequently had to opt for a fixed-rank design, and insert explicit DO-loops in the code which merely spanned the ranges of unprocessed index variables. We could have used data-parallel expressions with explicit array sections, but felt that that would obfuscate the algorithm even more than the extra indices. Figure 5 shows the FORTRAN version of the integrator, where all the j-loops had to be inserted into a code otherwise very similar to the one in Fig. 3.

The two parts of the linear solver had to be treated differently: the elimination stage was programmed as rank 1, see Fig. 5 whilst the back-substitution stage was made explicitly two-dimensional, Fig. 6.

On the positive side, the code is remarkably close to SAC, which demonstrates how low the barrier to the functional method would be for anyone involved in mainstream numerical computing. Such a programmer would only need to un-learn a few reflexes (avoidance of notation, variable declarations for nonessential objects, etc.) and perhaps learn a few SAC library functions.

6   Performance

We have measured the runtime of both FORTRAN and SAC versions of the poro-gram for varying problem sizes on three platforms: Intel XEON/Linux, AMD Athlon 64/Linux and Sun UltraSPARC/Solaris.

```fortran
   function pent(p,q,bet,den,a,f)
2     implicit none
      DOUBLE PRECISION , intent(in), dimension (0:XM-1) :: p
4     DOUBLE PRECISION , intent(in), dimension (0:XM-1) :: q
      DOUBLE PRECISION , intent(in), dimension (0:XM-1) :: bet
6     DOUBLE PRECISION , intent(in), dimension (0:XM-1) :: den
      DOUBLE PRECISION ,intent(in),dimension(0:XM-1,0:YM-1)::f
8     DOUBLE PRECISION , dimension (0:XM-1,0:YM-1) :: pent

10    do j=0,YM-1
         pent(0,j)=f(0,j)*bet(0)
12       pent(1,j)=(den(1)*pent(0,j)-f(1,j))*bet(1)
      end do
14
      do i=2, XM-1
16     do j=0,YM-1
         pent(i,j)=(a(i)*pent(i-2,j)+bet(i)*
18                  *pent(i-1,j)-f(i,j))*den(i)
       end do
20    end do
      do j=0,YM-1
22     pent(XM-2,j)=pent(XM-2,j)+p(XM-2)*pent(XM-1,j)
      end do
24    do i=XM-3,0,-1
       do j=0, YM-1
26      pent(i,j)=pent(i,j)+p(i)*pent(i+1,j)+q(i)*pent(i+2,j)
       end do
28    end do
   end function pent
```

Fig. 6. Back substitution in FORTRAN

For the Intel and AMD processors, the FORTRAN code was compiled using the Intel Fortran Compiler (or ifort for short) version 9.0. For the SAC program, the current research compiler sac2c v1.00-alpha has been used. To yield comparable results, the Intel C Compiler (or icc for short) version 9.0 served as the back-end compiler for sac2c. For both Intel compilers the -fast option was specified to switch on any speed optimisations. Since the -fast option is currently not supported for AMD Athlon processors, a lesser option -O3 was used when compiling for these.

The Sun UltraSPARC binaries were built using the Sun Studio Fortran compiler (or sfort for short) version 9.0. Again, for the sake of comparability, the Sun Studio C compiler (or scc for short) version 9.0 was used as the back-end compiler of sac2c. For both compilers, the -fast option was employed to obtain optimised binaries.

For all platforms the run-times of both implementations were measured in three consecutive runs and the average value was used. Values with a deviation higher than 5% were not considered.

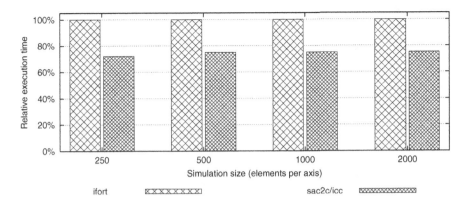

Fig. 7. Relative runtime of the two KPI implementations on a dual Intel XEON 3.0GHz machine. The runtime of the FORTRAN implementation is used as the base value.

Figure 7 shows the measured run-times on a dual Intel XEON 3.0GHz machine running Red Hat Enterprise Linux. The run-times of the SAC implementation are given relative to the FORTRAN run-times which serve as base values. The problem size is given in elements per axis of the data array which is the largest array size used within the algorithm. The results show that the SAC implementation outperforms the FORTRAN version by about 25%, despite its higher level of abstraction.

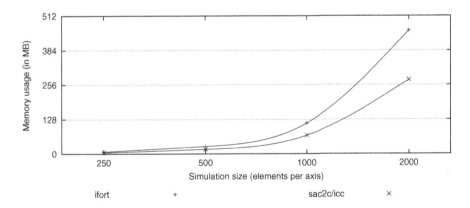

Fig. 8. Heap usage of the SAC and FORTRAN implementation in MB, measured on the Intel XEON machine

To find the reasons of the runtime advantage of the SAC implementation on the Intel XEON platform, we have measured the heap usage of both implementations for each problem size. Figure 8 gives the details. Obviously, the SAC implementation has a smaller memory footprint as the FORTRAN version, irrespective of the given problem size. A closer analysis reveals that the SAC

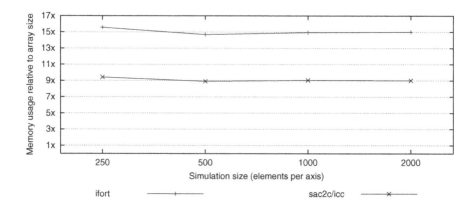

Fig. 9. Heap usage on the Intel XEON machine in multiples of data array size

heap usage is constantly 40% below the FORTRAN heap usage. This points to the SAC version of KPI handling memory reuse more efficiently and therefore requiring fewer simultaneous copies of the data array or intermediate arrays. To strengthen this assumption, we have calculated the overall heap usage in terms of multiples of the data array size. The results for both implementations of KPI are presented in Fig. 9.

The heap size of the FORTRAN implementation turns out to be about 15 times the size of the field array u. Given the declaration of 14 auxiliary arrays within the FORTRAN source code, this suggests that the FORTRAN compiler did not attempt to optimise array allocation. It seems that all arrays were allocated statically exactly as they have been declared by the programmer.

On the other side, the heap usage of the SAC version of KPI is approximately 9 times the size of the field array, despite liberal use of array expressions associated with auxiliary variables.

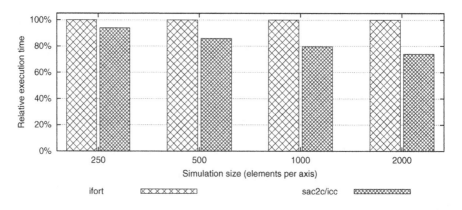

Fig. 10. Relative runtime of the two KPI implementations on a AMD Athlon 64 2.0GHz machine. The runtime of the FORTRAN implementation is used as the base value.

As a second benchmarking platform, an AMD Athlon 64 2.00GHz machine running SuSE Linux was used. Figure 10 gives the measured run-times. Similar to the results for the Intel XEON machine, the SAC implementation outperforms the FORTRAN version of KPI. Note that the advantage of the SAC version increases from about 7% for small problem sizes to 25% for a 2000 ×2000 data array.

This gave rise to the question whether low memory usage and high locality are more important to achieve good run times on the AMD machine than pure code efficiency. To investigate this further, we enabled a more aggressive version of With-loop Scalarisation [13] for the sac2c compiler to allow for optimisations that duplicate code to achieve higher locality and lower memory usage. Figure 11 shows the measured run times. The improvement is at least 10% for all tested problem sizes.

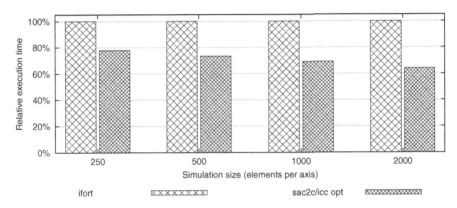

Fig. 11. Relative run time of the two KPI implementations on a AMD Athlon 64 2.0GHz machine. The SAC version was explicitly optimised for memory usage by the compiler. The runtime of the FORTRAN implementation is used as base value.

As our final benchmarking platform we used a SunFire 15k equipped with 72 UltraSparc III processors running at 900MHz under Sun Solaris. Figure 12 presents the measured run times. As on the AMD Athlon machine, we have measured two versions of the SAC implementation. The sac2c/scc version was compiled using the default settings of the sac2c compiler, whereas for the sac2c/scc opt version the more aggressive optimisations have been enabled.

To our surprise, the performance figures on the SunFire platform tell a different story compared to the cases discussed so far. For the conservatively optimised version of the SAC implementation, the FORTRAN version is between 50% and a factor of 2 faster. The more aggressively optimized version of the SAC implementation comes far closer to the FORTRAN version and even exceeds it in speed for large problem sizes. Compared to the results for the AMD Athlon machine, the differences between the two SAC versions is more striking. To investigate whether the performance difference is due to the better heap management of the

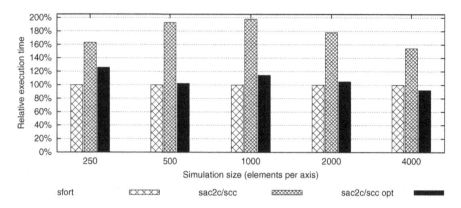

Fig. 12. Relative runtime of the two KPI implementations on a SunFire 15k. The SAC version denoted as `sac2c/icc opt` was explicitly optimised for memory usage by the compiler. The runtime of the FORTRAN implementation is used as the base value.

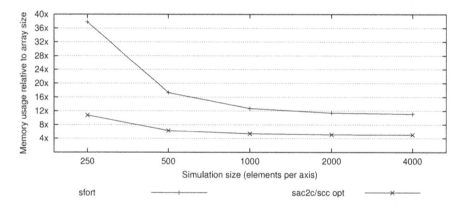

Fig. 13. Heap usage on the SunFire 15K in multiples of data array size

SAC compiler, we measured the heap usage of the aggressively optimised SAC version and the FORTRAN version. The results are given in figure 13. Here as well, we calculated the heap usage in multiplies of the size of the data array.

As the Figure shows, the heap usage of the SAC implementation converges at 5 times the data array size, whereas the FORTRAN implementation uses about eleven times the data array size. The huge difference in memory consumption for small problem sizes can be explained by memory used for initial setup.

An detailed investigation of why the Sun Studio Fortran compiler yields better runtime results while using more heap space would require close inspection of the object code and is as such beyond the scope of this paper. Due to the superscalar nature and large cache sizes of the SPARC processors being used, pipeline and cache effects may have a large impact on the runtime performance. As the SAC compiler does not generate machine code directly but instead uses the Sun C compiler as back end, pipeline and cache optimisations are out of its reach.

```
1 int main ()
  {
3    dx = 0.1; dy = 0.1; dt = 0.0002;
     n = 500; m = 400; x0 = 15.0;
5    alpha = [ 8.0/15.0, 2.0/15.0, 1.0/3.0] * dt;
     gamma = [ 8.0/15.0, 5.0/12.0, 3.0/4.0] * dt;
7    rho = [ -17.0/60.0, -5.0/12.0] * dt;
     eps = alpha / ( 4.0*dx*dx*dx);
9    u = with (ij)
           (. <= [i,j] <= .) : soliton( dx*tod( i) - x0,
11                                        dy*tod( i-199));
          genarray( [ n, m], undef);
13   a = genarray( [ n], -eps);
     a[0] = 0.0; a[1] = 0.0;
15   a[n-2] = 2.0*a[n-3]; a[n-1] = a[n-2];
     a = { [i,j] -> a[j,i]};
17   b = genarray( [n], 2.0*eps);
     b[0] = 0.0; b[1] = -b[2]; b[n-2] = 3.0*b[n-3];
19   b[n-1] = 2.0*b[n-3]; b = { [i,j] -> b[j,i]};
     c = genarray( [n], 1.0);
21   c[0] = c[0]+2.0*eps; c[1] = c[1]+6.0*eps;
     c[n-2] = c[n-2]-6.0*eps; c[n-1] = c[n-1]-2.0*eps;
23   c = { [i,j] -> c[j,i]};
     d = genarray( [n], -2.0*eps);
25   d[0] = 2.0*d[2]; d[1] = 3.0*d[2];
     d[n-2] = -d[n-3]; d[n-1] = 0.0; d = { [i,j] -> d[j,i]};
27   e = genarray( [n], eps);
     e[0] = 2.0*e[2]; e[1] = e[0];
29   e[n-2] = 0.0; e[n-1] = 0.0;
     e = { [i,j] -> e[j,i]};
31   p, q, bet, den = prepent( a, b, c, d, e);
     out = 0;
33   for ( iter=1; iter<100000; iter++) {
       out = display( u, iter, out);
35     Nubase = N( u, dx, dy);
       f = u + gamma[0]*Nubase +
37            alpha[0]*0.5*L(u,dx);
       u=pent( p[0], q[0], bet[0], den[0], a[0], f);
39     f = u + gamma[1]*N( u, dx, dy) +
              rho[0]*Nubase + alpha[1]*0.5*L(u,dx);
41     u = pent( p[1], q[1], bet[1], den[1], a[1], f);
       f = u + gamma[2]*N( u, dx, dy) +
43            rho[1]*Nubase+alpha[2]*0.5*L(u,dx);
       u = pent( p[2], q[2], bet[2], den[2], a[2], f);
45   }
     return( out);
47 }
```

Fig. 14. The main program of the SAC implementation

The conclusion to be drawn from these results is twofold. First of all, we have shown that the SaC compiler is capable of creating binaries in the same runtime league as two industrial-strength FORTRAN compilers. Secondly, we have seen that whether a FORTRAN implementation or SaC implementation yields better run times depends on the interplay of the SaC optimisations, the chosen C compiler and the executing machinery. To what extent the choice of these can be automated remains unclear and requires further research.

7   Conclusions

The results of a study of application programming in Single Assignment C has been presented. We have discussed the various design issues, principles and lessons arising from a programming exercise with a fairly mainstream equation, using several component methods: a linear solver, a Simpson space integrator and a Runge-Kutta time integrator. We have found Single Assignment C well-suited as a tool for developing numerical applications, especially when extensibility is required for future-proofness. We also found that the resulting code, although more flexible and easier to write than conventional FORTRAN, was not dramatically different in appearance, from which we conclude that SaC should present a low learning barrier to a busy computational scientist.

Finally we have contrasted the SaC code performance with that of an equivalent FORTRAN code using more than one compiler of commercial strength. We did that in order to establish whether the computational scientist might be discouraged from using the proposed methodology by unsatisfactory run-time efficiency, which could result from a liberal use of the functional programming method. The performance data we have obtained dispel this concern. In most cases they show SaC advantage in both speed and space utilisation thanks to a deeper level of optimisation that the SaC compiler is capable of.

Future work will focus on diversifying the benchmark code base by including component methods such as Monte-Carlo, sparse matrix algebra, etc. while continuing to provide whole application examples and supporting performance studies. The ultimate goal is to create a body of evidence for the advocacy of the functional method for computational science as well as the advocacy of the specific array manipulation methodology developed within the SaC project. Our hope is that this will help to convince the computation sector to adopt those methods and techniques in large-scale numerical modelling.

References

1. SaC development team: Single Assignment C. A definitive web site. (http://www.sac-home.org)
2. Grelck, C., Scholz, S.B.: Towards an efficient functional implementation of the nas benchmark ft. In: Proceedings of the 7th International Conference on Parallel Computing Technologies (PaCT'03), Nizhni Novgorod, Russia, LNCS 2763, Springer-Verlag (2003) 230–235

3. Hammes, J., Sur, S., Bohm, A.P.W.: On the effectiveness of functional language features: NAS benchmark FT. Journal of Functional Programming **7** (1997) 103–123

4. Serrarens, P.: Implementing the Conjugate Gradient Algorithm in a Functional Language. In Kluge, W., ed.: Implementation of Functional Languages, 8th International Workshop, Bad Godesberg, Germany, September 1996, Selected Papers. Volume 1268 of LNCS. Springer (1997) 125–140

5. Frens, J., Wise, D.: Auto-Blocking Matrix-Multiplication or Tracking BLAS3 Performance from Source Code. In: Proceedings of the 6th ACM SIGPLAN Symposium on Principles and Practice of Parallel Programming. Volume 32(7) of SIGPLAN Notices. ACM (1997) 206–216

6. E.A.Kuznetsov, Musher, S., Shafarenko., A.: Collapse of acoustic waves in dispersive media. In Sagdeev, R., ed.: Nonlinear and Turbulent Processes in Physics. Harward Academic Publishers (1984) 335–349

7. Kadomtsev, B.B., Petviashvili, V.I.: On the stability of solitary waves in weakly dispersive media. Sov. Phys. Dokl **15** (1970) 539–541

8. Singh, S., Honzawa, T.: Kadomtsevpetviashivili equation for an ion-acoustic soliton in a collisionless weakly relativistic plasma with finite ion temperature. Physics of Fluids B: Plasma Physics **5** (1993) 2093–2097

9. Gilbert, G.: The kadomtsev-petviashvili equations and fundamental string theory. Communications in Mathematical Physics **117** (1988) 331–148

10. Chen, X.N., Sharma, S.D.: Zero wave resistance for ships moving in shallow channels at supercritical speeds. J. Fluid Mech. **335** (1997) 305321

11. Lu, Z., Tian, E.M., Grimshaw, R.: Interaction of two lump solitons described by the kadomtsev-petviashvili equation. Technical report, Dept. Math. Sci., Loughborough University (2003)

12. Timmes, F.X.: A pentadiagonal linear equation solver. (`http://www.cococubed.com/code_pages/pent.shtml`)

13. Grelck, C., Scholz, S., Trojahner, K.: With-loop scalarization – merging nested array operations. In Michaelson, G., Trinder, P., eds.: Proceedings of IFL'03 (selected papers). Volume 3145 of LNCS., Springer-Verlag (2004) 118–134

With-Loop Fusion
for Data Locality and Parallelism

Clemens Grelck[1], Karsten Hinckfuß[1], and Sven-Bodo Scholz[2]

[1] University of Lübeck, Germany
Institute of Software Technology and Programming Languages
{grelck,hinckfus}@isp.uni-luebeck.de
[2] University of Hertfordshire, United Kingdom
Department of Computer Science
s.scholz@herts.ac.uk

Abstract. WITH-loops are versatile array comprehensions used in the functional array language SAC to implement aggregate array operations that are applicable to arrays of any rank and shape. We describe the fusion of WITH-loops as a novel optimisation technique to improve both the data locality of compiled code in general and the synchronisation behaviour of compiler-parallelised code in particular. Some experiments demonstrate the impact of WITH-loop-fusion on the runtime performance of compiled SAC code.

1 Introduction

SAC (Single Assignment C) [1] is a purely functional array processing language designed with numerical applications in mind. Image processing and computational sciences are two examples of potential application domains. The language design of SAC aims at combining generic functional array programming with a runtime performance that is competitive with low-level, machine-oriented languages both in terms of execution time and memory consumption.

The programming methodology of SAC essentially builds upon two principles: abstraction and composition [1,2,3]. In contrast to other array languages, e.g. APL [4], J [5], NIAL [6], or FORTRAN-90, SAC provides only a very small number of built-in operations on arrays. Basically, there are primitives to query for an array's shape, for its rank, and for individual elements. Aggregate array operations (e.g. subarray selection, element-wise extensions of scalar operations, rotation and shifting, or reductions) are defined in SAC itself. This is done with the help of WITH-loops, versatile multi-dimensional array comprehensions. SAC allows us to encapsulate these operations in abstractions that are universally applicable (i.e., they are applicable to arrays of any rank and shape). More complex array operations are not defined by WITH-loops, but by composition of simpler array operations. Again, they can be encapsulated in functions that may still abstract from concrete ranks and shapes of argument arrays.

Following this technique, entire application programs typically consist of various logical layers of abstraction and composition. This style of programming

A. Butterfield, C. Grelck, and F. Huch (Eds.): IFL 2005, LNCS 4015, pp. 178–195, 2006.

leads to highly generic implementations of algorithms and provides good opportunities for code reuse on each layer of abstraction. As a very simple example, consider a function MinMaxVal that yields both the least and the greatest element of an argument array. Rather than implementing this functionality directly using WITH-loops, our programming methodology suggests to define the function MinMaxVal by composition of two simpler functions MinVal and MaxVal that yield the least and the greatest element, respectively.

Direct compilation of programs designed on the principles of abstraction and composition generally leads to poor runtime performance. Excessive creation of temporary arrays as well as repeated traversals of the same array are the main reasons. Separately computing the minimum and the maximum value of an array A requires the processor to load each element of A into a register twice. If the array is sufficiently small, it may entirely be kept in the L1 cache and the second round of memory loads yields cache hits throughout. However, with growing array size elements are displaced from the cache before temporal reuse is exploited, and data must be re-fetched from off-chip L2 cache or even main memory. In fact, the time it takes to compute minimums and maximums of two values is completely negligible compared with the time it takes to load data from memory. Therefore, we must expect a performance penalty of a factor of two when computing the minimum and the maximum of an array in isolation rather than computing both in a single traversal through memory.

This example illustrates the classical trade-off between modular, reusable code design on the one hand and runtime performance on the other hand. Whereas in many application domains a performance degradation of a factor of 2 or more in exchange for improved development speed, maintainability, and code reuse opportunities may be acceptable, in numerical computing it is not. Hence, in our context abstraction and composition as software engineering principles are only useful to the extent to which corresponding compiler optimisation technology succeeds in avoiding a runtime performance penalty. What is needed is a systematic transformation of programs from a representation amenable to humans for development and maintenance into a representation that is suitable for efficient execution on computing machinery.

In the past, we have developed two complementary optimisation techniques that avoid the creation of temporary arrays at runtime: WITH-loop-folding [7] and WITH-loop-scalarisation [8]. In our current work we address the problem of repeated array traversals, as illustrated by the MinMaxVal example. We propose WITH-loop-fusion as a novel technique to avoid costly memory traversals at runtime. To make fusion of WITH-loops feasible, we extend the internal representation of WITH-loops in order to accomodate the computation of multiple values by a single WITH-loop, which we call *multi-operator* WITH-loop. We introduce WITH-loop-fusion as a high-level code transformation on intermediate SAC code. While the essence of fusion is formally defined in a very restricted setting, we introduce additional pre- and postprocessing techniques that broaden the applicability of fusion and improve the quality of fused code.

The remainder of this paper is organised as follows. Section 2 provides a brief introduction into WITH-loops. In Section 3 we extend the internal representation of WITH-loops to multi-operator WITH-loops. The base case for WITH-loop-fusion is described in Section 4. More complex cases are reduced to the base case using techniques described in Section 5 and post-fusion optimisations in Section 6. Section 7 illustrates the combined effect of the various measures on a small case study while Section 8 reports on a series of experiments. In Section 10 we draw conclusions and outline directions of future research.

2   With-Loops in SAC

As the name suggests, SAC is functional subset of C, extended by multi-dimensional arrays as first class citizens. We have adopted as much of the syntax of C as possible to ease adaptation for programmers with a background in imperative programming, the prevailing paradigm in our targeted application areas. Despite its C-like appearance, the semantics of SAC code is defined by context-free substitution of expressions. "Imperative" language features like assignment chains, branches, or loops are semantically explained and internally represented as nested let-expressions, conditional expressions, and tail-end recursive functions, respectively. Nevertheless, whenever SAC code is syntactically identical to C code, the functional semantics of SAC and the imperative semantics of C also coincide. Therefore, the programmer may keep his preferred model of thinking, while the SAC compiler may exploit the functional semantics for advanced optimisations. Space limitations prevent us from further elaborating on the design of SAC, but a rule of thumb is that everything that looks like C also behaves as in C. More detailed introductions to SAC and its programming methodology may be found in [1,2,3].

In contrast to other array languages SAC provides only a very small set of built-in operations on arrays. Basically, they are primitives to retrieve data pertaining to the structure and contents of arrays, e.g. an array's rank (dim(*array*)), its shape (shape(*array*)), or individual elements (*array*[*index-vector*]). Aggregate array operations are specified in SAC itself using powerful array comprehensions, called WITH-loops. Their syntax is defined in Fig. 1.

WithExpr	$\Rightarrow$	**with** *Generator* : *Expr Operation*
Generator	$\Rightarrow$	(*Expr* <= *Identifier* < *Expr* $\big[$ *Filter* $\big]$)
Filter	$\Rightarrow$	**step** *Expr* $\big[$ **width** *Expr* $\big]$
Operation	$\Rightarrow$	**genarray** (*Expr* $\big[$, *Expr* $\big]$)
	$\big|$	**fold** (*FoldOp* , *Expr*)

Fig. 1. Syntax of with-loop expressions

A WITH-loop is a complex expression that consists of three parts: a *generator*, an *associated expression* and an *operation*. The operation determines the overall meaning of the WITH-loop. There are two variants: `genarray` and `fold`. With `genarray( shp, default)` the WITH-loop creates a new array of shape *shp*. With `fold( foldop, neutral)` the WITH-loop specifies a reduction operation with *foldop* being the name of an appropriate associative and commutative binary operation with neutral element *neutral*.

The generator defines a set of index vectors along with an index variable representing elements of this set. Two expressions, which must evaluate to integer vectors of equal length, define lower and upper bounds of a rectangular index vector range. For each element of this set of index vectors the associated expression is evaluated. Depending on the variant of WITH-loop, the resulting value is either used to initialise the corresponding element position of the array to be created (`genarray`) or it is given as an argument to the fold operation (`fold`). In the case of a `genarray`-WITH-loop, elements of the result array that are not covered by the generator are initialised by the (optional) default expression in the operation part. For example, the WITH-loop

```
with ([1,1] <= iv < [3,4]) : iv[0] + iv[1]
genarray( [3,5], 0)
```

yields the matrix $\begin{pmatrix} 0\,0\,0\,0\,0 \\ 0\,2\,3\,4\,0 \\ 0\,3\,4\,5\,0 \end{pmatrix}$. The generator in this example WITH-loop defines the set of 2-element vectors in the range between `[1,1]` and `[3,4]`. The index variable `iv` represents elements from this set (i.e. 2-element vectors) in the associated expression `iv[0] + iv[1]`. Therefore, we compute each element of the result array as the sum of the two components of the index vector, whereas the remaining elements are initialised with the value of the default expression. The WITH-loop

```
with ([1,1] <= iv < [3,4]) : iv[0] + iv[1]
fold( +, 0)
```

sums up all non-zero elements of the above matrix and evaluates to 21. An optional filter may be used to further restrict generators to periodic grid-like patterns, e.g.,

```
with ([1,1] <= iv < [3,8] step [1,3] width [1,2]) : 1
genarray( [3,10], 0)
```

yields the matrix $\begin{pmatrix} 0\,0\,0\,0\,0\,0\,0\,0\,0\,0 \\ 0\,1\,1\,0\,1\,1\,0\,1\,0\,0 \\ 0\,1\,1\,0\,1\,1\,0\,1\,0\,0 \end{pmatrix}$.

3 Multi-operator With-Loops

The aim of WITH-loop-fusion is to avoid the repeated traversal of argument arrays by computing multiple values in a single sweep. Hence, a major prerequisite for fusion is the ability to represent the computation of multiple values by a single WITH-loop. Regular WITH-loops, as described in the previous section, define either a single array or a single reduction value. To overcome this limitation we extend the internal representation of WITH-loops to *multi-operator* WITH-loops, as illustrated in Fig. 2.

MultiOpWith	$\Rightarrow$	**with** $\lceil$ *Generator* : *Expr* $\lceil$, *Expr* $\rceil^*$ $\rceil+\lceil$ *Operation* $\rceil+$
Generator	$\Rightarrow$	(*Expr* <= *Identifier* < *Expr* $\lceil$ *Filter* $\rceil$)
Filter	$\Rightarrow$	**step** *Expr* $\lceil$ **width** *Expr* $\rceil$
Operation	$\Rightarrow$	**genarray** (*Expr*)
	$\mid$	**fold** (*FoldOp* , *Expr*)

Fig. 2. Pseudo syntax of multi-operator with-loop expressions

Internal multi-operator WITH-loops differ from language-level WITH-loops in various aspects:

- They have a non-empty sequence of operations rather than exactly one.
- They have a non-empty sequence of generators rather than exactly one.
- Each generator is associated with a non-empty, comma-separated list of expressions rather than a single one.
- There is no default expression in **genarray** operations.

In the internal representation of WITH-loops, the default case is made explicit by creating a full partition of the index space. If necessary, additional generators are introduced that cover those indices not addressed by the original generator. These generators are explicitly associated with the default expression. A side condition not expressed in Fig. 2 is that all generators must be associated with the same number of expressions, and this number must match the number of operations. More precisely, the first operation corresponds to the first expression associated with each generator, the second operation corresponds to each second expression, etc. For example, the function **MinMaxVal** from the introduction can be specified by the following multi-operator WITH-loop for argument arrays of any rank and shape:

```
int, int MinMaxVal( int[*] A)
{
  Min, Max = with (0*shape(A) <= iv < shape(A)) : A[iv], A[iv]
           fold( min, MaxInt())
           fold( max, MinInt());
  return( Min, Max);
}
```

The multi-operator WITH-loop yields two values, which are bound to two variables using simultaneous assignment. While this simple example only uses **fold** operations, **fold** and **genarray** operations are generally mixed. We do not feature multi-operator WITH-loops on the language level because they run counter the idea of modular generic specifications. We consider the above representation of **MaxMinVal** the desired outcome of an optimisation process, not a desirable implementation.

4   With-Loop-Fusion — The Base Case

In the following we describe WITH-loop-fusion as a high-level code transformation. The base case for optimisation is characterised by two WITH-loops that have the same sequence of generators and no data dependence (i.e., none of the variables bound to individual result values of the first WITH-loop is referred to within the second WITH-loop). A formalisation of WITH-loop-fusion for this base case is shown in Fig. 3. We define a transformation scheme

$$\mathcal{WLFS}[\![pattern]\!] \; = \; expr \mid guard$$

that denotes the context-free replacement of an intermediate SAC program fragment pattern *pattern* by the instantiated SAC expression *expr* provided that the guard expression *guard* evaluates to **true**.

WITH-loop-fusion systematically examines intermediate SAC code to identify pairs of suitable WITH-loops. The guard condition for applying $\mathcal{WLFS}$ is two-fold. Firstly, all operation parts of type **genarray** must refer to the same shape. Secondly, the two WITH-loops under consideration must be free of data dependences. For the formalisation of this property we employ a function $\mathcal{FV}$ that yields the set of free variables of a given SAC expression. The third prerequisite (i.e. the equality of the generator sequences) is expressed by using the same identifiers in the pattern part of the transformation scheme. Here, we ignore the fact that generators actually form a set rather than a sequence in order to simplify our presentation. In the implementation we resolve the issue by keeping generators sorted in a systematic way.

Since WITH-loop-fusion can be applied repeatedly, we define the transformation scheme $\mathcal{WLFS}$ on multi-operator WITH-loops. Hence, $Ids^{(a)}$ matches a non-empty, comma-separated list of identifiers rather than a single identifier. No special treatment of language-level WITH-loops is required. If all conditions are met, $\mathcal{WLFS}$ takes two assignments with WITH-loops on their right hand sides and concatenates

1. the sequences of assigned identifiers,
2. the sequences of expressions associated with each generator, and
3. the sequences of operations.

Intermediate SAC code is represented in a variant of static single assignment form [9]. Therefore, index variables used in the two WITH-loops to be fused have different names. In the transformation scheme $\mathcal{WLFS}$ we address this issue by keeping the index variable of the first WITH-loop. All associated expressions that originally stem from the second WITH-loop are systematically α-converted to use the index variable of the first WITH-loop, too. In Fig. 3, this is denoted by $[expr]^{iv^{(a)}}_{iv^{(b)}}$ meaning that all free occurrences of $iv^{(b)}$ in *expr* are replaced by $iv^{(a)}$.

The transformation scheme $\mathcal{WLFS}$ as presented in Fig. 3 is meaning-preserving as it preserves the one-to-one correspondence between associated expressions, WITH-loop operations, and bound variables. In the absence of data dependences, the associated expressions and operations of the second WITH-loop may safely be moved out of the scope of the identifiers bound by the first WITH-loop without penetrating the static binding structure.

$$\mathcal{WLFS} \left\|\left[\begin{array}{l} Ids^{(a)} \text{ = with} \\ \qquad (\ lb_1 \text{ <= } iv^{(a)} \text{ < } ub_1 \text{ step } s_1 \text{ width } w_1\ )\ : \\ \qquad\qquad expr^{(a)}_{1,1}, \ldots, expr^{(a)}_{1,m} \\ \qquad\qquad\qquad \ldots \\ \qquad (\ lb_k \text{ <= } iv^{(a)} \text{ < } ub_k \text{ step } s_k \text{ width } w_k\ )\ : \\ \qquad\qquad expr^{(a)}_{k,1}, \ldots, expr^{(a)}_{k,m} \\ \qquad operation^{(a)}_1\ \ldots\ operation^{(a)}_m\ ; \\ Ids^{(b)} \text{ = with} \\ \qquad (\ lb_1 \text{ <= } iv^{(b)} \text{ < } ub_1 \text{ step } s_1 \text{ width } w_1\ )\ : \\ \qquad\qquad expr^{(b)}_{1,1}, \ldots, expr^{(b)}_{1,n} \\ \qquad\qquad\qquad \ldots \\ \qquad (\ lb_k \text{ <= } iv^{(b)} \text{ < } ub_k \text{ step } s_k \text{ width } w_k\ )\ : \\ \qquad\qquad expr^{(b)}_{k,1}, \ldots, expr^{(b)}_{k,n} \\ \qquad operation^{(b)}_1\ \ldots\ operation^{(b)}_n\ ; \end{array}\right.\right\|$$

$$=\begin{cases} Ids^{(a)},\ Ids^{(b)} \text{ = with} \\ \qquad (\ lb_1 \text{ <= } iv^{(a)} \text{ < } ub_1 \text{ step } s_1 \text{ width } w_1\ )\ : \\ \qquad\qquad expr^{(a)}_{1,1}, \ldots, expr^{(a)}_{1,m}, \\ \qquad\qquad [expr^{(b)}_{1,1}]^{iv^{(a)}}_{iv^{(b)}}, \ldots, [expr^{(b)}_{1,n}]^{iv^{(a)}}_{iv^{(b)}} \\ \qquad\qquad\qquad \ldots \\ \qquad (\ lb_k \text{ <= } iv^{(a)} \text{ < } ub_k \text{ step } s_k \text{ width } w_k\ )\ : \\ \qquad\qquad expr^{(a)}_{k,1}, \ldots, expr^{(a)}_{k,m}, \\ \qquad\qquad [expr^{(b)}_{k,1}]^{iv^{(a)}}_{iv^{(b)}}, \ldots, [expr^{(b)}_{k,n}]^{iv^{(a)}}_{iv^{(b)}} \\ \qquad operation^{(a)}_1\ \ldots\ operation^{(a)}_m \\ \qquad operation^{(b)}_1\ \ldots\ operation^{(b)}_n \end{cases}$$

$$\begin{array}{l} \forall i \in \{1, \ldots, m\}\ :\ \forall j \in \{1, \ldots, n\}\ : \\ \qquad operation^{(a)}_i \equiv \texttt{genarray}(shape^{(a)}_i) \\ \qquad \land\ operation^{(b)}_j \equiv \texttt{genarray}(shape^{(b)}_j) \\ \qquad \implies\ shape^{(a)}_i = shape^{(b)}_j \\ Ids^{(a)}\ \cap\ \bigcup_{i=1}^{k}\ \bigcup_{j=1}^{n}\ \mathcal{FV}(expr^{(b)}_{i,j})\ =\ \emptyset \end{array}$$

Fig. 3. Basic WITH-loop-fusion scheme

5   Enabling With-Loop Fusion

The transformation scheme $\mathcal{WLFS}$, as outlined in the previous section, is only applicable in a very restricted setting. In particular, adjacency in intermediate code and the need for identical generator sets are difficult to meet in practice. Instead of extending our existing transformation scheme to cover a wider range of settings, we accompany $\mathcal{WLFS}$ by a set of preprocessing code transformations that create application scenarios.

Intermediate code between two WITH-loops under consideration for fusion must be moved ahead of the first WITH-loop if it does not reference any of the variables bound by it. The remaining code must be moved below the second WITH-loop if it does not bind variables referenced within the second WITH-loop. Any remaining code constitutes an indirect data dependence between the two WITH-loops and prevents their fusion. The referential transparency of a single assignment language like SAC substantially facilitates code reorganisation and is one prerequisite to make WITH-loop-fusion effective in practice.

$$\mathcal{IS}\left\llbracket \begin{array}{c} \texttt{with} \\ gen_1^{(a)} \; : \; exprs_1^{(a)} \\ \cdots \\ gen_k^{(a)} \; : \; exprs_k^{(a)} \\ operator_1^{(a)} \\ \cdots \\ operator_p^{(a)} \end{array} \right\rrbracket \left\llbracket \begin{array}{c} \texttt{with} \\ gen_1^{(b)} \; : \; exprs_1^{(b)} \\ \cdots \\ gen_l^{(b)} \; : \; exprs_l^{(b)} \\ operator_1^{(b)} \\ \cdots \\ operator_q^{(b)} \end{array} \right\rrbracket$$

$$= \left\{ \begin{array}{l} \texttt{with} \\ \quad \mathcal{GEN}\left\llbracket gen_1^{(a)} \; : \; exprs_1^{(a)} \right\rrbracket \left\llbracket gen_1^{(b)} \; \cdots \; gen_l^{(b)} \right\rrbracket \\ \qquad \cdots \\ \quad \mathcal{GEN}\left\llbracket gen_k^{(a)} \; : \; exprs_k^{(a)} \right\rrbracket \left\llbracket gen_1^{(b)} \; \cdots \; gen_l^{(b)} \right\rrbracket \\ \quad operator_1^{(a)} \\ \qquad \cdots \\ \quad operator_p^{(a)} \end{array} \right.$$

$$\mathcal{GEN}\left\llbracket gen^{(a)} \; : \; exprs \right\rrbracket \left\llbracket gen_1^{(b)} \; \cdots \; gen_l^{(b)} \right\rrbracket$$

$$= \left\{ \begin{array}{l} \mathcal{CUT}\left\llbracket gen^{(a)} \; : \; exprs \right\rrbracket \left\llbracket gen_1^{(b)} \right\rrbracket \\ \qquad \cdots \\ \mathcal{CUT}\left\llbracket gen^{(a)} \; : \; exprs \right\rrbracket \left\llbracket gen_l^{(b)} \right\rrbracket \end{array} \right.$$

$$\mathcal{CUT}\left\llbracket (lb^{(a)} \; \texttt{<=} \; iv^{(a)} \; \texttt{<} \; ub^{(a)}) \; : \; exprs \right\rrbracket \left\llbracket (lb^{(b)} \; \texttt{<=} \; iv^{(b)} \; \texttt{<} \; ub^{(b)}) \right\rrbracket$$

$$= \mathcal{ELIM}\left\llbracket (\texttt{max}(lb^{(a)}, lb^{(b)}) \; \texttt{<=} \; iv^{(a)} \; \texttt{<} \; \texttt{min}(lb^{(a)}, lb^{(b)})) \; : \; exprs \right\rrbracket$$

$$\mathcal{ELIM}\llbracket ([lb_1, \ldots, lb_n] \; \texttt{<=} \; iv \; \texttt{<} \; [ub_1, \ldots, ub_n]) \; : \; exprs \rrbracket$$

$$= \left\{ \begin{array}{ll} ./. & | \;\; \exists \, i \in \{1, \ldots n\} : lb_i \geq ub_i \\ ([lb_1, \ldots, lb_n] \; \texttt{<=} \; iv \; \texttt{<} \; [ub_1, \ldots, ub_n]) \; : \; exprs & | \;\; otherwise \end{array} \right.$$

Fig. 4. Intersection of generators

We unify generator sets of two WITH-loops by systematically computing intersections of each pair of generators from the first and from the second WITH-loop. This code transformation is formalised by the compilation scheme $\mathcal{IS}$, defined in

Fig. 4. $\mathcal{IS}$ takes two arguments: firstly, the WITH-loop whose generator set is to be refined and, secondly, the WITH-loop which is under consideration for later fusion. Each generator of the first WITH-loop is associated with the entire sequence of generators of the second WITH-loop. The auxiliary scheme $\mathcal{GEN}$ effectively maps the generator/expression pair that originates from the first WITH-loop to each generator originating from the second WITH-loop. Finally, the auxiliary scheme $\mathcal{CUT}$ defines the intersection between two individual generators. For the sake of clarity we restrict our presentation to generators without step and width specifications and refer to [10] for more details.

The resulting number of generators equals the product of the numbers of generators of the individual WITH-loops. However, in practice many of the potential generators refer to empty index sets. Therefore, we add another auxiliary scheme $\mathcal{ELIM}$ that identifies and eliminates these generators. In addition, we use a compile time threshold on the number of generators in fused WITH-loops to prevent accidental code explosion in rare cases. We illustrate the unification of generator sets in Fig. 5. We start with two language-level WITH-loops and as a first step introduce additional generators that make each WITH-loop's default rule explicit. In a second step, we unify the two generator sets by computing all pairwise intersections between generators, and, eventually, we apply WITH-loop-fusion itself.

Another common obstacle to WITH-loop-fusion are data dependences between WITH-loops. If the sets of generators are sufficiently simple or similar to make fusion feasible, it is often beneficial to eliminate the data dependence by a forward substitution of associated expressions of the first WITH-loop into the second WITH-loop. More precisely, we analyse the second WITH-loop and replace every reference to an element of an array defined by the first WITH-loop with the corresponding defining expression.

Technically, the forward substitution of expressions from one WITH-loop into another resembles WITH-loop-folding. However, it is of little help here as WITH-loop-folding only performs the forward substitution of an associated expression if the original WITH-loop eventually becomes obsolete in order to avoid duplication of work. Exactly this prerequisite is not met in a fusion scenario because the values defined by both WITH-loops under consideration are necessarily needed in subsequent computations. However, if we are sure to apply WITH-loop-fusion as well and if the second WITH-loop solely references elements of the first WITH-loop at the position of the index variable, we can guarantee that the duplication of work introduced by forward substitution will be undone by subsequent transformations. This is demonstrated by means of a more realistic example, which we discuss in Section 7.

6   Post-fusion Optimisations

After successful fusion of WITH-loops, generators are associated with multiple expressions. The expressions themselves, however, are left unmodified. Taking the definition of the function `MinMaxVal` introduced in Section 3 as an example,

```
A = with ([1,1] <= iv < [6,6]) : 0
    genarray( [9,9], 1);

B = with ([2,3] <= iv < [6,6]) : 2
    genarray( [9,9], 3);
```

⇓ Making default rule explicit ⇓

```
A = with ([0,0] <= iv < [1,9]) : 1
         ([1,0] <= iv < [6,1]) : 1
         ([1,1] <= iv < [6,6]) : 0
         ([1,6] <= iv < [6,9]) : 1
         ([6,0] <= iv < [9,9]) : 1
    genarray( [9,9]);

B = with ([0,0] <= iv < [2,9]) : 3
         ([2,0] <= iv < [6,3]) : 3
         ([2,3] <= iv < [6,6]) : 2
         ([2,6] <= iv < [6,9]) : 3
         ([6,0] <= iv < [9,9]) : 3
    genarray( [9,9]);
```

⇓ Computing intersections ⇓

```
A = with ([0,0] <= iv < [1,9]) : 1
         ([1,0] <= iv < [6,1]) : 1
         ([1,1] <= iv < [2,6]) : 0
         ([1,6] <= iv < [6,9]) : 1
         ([2,1] <= iv < [6,3]) : 0
         ([2,3] <= iv < [6,6]) : 0
         ([6,0] <= iv < [9,9]) : 1
    genarray( [9,9]);

B = with ([0,0] <= iv < [1,9]) : 3
         ([1,0] <= iv < [6,1]) : 3
         ([1,1] <= iv < [2,6]) : 3
         ([1,6] <= iv < [6,9]) : 3
         ([2,1] <= iv < [6,3]) : 3
         ([2,3] <= iv < [6,6]) : 2
         ([6,0] <= iv < [9,9]) : 3
    genarray( [9,9]);
```

⇓ Fusing WITH-loops ⇓

```
A,B = with ([0,0] <= iv < [1,9]) : 1, 3
           ([1,0] <= iv < [6,1]) : 1, 3
           ([1,1] <= iv < [2,6]) : 0, 3
           ([1,6] <= iv < [6,9]) : 1, 3
           ([2,1] <= iv < [6,3]) : 0, 3
           ([2,3] <= iv < [6,6]) : 0, 2
           ([6,0] <= iv < [9,9]) : 1, 3
      genarray( [9,9])
      genarray( [9,9]);
```

Fig. 5. Example illustrating the systematic intersection of generators

fusion has changed the order in which elements of the argument array A are accessed, but the number of accesses is still the same. This change in the order of memory accesses improves temporal locality. In fact, every second access is guaranteed to be an L1 cache hit. Nevertheless, it would be even more desirable to avoid the second memory access at all and to directly take the value from the destination register of the first memory load.

```
Min, Max = with (0*shape(A) <= iv < shape(A)) : A[iv], A[iv]
             fold( min, MaxInt())
             fold( max, MinInt());

        ⇓  Abstraction into local assignment block  ⇓

Min, Max = with (0*shape(A) <= iv < shape(A)) : { tmp1 = A[iv];
                                                  tmp2 = A[iv];
                                                 }: tmp1, tmp2
             fold( min, MaxInt())
             fold( max, MinInt());

        ⇓  Conventional optimisations  ⇓

Min, Max = with (0*shape(A) <= iv < shape(A)) : { tmp1 = A[iv];
                                                 }: tmp1, tmp1
             fold( min, MaxInt())
             fold( max, MinInt());
```

Fig. 6. Illustration of post-fusion optimisation

Unfortunately, our current representation, which associates a sequence of unrelated expressions with each generator, effectively hinders our standard optimisations to further improve the code. Therefore, we introduce a block of local variable bindings between each generator and its associated expressions. At the same time, we restrict these expressions to be identifiers bound in that block. Fig. 6 illustrates this transformation by means of the MinMaxVal example. Here, we assume tmp1 and tmp2 to be fresh, previously unused identifiers. This rather simple postprocessing step allows us to apply the full range of optimisation techniques available in SAC. In the example common subexpression elimination and variable propagation succeed in reducing the effective number of memory references by one half.

7   Case Study

We illustrate the various code transformation steps involved in WITH-loop-fusion by means of a small case study. Fig. 7 shows a dimension-invariant SAC implementation of a simple convolution algorithm with periodic boundary conditions and convergence test. Within the function convolution we iteratively compute a single relaxation step (relax) and evaluate a convergence criterion (continue). Relaxation with periodic boundary conditions is realised by rotating the argument array one element clockwise and one element counterclockwise in each dimension. The convergence criterion `continue` yields `true` iff there is an index position for which the absolute difference of the corresponding values in argument arrays A and B exceeds the given threshold `eps`. All array operations are imported from the SAC standard array library and are themselves implemented in SAC by means of WITH-loops.

```
double[+] relax (double[+] A)
{
  for (i=0; i<dim(A); i+=1) {
    R = R + rotate( i, 1, A) + rotate( i, -1, A);
  }
  return( R / (2 * dim(A) + 1));
}

bool continue (double[+] A, double[+] B, double eps)
{
  return( any( abs( A - B) > eps));
}

double[+] convolution (double[+] A, double eps)
{
  do {
    B = A;
    A = relax( B);
  }
  while (continue( A, B, eps));
  return( A);
}
```

Fig. 7. Dimension-invariant specification of convolution

Specialisation of the dimension-invariant code to a concrete shape of argument arrays and preceding optimisations, mostly function inlining and WITH-loop folding, lead to the intermediate SAC code shown on top of Fig. 8. In each iteration of the convolution algorithm we essentially compute the relaxation step by a single `genarray`-WITH-loop and the convergence test by a single `fold`-WITH-loop. For illustrative purposes we assume a specialisation to 9-element vectors.

Fig. 8 illustrates the various steps required for even this simple example to achieve successful fusion of the two WITH-loops. The first step is the unification of the two generator sequences. The single generator of the `fold`-WITH-loop is split into three parts and the associated expression is duplicated accordingly, as described in Section 5. Unfortunately, the result of the relaxation step is required for evaluating the convergence test. This data dependence still prevents WITH-loop fusion. We eliminate it by replacing the reference to array A in the `fold`-WITH-loop by the corresponding expression that defines the value of this element of A in the `genarray`-WITH-loop. As the corresponding generators from both WITH-loops are treated in the same way from here on, we show only one.

```
A = with ([0]<=iv<[1]): (B[iv+8]+B[iv]+B[iv+1])/3
         ([1]<=iv<[8]): (B[iv-1]+B[iv]+B[iv+1])/3
         ([8]<=iv<[9]): (B[iv-1]+B[iv]+B[iv-8])/3
    genarray( [9]);
c = with ([0]<=jv<[9]): abs(A[jv]-B[jv])>=eps
    fold( ||, false);
```

⇓ Generator unification ⇓

```
A = with ([0]<=iv<[1]): (B[iv+8]+B[iv]+B[iv+1])/3
         ([1]<=iv<[8]): (B[iv-1]+B[iv]+B[iv+1])/3
         ([8]<=iv<[9]): (B[iv-1]+B[iv]+B[iv-8])/3
    genarray( [9]);
c = with ([0]<=jv<[1]): abs(A[jv]-B[jv])>=eps
         ([1]<=jv<[8]): abs(A[jv]-B[jv])>=eps
         ([8]<=jv<[9]): abs(A[jv]-B[jv])>=eps
    fold( ||, false);
```

⇓ Data dependence elimination ⇓

```
A = with ...
         ([1]<=iv<[8]):(B[iv-1]+B[iv]+B[iv+1])/3
    genarray( [9]);
c = with ...
         ([1]<=jv<[8]): abs(((B[jv-1]+B[jv]+B[jv+1])/3)-B[jv])>=eps
    fold( ||, false);
```

⇓ With-loop fusion ⇓

```
A,c = with ...
         ([1]<=iv<[8]): (B[iv-1]+B[iv]+B[iv+1])/3,
                        abs(((B[iv-1]+B[iv]+B[iv+1])/3)-B[iv])>=eps
    genarray( [9])
    fold( ||, false);
```

⇓ Abstraction into local assignment block ⇓

```
A,c = with ...
         ([1]<=iv<[8]):
             { tmp1 = (B[iv-1]+B[iv]+B[iv+1])/3;
               tmp2 = abs(((B[iv-1]+B[iv]+B[iv+1])/3)-B[iv])>=eps
             }: tmp1, tmp2
    genarray( [9])
    fold( ||, false);
```

⇓ Conventional optimisations ⇓

```
A,c = with ...
         ([1]<=iv<[8]):
             { tmp0 = B[iv];
               tmp1 = (B[iv-1]+tmp0+B[iv+1])/3;
               tmp2 = abs(tmp1-tmp0)>=eps;
             }: tmp1, tmp2
    genarray( [9])
    fold( ||, false);
```

Fig. 8. Illustration of fusion steps for convolution example

We now apply WITH-loop fusion as defined in Section 4. Abstraction of subexpressions into a joint block of local variable bindings, as described in Section 6, follows next. This opens up a plethora of further optimisation opportunities. Most notable, common subexpression elimination avoids the repeated computation of the relaxation step introduced when eliminating the data dependence between the two initial WITH-loops. The overall outcome of this sequence of code transformations is an intermediate code representation that computes both the relaxation step and the convergence test in a single sweep.

8 Experimental Evaluation

We have conducted several experiments in order to quantify the impact of WITH-loop-fusion on the runtime performance of compiled SAC code. Our test system is a 1100MHz Pentium III based PC running SuSE LINUX, and we used gcc 3.3.1 as backend compiler to generate native code.

The first experiment involves our initial motivating example: computing minimum and maximum values of an array. Fig. 9a shows runtimes for three different problem sizes with and without application of WITH-loop-fusion. As expected, there is almost no improvement for very small arrays. The benefits of fusion in this example are two-fold. We do save some loop overhead, but our experiments show this to be marginal. Therefore, the main advantage of fusion in this example is that we can avoid one out of two memory accesses. However, as long as an argument array easily fits into the L1 cache of the processor, the penalty turns out to be negligible. As Fig. 9a shows, this situation changes in steps as the array size exceeds L1 and later L2 cache capacities. In the latter case, WITH-loop-fusion reduces program execution time by almost 50%.

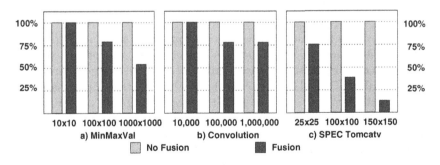

Fig. 9. Impact of WITH-loop-fusion on program execution times for computing minimum and maximum element values (left), convolution with periodic boundaries and convergence test (centre), and the SPEC benchmark `tomcatv` (right) for varying problem sizes

Our second benchmark is the convolution algorithm used as a case study in Section 7. Fig. 9b shows our measurements. For a small problem size fusion again has no visible impact on performance, but with growing problem size a nearly 25% reduction can be observed. While this is truly a substantial performance gain, we had anticipated more. For the given example, WITH-loop-fusion should reduce the number of memory load operations in the inner loop from 5 (3 in the relaxation kernel and 2 in the convergence criterion) to only 3. Keeping in mind that this numerical kernel is fully memory bound, one would expect a speedup of 40% rather than only 25%. However, a closer look at the generated assembly code revealed that both short and simple loop kernels in the non-fused case exclusively operate on registers, whereas the larger and more complex loop kernel derived from the fused code partially operates on the stack. This explains the sub-optimal performance gain observed.

The last experiment is based on a SAC implementation of the SPEC benchmark tomcatv. As shown in Fig. 9c, substantial performance gains can be observed for this benchmark with growing problem size. Improvements of up to 80% must be attributed to the fact that unlike in the previous examples more than two WITH-loops are fused at a time.

Having demonstrated the significant performance impact of WITH-loop-fusion, it would be similarly interesting to see how many application cases exist across a representative suite of programs. However, the answer critically depends on programming style. In fact, we consider WITH-loop-fusion, as WITH-loop-folding and WITH-loop-scalarisation, an enabling technology to make our propagated programming methodology based on the principles of abstraction and composition feasible in practice. Rather than generally improving the runtime behaviour of existing programs, WITH-loop-fusion eliminates the performance penalty of compositional specifications and, thus, enables us to write code that is easier to maintain and to reuse without sacrificing performance.

9   Related Work

WITH-loop-fusion is the third and last missing optimisation technique to systematically transform generic SAC programs into efficiently executable code. It is orthogonal to our previously proposed optimisations, WITH-loop-folding [7] and WITH-loop-scalarisation [8], in the sense that each of the three optimisations addresses a specific type of composition. WITH-loop-folding resolves vertical compositions of WITH-loops, where the result of one array operation becomes the argument of subsequent array operations (i.e., program organisation follows a producer-consumer pattern). WITH-loop-scalarisation addresses nested compositions of WITH-loops, where for each element of the set of indices of an outer WITH-loop a complete inner WITH-loop is evaluated (i.e., in each iteration of the outer WITH-loop a temporary array is created). Thus, both WITH-loop-folding and WITH-loop-scalarisation aim at avoiding the actual creation of temporary arrays at runtime. In contrast, WITH-loop-fusion addresses WITH-loops that are unrelated in the data flow graph or that can be made so by preprocessing techniques. In this case, fusion of WITH-loops does not change the number of data structures created at runtime, but it reduces some loop overhead and — most important — it changes the order of references into existing arrays in a way that improves data locality in memory hierarchies.

The wish to avoid the repeated traversal of large data structures is neither specific to generic array programming in general nor to SaC in particular. In the context of algebraic data types tupling [11] has been proposed to avoid repeated traversals of list- and tree-like data structures. Rather than gathering two values from the same data structure one after the other, tupling aims at gathering the tuple of values in a single traversal, hence the name. Whereas, the underlying idea essentially is the same in tupling and WITH-loop-fusion the different settings make their concrete appearances fairly different.

Fusion techniques have a long tradition in research on implementation of functional languages [12,13,14,15]. The growing popularity of generic programming techniques [16,17] has created additional optimisation demand [18]. All these approaches follow the mainstream of functional languages in that they focus on lists or on algebraic data types. Much less work has been devoted to arrays, one exception being *functional array fusion* [19]. All these techniques aim at identifying and eliminating computational pipelines, where a potentially complex intermediate data structure is synthesised by one function for the sole purpose to be analysed by another function later on. In contrast, the objective of WITH-loop-fusion is not the elimination of intermediate data structures, which in SaC is taken care of by WITH-loop-folding [7]. The essence of WITH-loop-fusion is more similar to the aims of traditional loop fusion in high performance computing in reducing loop overhead and the size of memory footprints.

There is a plethora of work on fusion of FORTRAN-style do-loops [20,21,22,23]. While the intentions are similar to the objectives of WITH-loop-fusion, the setting is fairly different. Despite their name, our WITH-loops represent potentially complex array comprehensions with abstract descriptions of multi-dimensional index spaces rather than conventional loops. Whereas WITH-loops define the computation of an aggregate value in an abstract way, do-loops merely define a control flow that leads to a specific sequence of read and write operations. Since the fusion of do-loops changes this sequence a compiler must be sure that both the old and the new sequence are semantically equivalent and that the new sequence is beneficial with respect to some metric. Both require the compiler to develop a deeper understanding of the programmer's intentions. Consequently, much of the work on loop fusion in FORTRAN is devoted to identification of dependences and anti-dependences on a scalar or elementary level. In contrast, the functional setting of SaC rules out anti-dependences and discloses the data flow. Rather than reasoning on the level of scalar elements, WITH-loop-fusion addresses the issue on the level of abstract representations of index spaces.

10   Conclusion and Future Work

Engineering application programs based on the principles of abstraction and composition as in SaC leads to well-structured and easily maintainable software. However, the downside of this approach is that it requires non-trivial compilation techniques which systematically restructure entire application programs into a form that allows for efficient execution on real computing machinery.

In the current work, we have described WITH-loop-fusion as one mosaic stone of this code restructuring compiler technology. WITH-loop-fusion takes two WITH-loops and transforms them into a single generalised variant named multi-operator WITH-loop, which we have introduced as a compiler internal intermediate code representation for exactly this purpose. The positive effect of WITH-loop fusion is to avoid repeated traversals of the same array and replace memory load and store operations by equivalent but much faster register accesses. In several experiments we have demonstrated the potential of WITH-loop-fusion to achieve substantial reductions of execution times. In fact, it has proved to be a major prerequisite to make the modular programming style of SAC feasible in practice.

Individual WITH-loops also form the basis of compiler-directed parallelisation of SAC programs following a data parallel approach [24]. Like folding and scalar-isation WITH-loop-fusion has the effect to concentrate computational workload scattered throughout multiple WITH-loops within a single one. Therefore, WITH-loop-fusion also improves the quality of parallelised code by reducing the number of synchronisation barriers and the need for communication. Furthermore, dealing with larger computational workload improves both the quality and the efficiency of scheduling workload to processing units.

In the future, we plan to extend WITH-loop-fusion to handle **genarray**-WITH-loops that define arrays of non-identical shape. The idea is to create a joint WITH-loop whose generators cover the convex hull of the individual WITH-loop's index spaces. Index positions not existing in one or another result array would be associated with a special value **none** and ignored by compiled code. Another area of future research is the selection of WITH-loops for fusion. As fusion of two WITH-loops may prevent further fusion with a third WITH-loop, we may want to identify the most rewarding optimisation cases on the basis of heuristics.

References

1. Scholz, S.B.: Single Assignment C — Efficient Support for High-Level Array Operations in a Functional Setting. J. Functional Programming **13** (2003) 1005–1059
2. Grelck, C.: Implementing the NAS Benchmark MG in SAC. In: Proceedings of the 16th International Parallel and Distributed Processing Symposium (IPDPS'02), Fort Lauderdale, USA, IEEE Computer Society Press (2002)
3. Grelck, C., Scholz, S.B.: Towards an Efficient Functional Implementation of the NAS Benchmark FT. In: Proceedings of the 7th International Conference on Parallel Computing Technologies (PaCT'03), Nizhni Novgorod, Russia. LNCS 2763, Springer-Verlag (2003) 230–235
4. Iverson, K.: A Programming Language. John Wiley, New York, USA (1962)
5. Iverson, K.: Programming in J. Iverson Software Inc., Toronto, Canada. (1991)
6. Jenkins, M.: Q'Nial: A Portable Interpreter for the Nested Interactive Array Language Nial. Software Practice and Experience **19** (1989) 111–126

7. Scholz, S.B.: With-loop-folding in SAC — Condensing Consecutive Array Operations. In: Proceedings of the 9th International Workshop on Implementation of Functional Languages (IFL'97), St. Andrews, Scotland, UK, Selected Papers. LNCS 1467, Springer-Verlag (1998) 72–92

8. Grelck, C., Scholz, S.B., Trojahner, K.: With-Loop Scalarization: Merging Nested Array Operations. In: Proceedings of the 15th International Workshop on Implementation of Functional Languages (IFL'03), Edinburgh, UK, Revised Selected Papers. LNCS 3145, Springer-Verlag (2004)

9. Appel, A.: SSA is Functional Programming. ACM SIGPLAN Notices **33** (1998)

10. Hinckfuß, K.: With-Loop Fusion für die Funktionale Programmiersprache SAC. Master's thesis, University of Lübeck, Institute of Software Technology and Programming Languages, Lübeck, Germany (2005)

11. Chin, W.: Towards an Automated Tupling Strategy. In: Proceedings of the ACM SIGPLAN Symposium on Partial Evaluation and Semantic-Based Program Manipulation (PEPM'97), Copenhagen, Denmark, ACM Press (1993) 119–132

12. Wadler, P.: Deforestation: Transforming Programs to Eliminate Trees. Theoretical Computer Science **73** (1990) 231–248

13. Gill, A., Launchbury, J., Peyton Jones, S.: A Short Cut to Deforestation. In: Proceedings of the Conference on Functional Programming Languages and Computer Architecture (FPCA'93), Copenhagen, Denmark, ACM Press (1993) 223–232

14. Chin, W.: Safe Fusion of Functional Expressions II: Further Improvements. J. Functional Programming **4** (1994) 515–550

15. van Arkel, D., van Groningen, J., Smetsers, S.: Fusion in Practice. In: Proceedings of the 14th International Workshop on Implementation of Functional Languages (IFL'02), Madrid, Spain, Selected Papers. LNCS 2670, Springer-Verlag (2003)

16. Alimarine, A., Plasmeijer, R.: A Generic Programming Extension for Clean. In: Proceedings of the 13th International Workshop on Implementation of Functional Languages (IFL'01), Stockholm, Sweden, Selected Papers. LNCS 2312, Springer-Verlag (2002) 168–186

17. Löh, A., Clarke, D., Jeuring, J.: Dependency-style Generic Haskell. In: Proceedings of the 8th ACM SIGPLAN Conference on Functional Programming (ICFP'03), Uppsala, Sweden, ACM Press (2003) 141–152

18. Alimarine, A., Smetsers, S.: Improved Fusion for Optimizing Generics. In: Proceedings on the 7th International Symposium on Practical Aspects of Declarative Languages (PADL'05), Long Beach, USA. LNCS 3350, Springer-Verlag (2005)

19. Chakravarty, M.M., Keller, G.: Functional Array Fusion. In: Proceedings of the 6th ACM SIGPLAN International Conference on Functional Programming (ICFP'01), Florence, Italy, ACM Press (2001) 205–216

20. McKinley, K., Carr, S., Tseng, C.W.: Improving Data Locality with Loop Transformations. ACM Transactions on Programming Languages and Systems **18** (1996)

21. Manjikian, N., Abdelrahman, T.: Fusion of Loops for Parallelism and Locality. IEEE Transactions on Parallel and Distributed Systems **8** (1997) 193–209

22. Roth, G., Kennedy, K.: Loop Fusion in High Performance Fortran. In: Proceedings of the 12th ACM International Conference on Supercomputing (ICS'98), Melbourne, Australia, ACM Press (1998) 125–132

23. Xue, J.: Aggressive Loop Fusion for Improving Locality and Parallelism. In: Parallel and Distributed Processing and Applications: 3rd International Symposium, ISPA 2005, Nanjing, China. LNCS 3758, Springer-Verlag (2005) 224–238

24. Grelck, C.: Shared memory multiprocessor support for functional array processing in SAC. J. Functional Programming **15** (2005) 353–401

A Document-Centered Environment for Haskell

Keith Hanna

University of Kent
fkh@kent.ac.uk

Abstract. This paper describes a document-centered environment for
Haskell that is aimed at making the language accessible to a broad range
of end users. In this environment (named Vital), Haskell modules are
presented as documents with the values they define displayed in place
textually or graphically (as 'views'). An end user, who may have only a
superficial knowledge of Haskell, is able to edit a program (for example,
manipulating literal values of complex, user-defined ADTs) by interact-
ing with these views. The representation of an ADT and the range of
interactions possible with it (that is, its 'look and feel') are open-ended
and are defined (by an expert user) in terms of Haskell type classes
and implemented by a mechanism that employs a specialised form of
reflection.

1 Introduction

A *document-centered environment* (DCE) is one in which both the program and
the results it produces are presented to the user in the form of an integrated
document that supports *direct manipulation*. This term means that editing operations are carried out on visual representations of the data, that they take
effect immediately and that they are easily reversible.

Usually the underlying language used in a DCE is declarative in nature. This
means that there is no hidden state to take account of and there is no layout-
defined order in which the individual program declarations or expressions need
to be evaluated.

The canonical example of a DCE system is the spreadsheet. A spreadsheet
program is implicitly defined by the 'formulae' in its cells and has a purely
declarative semantics. The order in which its cells are evaluated is determined
only by the dependancy relations between the cells. Many spreadsheet systems
provide a means for high-level visualisation of the contents of a spreadsheet, for
example, as a graph and support direct manipulation of the graph (for example,
dragging the ordinates of a graph causes the corresponding spreadsheet formulae
to be updated).

Other example of DCEs are the so-called 'technical' computing systems (such
as Mathcad, Mathematica or Maple). These allow a free-format for the layout of
expressions and data and support a limited range of types (typically numbers,
strings, lists and arrays).

But present-day realisations of DCEs are severely limited by the impoverished
semantics of their underlying languages. Typically these languages have largely

A. Butterfield, C. Grelck, and F. Huch (Eds.): IFL 2005, LNCS 4015, pp. 196–211, 2006.

first-order semantics with the declarative core of the language being bolstered by imperative features (assignment statements, loops, etc.) to make up for their limited expressiveness. These limitations and *ad hoc* extensions, together with the lack of user-defined types and strong type-checking, severely limit the ability of programmers (even expert ones) to construct reliable, correct, maintainable programs — with well-known consequences.

1.1 A Document-Centered Environment for Haskell

In this paper we describe an approach, based on the use of Haskell, that overcomes these limitations. In particular, it allows a graphical representation to be defined for any type together with an associated set of kinds of direct manipulation that a user can carry out on values of that type. The approach (described in §2) is based on the use of Haskell's type classes coupled with a mechanism that, using reflection, provides controlled updating of the source text of the user program.

A prototype implementation [9] of the approach, named Vital, has been developed and significant aspects of its implementation and performance are described in §3. As with other systems intended to support end-user computing, two classes of user are envisaged. Firstly, there are expert Haskell programmers, who will design and implement libraries of domain-specific abstractions, (including the graphical representation and direct manipulation of these abstractions). Secondly, there are the end users (engineers, scientists, financial analysts, etc.) who, possibly with only a superficial knowledge of Haskell, will program in terms of these abstractions (mainly using direct manipulation on their graphical representation).

Here, as an illustration, here is an example (taken from the prototype implementation described in §3) of this approach in action:

- Consider an applied mathematican (as an end user) working on a problem involving binary relations. He can load a module that implements an ADT representing binary relations (in this case, defined on sets of size 8) whose values are displayed as directed graphs. Then, possibly starting from a null relation, he can, using only mouse gestures, define a desired relation simply by editing edges into its graph or he can carry out high-level operations (see Fig. 1) such as transitive closure or intersection with a relational value on the clipboard.

Whilst the operations that a user carries out *appear* to be operating directly on the displayed values, they actually operate on the text of the Haskell source program the user has implicitly constructed (and hence they indirectly update the values displayed). This indirection brings several benefits:

- It allows values that may not have a defined textual representation (such as functions or infinite data structures) to be manipulated.
- It means that the solution the user has developed (by direct manipulation) is *portable*, since it takes the form of an ordinary Haskell program (with some meta-data embedded as comments).

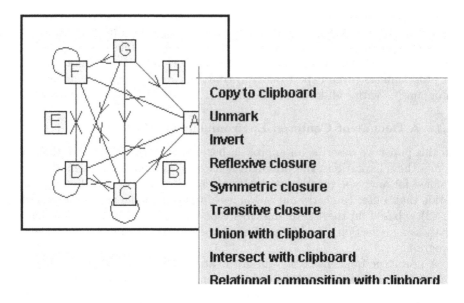

Fig. 1. Visualisation of a binary relation. Clicking on one of the nodes drops down a menu that allows edges to be inserted or deleted. Clicking elsewhere, as shown here, drops down a menu that allows operations to be applied to the relation, or (for binary operations) between it and a relation that has been copied to the clipboard.

– It achieves *persistence*, that is, it allows documents to be saved and restored to an identical state.

2   Principles of Direct Manipulation

In this section we will describe the principles of a document-centered environment that supports direct manipulation. We will cast the description in terms of Haskell but the principles are equally applicable for any other purely declarative higher-order language that supports type classes. So as to be able to focus on principles, we elide all inessential detail (but include some screenshots from the implementation described in §3 to aid the explanation).

2.1   Document-Centered Environment

By a *document-centered environment* for Haskell, we mean an environment in which Haskell modules are displayed as *documents* within which the individual declarations are freely located with the value defined by each value declaration optionally displayed adjacent to it. Fig. 2 shows part of a typical document.

Values may be displayed either textually or graphically. The way that a value is displayed is determined by its type and by the corresponding instance declarations for one or other of the predefined type classes:

☐ | A function (due to Gibbons) that, applied to the arguments 1, 0, 1 and 1, yields the infinite decimal expansion of pi.

```
☐  f q r t k =
       let n = (3*q+r) `div` t in
       if (4*q+r) `div` t == n    then
           n : f (10*q) (10*(r-(n*t))) t k
       else
           f (q*k) ((q*(4*k+2)) + (r*(2*k+1))) (t*(2*k+1)) (k+1)
```

☐ | Decimal expansion of pi | ☐ (More about this algorithm)

```
☐  f 1 0 1 1
```

| 3 | 1 | 4 | 1 | 5 | 9 | 2 | 6 | 5 | 3 | 5 | 8 | 9 | 7 | 9 |

Fig. 2. A document containing a declaration for a function, **f**, an expression involving **f** (whose value is an infinite list of integers), a couple of comments and a hypertext link to another document

```
class Show a where              class Display a where
    show :: a -> String             display :: a -> Pic
    . . .                               . . .
```

The `Show` class is the usual means that Haskell interpreters employ to map values to their textual representation as strings. The `Display` class, introduced here, is an analogous class that maps values to their graphical representation as *pictures*, that is, as elements of type `Pic`. Both type classes are on an equal footing: the two types, `String` and `Pic`, are pervasive and are supported by primitives that automatically render strings or pictures in place in a document. We will refer to the graphical representation (as produced by the `Display` class) of a value as a *view* of the value.

For example, the particular graphical representation used for binary relations (as in Fig. 1) is defined by an instance declaration of the form

```
instance Display Rel where
    display rel = . . .
```

(where `Rel` is an abstract type, declared elsewhere, of binary relations).

The type `Pic` is an algebraic datatype that provides constructors for a variety of different kinds of picture together with a constructor for composition (superposition):

```
data Pic
  = NoPic
  | Rect Int Int Color Color              -- Rectangles
```

```
     . . .
   | Trans Int Int Pic                       -- Linear translation
   | Super Pic Pic                           -- Superposition
   | PicText Format String                   -- Text
   | PicImage Image                          -- Images

   | Animation (Time -> Pic)
   | forall s. Interaction s
                    (Time -> Int -> Int -> Bool -> s -> (s, Pic))
   | PicAction Int Int Color Color (IO ())
```

Expressions in a document are, in accordance with standard Haskell semantics, evaluated lazily. The process of evaluation is driven by the rendering mechanism which forces evaluation of only those parts of a string or a picture that are visible within the current *viewport*. (A more detailed description of the rendering mechanism, which allows (finite prefixes of) infinite values to be rendered without risk of boundless recursion, is given in [8].)

2.2   Direct Manipulation

We now describe a mechanism that will allow an end-user to manipulate ADT values by *direct manipulation*. This term[14] means that a user can interact with a visual representation of a value by intuitively meaningful gestures, and that any changes should be immediately displayed and should be reversible.

User's perspective Seen from a user's perspective, the system behaves as follows:

– The user clicks on the part (of the view of) the value that he wishes to change. For example (see Fig. 1), the user might click on one of the elements of the set (perhaps to add or remove a link to that element) or (as shown) might click on the background of the picture (perhaps to perform an operation such as reflexive closure on the overall relation).
– The system responds by displaying a menu (specific both to the type of the value and to the location in the view where the user clicked) of allowable operations.
– The user responds by selecting one of these operations.
– The system then updates the document so that it shows the result of the operation.

A value-based approach. One approach to implementing this behaviour would be to arrange for the selected operation (in the form of a user-defined Haskell function) to be applied directly to the value itself. But, whilst simple to implement, this approach would have two major disadvantages. Firstly, the displayed value would be inconsistent with the Haskell declaration in the document. Secondly, in order to be able to save and restore a document, it would be necessary to provide some means of serialising values (for instance, [4]), and this would limit the portability of the Haskell program.

Reflection. Instead, we propose adopting an indirect approach involving the use of reflection. When a user interacts with the graphical representation of the value of a declaration, the effect is not directly to modify the value itself but rather it is *to invoke a Haskell function that will modify the Haskell source code of the relevant declaration in such a way that it will, when evaluated, embody the desired changes.* (This is similar to the way that direct manipulation is handled in spreadsheet systems: mouse gestures alter the formulae in the cells rather than directly alter the displayed values.)

The mechanism required for supporting this approach to direct manipulation can be split into two aspects:

- A *type-specific* aspect that defines the particular set of direct manipulation operations (if any) that can be applied to values of each particular type. This aspect can nicely be handled using the Haskell type class mechanism.
- A *generic* aspect that implements the services necessary for invoking the type-specific component. This will involve a selection mechanism (allowing a user to select a particular element in the graphical representation of a value), a menu mechanism (that displays a menu of allowable operations for values of a particular type) and a reflection mechanism (that allows controlled updating of the Haskell source text of the user program).

This, then, is the overall approach. We now describe aspects of the approach in more detail.

The Selection mechanism. Some operations applied by a user may take, as a parameter, a *location* defined by the user clicking to select a particular component (eg, a `Rect` component) within the view of a value. Views (that is, values of type Pic, defined by the `display` method of the `Display` class) have a tree structure, and so the location of the selected component can be defined by a list of integer-valued selectors that define a path from the root of the tree to the component. We introduce a type synonym for paths

```
type Path = [Int]
```

The type-specific operations. The repetoire of operations applicable to a given value will, in general, depend both on its type and on the form of its graphical representation (which, via the `Display` class, also depends on its type). Thus, it is natural to make use of the `Display` class for defining this repetoire.

We need to cater for two distinct categories of direct manipulation operations:

- *Discrete* operations (for example, ones such as cut/copy/paste/update/ increment, etc.) where an operator is applied exactly once.
- *Continuous* operations (for example, ones such as dragging a slider to change a colour or dragging a vertex of a shape to change a dimension) where an operation is applied repeatedly (at a sufficient high rate to give an impression of continuous adjustment).

A given type may include operations of either or both categories.

For each operation (of either category) in the repetoire of a given type, we need to be able to define both a name (for display to the user) for the operation and a Haskell function (for implementing the operation). To this end, the `Display` class includes these two methods:

- `edit`, for defining the repetoire of discrete operations, and
- `adjust`, for defining the repetoire of continuous operations (not further discussed here).

The full definition of the `Display` class is:

```
class Display a where
    display :: a -> Pic
    edit    :: a -> Path -> [(String, EditFn a)]
    adjust  :: a -> Path -> [(String, AdjustFn a)]

    edit x path    = []          -- default methods
    adjust x path = []
```

Both of these edit methods take both the value itself and also the path to the component of the value that the user selected; this allows the set of operations offered to the end user to be *context dependent*. Each method yields a list of pairs, each consisting of:

- a string defining the name of the operation (that will appear in the menu of operations offered to the user), and
- a function that will implement the operation by (reflectively) updating the source text of the program

The operation-selection mechanism. When the user clicks within a document, the system determines whether the location defined is within a component of (the graphical representation of) a value. If it is, the system determines the path corresponding to that location and then applies the relevant instances of both the `edit` and the `adjust` methods to the value and its path. This yields a list of (name, implementation) pairs defining the operations that (from a user's perspective) may validly be applied to the selected component of the displayed value. The system displays these names as a menu, so allowing the user to select the particular operation to be applied.

The selection by the user of a particular operation causes the system to apply (reflectively) its associated implementation function.

Discrete operations. For an operation associated with the `edit` method (ie, for a discrete operation), the implementation function is of type

```
type EditFn a  =  a -> Path -> String -> String
```

The system marshals the following arguments:

- the value the user selected;
- the path to the selected graphical component of that value;
- the righthand side of the Haskell source code of the declaration that defined that value.

To these arguments it applies the implementation function. The system then updates the righthand side of the declaration with the resultant string, and then triggers a re-display of the document (which in turn triggers the necessary recompilation and reevaluation of the Haskell program). Assuming the implementation function has been correctly written, the overall effect will appear, to the end user, as if the value itself had simply been updated in the desired way.

2.3   An Example

A simple example will help clarify the *modus operandi* of the system. Assume that a library module is required that will provide an end user with the ability to create, visualise and manipulate *finite predicates on the natural numbers*.

The first step is to define the signature and an implementation for an ADT (named `Pred`) for such predicates. The signature could be defined as:

```
data Pred

nullPred       :: Pred
complement     :: Pred -> Pred
get            :: Int -> Pred -> Bool
set            :: Int -> Bool -> Pred -> Pred

predToString :: Pred -> String
stringToPred :: String -> Pred
```

where:

- `nullPred` is the null predicate;
- `complement` yields the complement of a predicate;
- `get` determines the truth value of a predicate at a given domain value;
- `set` specifies the truth value of a predicate at a given domain value;
- `predToString` yields a compact textual representation [1] of a predicate
- `stringToPred` is the left-inverse of the above function.

Next, an instance of the `Display` class is defined to specify what we can call the desired *look and feel* for values of type `Pred`:

```
instance Display Pred where
    display = displayPred        -- defined below
    edit    = editPred           -- defined below
```

---

[1] Although the domain of the predicates is infinite, any particular predicate is constructed with a finite number of operations and so a textual representation is possible.

Defining the 'look' of the ADT. We will assume that a predicate should be displayed to an end user as (see Fig. 3) a row of squares containing ticks or crossses (representing True/False values of the predicate for n = 0, 1, ..), superimposed on a shaded background.

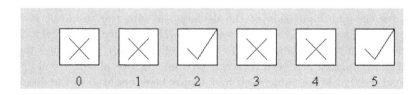

Fig. 3. Visualisation of a value of type Pred

This is achieved by defining the rendering function

```
displayPred :: Pred -> Pic
displayPred pred = . . .
```

(Since the domain of Pred is infinite, the pictorial representation of a predicate is likewise of unbounded extent[2].)

When the user selects (by clicking) a component of such a picture, the system generates the path that identifies that component. This path (since it depends intimately on the `displayPred` function) is a low-level representation of the index position of an element of a predicate. For manipulating predicates, we will need a high-level representation, that is, one that is compatible with the index type used in the signature of the ADT. To this end, we define a path abstraction function

```
decode :: Path -> Maybe Int
decode path = . . .
```

that yields the value `Just i` if the user clicks within the ith square of a predicate picture, or the value `Nothing` if the user clicks elsewhere.

Defining the 'feel' of the ADT. We will assume that the following set of operations on views of predicates should be available to an end user:

- *Tick* (ie, set the value of a selected element to True);
- *Cross* (ie, set the value of a selected element to False);
- *Flip* (ie, complement the value of every element);
- *Evaluate* (ie, define a string literal that represents the predicate).

These operations should be presented to the user in a context-dependent fashion: the first two if the user selects an element of a predicate (by clicking within a square), the second two if the user selects the overall predicate (by clicking within

---

[2] As noted in earlier, the underlying display mechanism evaluates `Pic` values lazily and displays only the elements that lie within the (scrollable) viewport.

its background). In all four cases, the operations are discrete in nature (since they should be applied once only not continuously).

This behaviour is achieved by defining the editPred function as:

```
editPred :: Pred -> Path -> [(String, EditFn Pred)]

editPred pred path =
  case decode path of
    Nothing -> [("Flip", complementFn),
                ("Evaluate", evalFn)]
    Just i  -> [("Tick",  setTrueFn i),
                ("Cross", setFalseFn i)]
```

With this definition, if the user clicks within one of the elements of a view of a predicate, then a menu appears offering a choice of *Tick* or *Cross*. If, alternatively, the user clicks on the background of the view, then a menu appears offering a choice of *Flip* or *Evaluate*. (Since there is no instance defined for the adjust method in the Display class, there are no menu entries present for continuous operations.)

Finally, the actual editing functions need to be defined. These are of type

```
complementFn, evalFn, setTrueFn, setFalseFn ::
    Pred -> Path -> String -> String
```

When one of these functions is invoked by the system, it will be supplied with arguments representing:

- the value of the predicate
- the path to the selected picture component
- the righthand side of the declaration that defines the predicate

The task of an editing function is to synthesise a string that will be used, by the system, to update the righthand side of the selected declaration so that it will, when evaluated, yield the desired result. Here are their definitions:

```
complementFn _ _ rhs = "complement (" ++ rhs ++ ")"

evalFn pred _ _ = "stringToPred " ++ predToString pred

setTrueFn i _ _ rhs =
    "set " ++ show i ++ " True  (" ++ rhs ++ ")"

setFalseFn i _ _ rhs =
    "set " ++ show i ++ " False (" ++ rhs ++ ")"
```

Example. As an example of the system in operation, assume that the initial Haskell program is:

```
p, q :: Pred
p = set 3 True nullPred
q = set 1 p
```

The system will display the value defined by the declaration for q as a row of squares with ticks in the 1st and 3rd squares and crosses elsewhere.

Here is a typical sequence of interactions that might occur:

- The user clicks on the predicate background. The system applies the path abstraction function to the path and obtains a Nothing value. This indicates that the predicate as a whole is being selected and so the system displays a menu with entries for *Flip* and *Evaluate*.
- The user selects the *Flip* entry. The system then applies the complementFn function to the righthand side of the declaration for q, obtaining the string

```
complement (set 1 p)
```

with which it updates the declaration and then recompiles the program and redisplays document.
- The user clicks on the 6th element of the predicate. This time, the path abstraction function yields the value Just 6 and so the system displays a menu with entries for *Tick* and *Cross*.
- The user selects the *Cross* entry and so the system applies the setFalse function, obtaining the string

```
set 6 False (complement (set 1 p))
```

with which it updates the declaration, recompiles and redisplays the document.

Following these operations, the declaration for q is

```
q = set 6 False (complement (set 1 p))
```

and the resultant predicate is displayed as a row of squares with crosses in the 1st, 3rd and 6th squares and ticks elsewhere.

Notice that, in the final document:

- the value of q still depends upon the value of p (if the latter was subsequently changed by editing, then the value of the former would reflect the change.)
- the form of the declaration for q provides a trace of the sequence of editing operations by which the resultant predicate was created.

Depending on the context, either of these properties may be an advantage. But, if more than a small number of editing operations are carried out on a declaration, it will begin to get unwieldy (and computationally inefficient). The *Evaluate* operation provides a remedy for this; unlike the other operations (which augment the original text of the righthand side of the declaration), this operation replaces the expression on the righthand side by a literal that represents its value. In the resultant Haskell program:

- the value of p becomes independent of all other bindings;
- depending on the actual value of the declaration and the actual way in which this value is encoded (by the predToString function), the resultant declaration may be more or less bulky than the original one.

3   The 'Vital' Implementation

A prototype implementation[3], named Vital[4], has been created to explore the practical realisation of the scheme described above. In this section we discuss distinctive aspects of this system.

3.1   Pictures and the `Pic` Datatype

Pictures are pervasive in Vital. The `Pic` datatype, described in §2, is a primitive of the system; values of type `Pic` are automatically rendered (in place) as *pictures*. The constructors of the datatype allow complex pictures to be defined in terms of simple geometric shapes, text and images, and pictures may also involve *animation, user interaction* and *event initiation*.

Animation. The ability to incorporate animations as an integral part of a document is particular useful in many end-user application areas. Typical uses range from simple animated text (for instance, showing a continuously updated time of day) to animated diagrams of complex mechanisms.

There are several possible approaches that could be used to implement animation but here the overriding concern is one of simplicity (for end users) — and, in particular, avoiding the use of monadic constructions. Thus, an animated picture is represented by a picture-valued function, `fn :: Time -> Pic` (supplied as an argument to the `Animation` constructor). The system repeatedly (at the display frame rate) applies the function to the current value of real time (measured in ms) and triggers a redisplay of the document[5].

User interaction. Pictures involving user interaction via the mouse may be formed using the `Interaction` constructor and supplying it with the definition of a finite-state machine, in the form of an initial state `s0 :: s` and a function

```
fn :: Time -> Int -> Int -> Bool -> s -> (s, Pic)
```

that yields a next state and a picture when supplied the current time, the current x and y coordinates of the mouse cursor, the state of depression of the

---

[3] This implementation is available at `http://www.cs.kent.ac.uk/projects/vital/` and may be run via the web. It implements a representative subset of Haskell and (at present) carries out type-checking at run time.

[4] Vital: an acronym for 'Visual Interactive Typed Applicative Language'.

[5] Initially, it was assumed that a straightforward approach like this would be too inefficient and, instead, a more elaborate scheme, limited to being able to display only strictly periodic animations and involving the pre-computation and caching of sequences of images, was implemented. Experience, however, showed that the majority of the computational burden involved in typical animations is incurred at the rendering stage, and so caching has a relatively minor effect. But, this is not universally true; there is an important class of animation, those involving synthetic images defined as spatial functions (as in [6]), where caching would be essential. This could, however, be handled by having the user program pre-compute the sequence of images and arranging for the animation function to select from the sequence in a time-dependent way.

mouse button and the current state. As with the `Animation` constructor, when an `Interaction` constructor is encountered, the system repeatedly applies the function to the current value of its arguments and triggers a redisplay of the document. (Notice that these values of these arguments are *not* accessible from the main program namespace and so the purely declarative semantics of Haskell are not compromised.)

As with simple animation, this more general form of interaction is useful in many end-user application areas. Typical uses range from controlling the viewpoint used when rendering 3-D objects to simulating arcade-type games. In practice, libraries of higher-level functions (for example, for the numerical solution and display of discrete dynamical systems defined by differential equations) can easily be defined in terms of the `Animation` constructor. There appears to be no reason why the approach embodied by the Fran system [15], which nicely combines efficiency with user simplicity, should not also be implemented.

4   Related Work

As noted in the introduction, commercial spreadsheet systems support direct manipulation, with mouse gestures being mapped to editing operations on the formulae in the spreadsheet cells. It was this pattern of interaction that provided the original motivation for the Vital scheme.

Functional language spreadsheets. The formulae in the traditional spreadsheet system are first-order expressions and a spreadsheet can be regarded as implicitly defining a program in a purely declarative, first-order language. Two groups have explored generalisation of this paradigm: a spreadsheet system implemented in Clean is described in [5] and, more recently, a spreadsheet-like interface for Haskell in [11]. In both cases, the first-order language conventionally used for cell formulae is replaced by a higher-order, strongly typed language with the aim of retaining the advantage of direct manipulation offered by the spreadsheet approach whilst overcoming the limitations of an inexpressive first-order language.

Graphical presentation of functional programs. Several authors[13,3,10] have explored the representation of functional programs using a graphical syntax but, whilst such an approach would be compatible with a document-centered interface, it appears that it would have few advantages (it is generally agreed that the conventional text-based representation of programs is both more compact and more convenient to use than graphical representation).

The Forms/3 system. The Forms/3 system[1,7], an innovative generalisation of the spreadsheet paradigm, introduces data abstraction and direct manipulation of the formulae defining such abstractions. The approach adopted by Vital has been significantly influenced by concepts introduced in this system.

Data abstraction is implemented by allowing a 'form' (a freely-arranged collection of 'cells' holding Lisp formulae) to be displayed either as a document or represented graphically in a programmer-defined manner. For example, a data abstraction could be introduced to represent binary trees and such values displayed as tree diagrams. Further, a range of mouse *gestures* may be associated with a data abstraction such that making the gesture (or pointing to an image of the gesture) will modify the formulae in the cells of the associated form in a programmer-defined way. For instance, the gesture of sketching a circle could be associated with the act of creating an instance of a form to represent a circle with the corresponding radius, or selecting a displayed string and sketching a vertical stroke could be associated with replacing the formula that defines the point size of the displayed string.

Values in Forms/3 are potentially time-varying and are represented by sparse sequences; this allows user-interaction to be handled declaratively; in particular, it allows user-input sequences to be captured and replayed.

5 Conclusions and Future Possibilities

This paper has described an approach to providing a document-centered interface to Haskell with the aim of making the expressiveness and robustness that this language offers available to non-expert end users (with supporting domain-specific libraries written by expert users).

The interface presents the individual modules of a Haskell program as documents and the values declared in these modules as pictures (with text as a special case). The interface supports direct manipulation, that is, values are continuously displayed and can be manipulated in high-level (ie, visual) terms.

The key features of the approach are:

- The introduction of a `Display` class (an analog of the standard, text-based `Show` class) with a `display` method that allows a pictorial representation to be defined for each type.
- Picture values include both static and interactive pictures (defined by functions modelling finite-state machines) and also event-sensitive pictures[6] that allow arbitrary imperative actions (defined by monadic values) to be initiated.
- The `Display` class also includes methods allowing arbitrary programmer-defined editing operations (discrete or continuous) to be defined on the pictorial representation of values. This co-location of the display and editing methods within the `Display` class allows the choice of pictorial representation adopted for each type to be encapsulated within the corresponding instance declaration — which aids code maintainability.
- These editing operations, although they appear to the user to operate directly on the pictorial values, in fact operate indirectly on the Haskell source text of the corresponding declaration. This gives both persistence (ie, the ability for the user program to be unloaded and subsequently restored) and portability. It also allows editing operations to involve infinite or functional values.

---

[6] Event-sensitive pictures are not discussed in this paper.

5.1 Future Developments

There are many interesting and potentially useful directions in which this approach can be further developed including, in particular, type-safe manipulation and a Haskell-based implementation.

The graphical selection mechanism (that the user employs during direct manipulation) can be tightly coupled to the type checker so as to prevent (*a priori*) type-unsafe gestures from even being expressed. (Preliminary results on this technique have recently been presented by Callanan[2].)

The existing Vital prototype is a free-standing implementation of a Haskell compiler. However, the recently-developed 'Plugin' library for Haskell[12], which allows the dynamic, type-safe compilation and execution of Haskell code from within a Haskell program, offers the exciting prospect of being able to implement a document-centered interface for Haskell entirely within Haskell itself. A prototype system[7], named Pivotal, based on this approach is presently being explored.

References

1. M. Burnett et al. Forms/3: A first-order visual language to explore the boundaries of the spreadsheet paradigm. *J. Functional Programming*, 11(2):155–260, March 2001.
2. M. Callanan. Type-safe clipboard operations for document-centered functional programs. In *21st British Colloquium for Theoretical Computer Science, Nottingham*, 2005.
3. L. Dami and D. Vallet. Higher-order functional composition in visual form. In D. Tsichritzis, editor, *Object Applications*, pages 139–154. Univ. of Geneva, 1996.
4. T. Davie, K. Hammond, and J. Quintela. Efficient persistent Haskell. Technical report, Univ. St. Andrews, 2000.
5. W. A. C. A. J. de Hoon, L. M. W. J. Rutten, and M. C. J. D. van Eekelen. Implementing a functional spreadsheet in Clean. *J. Functional Programming*, 5(3):383–414, July 1995.
6. C. Elliott. Functional images. In J. Gibbons and O. de Moor, editors, *The fun of programming*. Palgrave MacMillan, 2003.
7. H. J. Gottfried and M. Burnett. Graphical definitions: making spreadsheets visual through direct manipulation and gestures. In *Proc VL'97, Capri, Italy*. IEEE, 1997.
8. K. Hanna. Interactive visual functional programming. In *Proc. Seventh ACM SIGPLAN Intnl. Conf. on Functional Programming*, pages 145–156. ACM, 2002.
9. K. Hanna. *Vital: a document-centered implementation of Haskell*. University of Kent, 2005. Includes tutorial, reference manual and download. Available from http://www.cs.kent.ac.uk/projects/vital/.
10. J. Kelso. Visual representation for functional programs. Technical Report CS-95-01, Dept of Comp. Sc., Murdoch University, 1995.
11. B. Lisper and J. Malmstrom. Haxcel: a spreadsheet interface to Haskell. In *14th Int. Workshop on Impl. of Functional Languages*, pages 206–222, 2002.

---

[7] Preliminary notes on, and screenshots from, a skeletal implementation of Pivotal are available at http://www.cs.kent.ac.uk/projects/pivotal/

12. A. Pang, D. Stewart, S. Seefried, and M. M. T. Chakravarty. Plugging Haskell in. In *Proc ACM SIGPLAN workshop on Haskell, Snowbird, USA*, pages 10–21. ACM Press, 2004.
13. H. J. Reekie. Visual Haskell: a first attempt. Technical Report 94.5, Centre for Adv. Comp. Sc., Univ. of Tech., Sydney, 1994.
14. B. Shneiderman. Direct Manipulation: a step beyond programming languages. *IEEE Computer*, 16(8):57–67, 1983.
15. S. Thompson. A functional reactive animation of a lift using Fran. *J. Functional Programming*, 10:245–268, 2000.

A Binding Scope Analysis for Generic Programs on Arrays

Clemens Grelck[1], Sven-Bodo Scholz[2], and Alex Shafarenko[2]

[1] Inst. of Software Technology and Programming Languages, University of Lübeck, Germany
Grelck@isp.uni-luebeck.de
[2] Dept of Computer Science, University of Hertfordshire, United Kingdom
{S.Scholz,A.Shafarenko}@herts.ac.uk

Abstract. Performance of generic array programs crucially relies on program specialisation wrt. shape information. Traditionally, this is done in a rather ad hoc fashion by propagating all shape information that is available. When striving for a compositional programming style that adheres to good software engineering principles this approach turns out to be insufficient. Instead, static value information needs to be propagated as well which introduces all the well known problems of partial evaluation in general.

In this paper, we propose a static analysis that identifies to what extent specialisation needs to be employed in order to achieve a certain level of shape information. This narrows the scope of specialisation far enough to make specialisation for shape information feasible despite a compositional programming style. Some examples to this effect are presented.

1 Introduction

Compiling abstract high-level specifications into efficiently executable code is well-known to be a challenging task. Usually, a whole set of complementing optimisations need to be orchestrated properly in order to achieve excellent run-time performance. In the area of array programming, the effectiveness of many optimisations relies on static knowledge of array rank (dimension) and array shape (extent wrt. individual axes). Not only does static knowledge of shapes facilitate many loop related optimisations, it is also essential for eliminating intermediate arrays[LLS98, Sch03] as well as compiler-introduced memory reuse [Can89, GT04].

For most applications in array programming, the majority of array operations are such that the shape of the result can be computed from the shapes, rather than full values, of the arguments. Such operations often are referred to as *uniform operations* [Hui95]. Uniformity enables a straight-forward approach to an effective utilisation of static shape information: Whenever a shape information is statically available it is propagated into all existing function calls by specialising these according to the given shapes. Since most array programs operate on a

A. Butterfield, C. Grelck, and F. Huch (Eds.): IFL 2005, LNCS 4015, pp. 212–230, 2006.

small set of different shapes only, non-termination of specialisation in practice is rarely hit or otherwise can be detected by a compiler fairly easily [Kre03]. For these reasons, array languages such as FISH [JMB98, JS98] or SAC [Sch03] follow that approach.

Unfortunately, uniformity is at odds with a compositional programming style. In contrast to FISH, SAC allows the programmer to successively break down complex (and usually uniform) array operations into compositions of small, rather generic operations similar to those available in APL. These small array operators typically separate concerns such as inspecting structural properties, selecting parts of an array, or combining arrays into new ones. Unfortunately, the separation of concerns in most cases makes these small operators non-uniform, i.e., the shapes of their results depend on argument values rather than argument shapes only. Typical examples are operations such as **take** or **drop**. These operations select parts of an array by taking or dropping a certain amount of elements, respectively. The number of elements to be dropped or taken is specified as an explicit parameter of these operations which renders the shape of the result dependent on that parameter's value.

Although such a programming style is desirable from a software engineering perspective, it has a strong impact on the performance of such specifications. A specialisation strategy as described above, i.e., based on specialisations to shapes only, leads to a loss of shape information whenever non-uniform operations such as **take** or **drop** are used. As shown in [Kre03], the loss of static shape information can have a significant effect on the overall performance.

One alternative to avoid this potential source of performance degradation would be to specialise functions to argument values whenever these are statically available. However, this would in fact fully embrace the online approach to partial evaluation and, with it, its well-known difficulties: recursive functions introduce undecidability, and the resulting code expansion may outweigh the potential gain in performance (for surveys see [JGS93, Jon96]).

In order to avoid these difficulties, we propose a static program analysis that for each function of a given program infers what level of argument specialisation is required in order to compute the shape of the result. With this information, we can restrict specialisation to argument values to those situations, where this information is crucial for shape inference. In all other situations, a less aggressive specialisation scheme, e.g. specialisation to argument shapes, can be applied. Since APL-style program compositions usually contain only a small percentage of non-uniform operations it turns out that, by and large, only a few specialisations to argument values are required in order to statically infer all shapes within a large application program.

More generally, the proposed analysis can serve as a "specialisation oracle" that guides the entire specialisation process as the inference algorithm does not only compute the requirements for static shape knowledge, but it also determines the requirements for other levels of static shape information such as static rank knowledge. This additional information can be used for adjusting the specialisation oracle so that it can predict the minimum level of specialisation that is required for a predefined level of overall shape information. Once the scope of the specialisation has been determined, an online approach towards specialisation suffices for specialising most programs to the predefined level irrespective of whether they have been written in a compositional style or not.

The inference algorithm is described in terms of a subset of SAC [Sch03], which has been adjusted to a fairly generic λ-calculus syntax. This measure allows us to concentrate on the language essentials and it may facilitate transferability of results to other languages. Besides a formal description of the inference, its effectiveness is demonstrated by means of several examples.

The paper is organised as follows: the next section introduces a stripped-down version of SAC, called SAC$_\lambda$. Section 3 discusses the issues of compositional programming and function specialisation by means of a few examples. The main idea of the analysis is presented in Section 4, before Section 5 and Section 6 provide the formal details of it. In Section 7 the formalism is applied to the examples of Section 3. Section 8 relates the work to other approaches towards the specialisation og generic program specifications before some conclusions are drawn in Section 9.

2   SAC$_\lambda$

This paper is based on a stripped-down version of SAC. It contains only the bare essentials of the language and its syntax has been adjusted to a λ-calculus style in order to facilitate transferability of results.

Fig. 1 shows the syntax of SAC$_\lambda$. A program consists of a set of mutually recursive function definitions and a designated main expression. Essentially, ex-

$$
\begin{array}{ll}
Program & \Rightarrow \big[\, FunId \;=\; \lambda Id \big[\, ,\, Id \,\big]^{*} . \, Expr \;;\; \big]^{*} \\
& \mathbf{main} \;=\; Expr \;; \\
\\
Expr & \Rightarrow Const \\
& \mid\; Id \\
& \mid\; FunId \,(\, \big[\, Expr \,\big[\, ,\, Expr \,\big]^{*}\, \big]\,) \\
& \mid\; Prf \,(\, \big[\, Expr \,\big[\, ,\, Expr \,\big]^{*}\, \big]\,) \\
& \mid\; \mathbf{if}\; Expr \;\mathbf{then}\; Expr \;\mathbf{else}\; Expr \\
& \mid\; \mathbf{let}\; Id = Expr \;\mathbf{in}\; Expr \\
& \mid\; \mathbf{with}(\, Expr <= Id < Expr \,) \;:\; Expr \\
& \quad \mathbf{genarray}(\, Expr \,,\, Expr \,) \\
\\
Prf & \Rightarrow \mathbf{shape} \\
& \mid\; \mathbf{dim} \\
& \mid\; \mathbf{sel} \\
& \mid\; * \\
& \mid\; ...
\end{array}
$$

Fig. 1. The syntax of SAC$_\lambda$

pressions are either constants, variables or function applications. As SAC does neither support higher-order functions nor name-less functions, abstractions occur at top-level only. Function applications are written in C-style, i.e., with parenthesis around arguments rather than entire applications. It should be noted here that all constants are in fact arrays. Therefore, we use (nestings of) vectors in square-brackets alongside with scalars as notation for constants. SAC_λ provides a few built-in array operators, referred to as primitive functions. Among these are **shape** and **dim** for computing an array's shape and dimensionality (rank), respectively. Furthermore, a selection operation **sel** is provided which takes two arguments: an index vector that indicates the element to be selected and an array to select from. These very basic array operations are complemented by element-wise extensions of arithmetic and relational operations such as *∗* and *>=*, respectively. For improved readability, we use the latter in infix notation throughout our examples.

On top of this language kernel, SAC provides a special language construct for defining array operations in a generic way which is called WITH-loop. For the purpose of this paper, it suffices to consider a restricted form of WITH-loop only. Fully-fledged WITH-loops are described elsewhere, e.g. in [Sch03]. They provide several extensions which primarily relate to programming convenience. Since these extensions do not affect the analysis in principle but would substantially blow up the formal apparatus, we refrain from the fully-fledged version.

As can be seen from Fig. 1, WITH-loops in SAC_λ take the general form

> **with** (*lower* **<=** *idx_vec* **<** *upper*) : *expr*
> **genarray**(*shape, default*)

where *idx_vec* is an identifier, *lower*, *upper*, and *shape* denote expressions that should evaluate to vectors of identical length and *expr* and *default* denote arbitrary expressions that need to evaluate to arrays of identical shape. Such a WITH-loop defines an array of shape *shape*, whose elements are either computed from the expression *expr* or from the default expression *default*. Which of these two values is chosen for an individual element depends on the element's location, i.e., it depends on its index position. If the index is within the range specified by the lower bound *lower* and the upper bound *upper*, *expr* is chosen, otherwise *default* is taken. As a simple example, consider the WITH-loop

```
with ([1] <= iv < [4]) : 2
genarray( [5], 0)
```

It computes the vector [0, 2, 2, 2, 0]. Note here, that the use of vectors for the shape of the result and the bounds of the index space (also referred to as the "generator"') allows WITH-loops to denote arrays of arbitrary rank. Furthermore, the "generator expression" *expr* may refer to the index position through the "generator variable" *idx_vec*[1]. For example, the WITH-loop

---

[1] Most of our examples use **iv** as variable name for the generator variable.

```
with ([1,1] <= iv < [3,4]) : sel([0], iv) + sel([1], iv)
genarray( [3,5], 0)
```

yields the matrix $\begin{pmatrix} 0\ 0\ 0\ 0\ 0 \\ 0\ 2\ 3\ 4\ 0 \\ 0\ 3\ 4\ 5\ 0 \end{pmatrix}$.

We can formalise the semantics of SAC_λ by a standard big-step operational semantics for λ-calculus-based applicative languages as defined in several textbooks, e.g., [Pie02]. The core relations, i.e., those for conditionals, abstractions, and function applications can be used in their standard form. Hence, only those relations pertaining to the array specific features of SAC_λ are shown in Fig. 2.

CONST : $\dfrac{}{n \Downarrow < [], [n] >}$

VECT : $\dfrac{\forall i \in \{1, \ldots, n\} : e_i \Downarrow < [\, s_1, \ldots, s_m], [\, d_1^i, \ldots, d_p^i] >}{[\, e_1, \ldots, e_n] \Downarrow < [\, n,\ s_1, \ldots, s_m], [\, d_1^1, \ldots, d_p^1, \ldots, d_1^n, \ldots, d_p^n] >}$

DIM : $\dfrac{e \Downarrow < [\, s_1, \ldots, s_n], [\, d_1, \ldots, d_m] >}{\text{dim}(\ e) \Downarrow < [], [n] >}$

SHAPE : $\dfrac{e \Downarrow < [\, s_1, \ldots, s_n], [\, d_1, \ldots, d_m] >}{\text{shape}(\ e) \Downarrow < [\, n], [\, s_1, \ldots, s_n] >}$

SEL : $\dfrac{iv \Downarrow < [\, n], [\, i_1, \ldots, i_n] > \qquad e \Downarrow < [\, s_1, \ldots, s_n], [\, d_1, \ldots, d_m] >}{\text{sel}(\ iv,\ e) \Downarrow < [], [\, d_l] >}$
$$\text{where } l = \sum_{j=1}^{n} (i_j * \prod_{k=j+1}^{n} s_k)$$
$$\Longleftrightarrow \forall k \in \{1, \ldots, n\} : 0 \leq i_k < s_k$$

$*$: $\dfrac{\begin{array}{c} e_1 \Downarrow < [\, s_1, \ldots, s_n], [\, d_1^1, \ldots, d_m^1] > \\ e_2 \Downarrow < [\, s_1, \ldots, s_n], [\, d_1^2, \ldots, d_m^2] > \end{array}}{*(\ e_1,\ e_2) \Downarrow < [\, s_1, \ldots, s_n], [\, d_1^1 * d_1^2, \ldots, d_m^1 * d_m^2] >}$

WITH : $\dfrac{\begin{array}{c} e_l \Downarrow < [\, n], [\, l_1, \ldots, l_n] > \\ e_u \Downarrow < [\, n], [\, u_1, \ldots, u_n] > \\ e_{shp} \Downarrow < [\, n], [\, shp_1, \ldots, shp_n] > \\ e_{def} \Downarrow < [\, s_1, \ldots, s_m], [\, d_1, \ldots, d_p] > \\ \forall i_1 \in \{l_1, ..., u_1 - 1\} \ldots \forall i_n \in \{l_n, ..., u_n - 1\} : (\lambda \, Id . e_b \ [\ i_1, \ldots, i_n]) \\ \Downarrow < [\, s_1, \ldots, s_m], [\, d_1^{[i_1, \ldots, i_n]}, \ldots, d_p^{[i_1, \ldots, i_n]}] > \end{array}}{\begin{array}{c} \text{with}(\ e_l\ \text{<=}\ Id\ \text{<}\ e_u) :\ e_b \ \text{genarray}(\ e_{shp},\ e_{def}) \\ \Downarrow < [\ shp_1, \ldots, shp_n,\ s_1, \ldots, s_m], \\ [\ d_1^{[0, \ldots, 0]}, \ldots, d_p^{[0, \ldots, 0]}, \ldots, d_1^{[shp_1 - 1, \ldots, shp_n - 1]}, \ldots, d_p^{[shp_1 - 1, \ldots, shp_n - 1]}] > \end{array}}$
$$\text{where } d_i^{[x_1, \ldots, x_n]} = d_i \text{ iff } \exists j \in \{1, ..., n\} : x_j \in \{0, ..., l_j - 1\} \cup \{u_j, ..., shp_j - 1\}$$

Fig. 2. An operational semantics for SAC_λ

As a unified representation for n-dimensional arrays we use pairs of vectors $< [\ shp_1, \ldots, shp_n], [\ data_1, \ldots, data_m\ ] >$ where the vector $[\ shp_1, \ldots, shp_n]$ denotes the shape of the array, i.e., its extent with respect to the n individual axes, and the vector $[\ data_1, \ldots, data_m]$ contains all elements of the array in a linearised form. Since the number of elements within an array equals the product of the number of elements per individual axes, we have $m = \prod_{i=1}^{n} shp_i$.

The first two evaluation rules of Fig. 2 show how scalars as well as vectors are transformed into the internal representation. Note with the rule VECT, that all elements need to be of the same shape which ensures shape consistency in the overall result.

The next three rules formalise the semantics of the main primitive operations on arrays: dim, shape, and sel. Element-wise extensions of standard operations such as the arithmetic and relational operations are demonstrated by the example of the rule for multiplication (*).

The last rule gives the formal semantics of the WITH-loop in SAC_λ. The first three conditions require the lower bound, the upper bound and the shape expression to evaluate to vectors of identical length. The next two conditions relate to the default expression e_{def} and the generator expression e_b, respectively. They ensure, that the default expression evaluates to an array of the same shape as the generator expression does. Since the generator expression may refer to the index variable, this is formalised by transforming the generator expression into an anonymous function and by evaluating a pseudo-application of this function to all indices specified in the generator. The lower part of the WITH-loop-rule shows how the values from the individual generator expression evaluations and the value of the default expression are combined into the overall result. The shape of the result stems from concatenating the shape expression with the shape of the default element. Its data vector consists of a concatenation of the data vectors from the individual generator expression evaluations. Since the generator does not necessarily cover the entire index space, the default expression values need to be inserted whenever at least one element of the index vector $[i_1, \ldots, i_n]$ is outside the generator range, i.e., $\exists j \in \{1, ..., n\} : x_j \in \{0, ..., l_j - 1\} \cup \{u_j, ..., shp_j - 1\}$. Formally this is achieved by the "where clause" of the rule WITH.

3   A Motivating Example

The core language introduced in the previous section suffices to define generic array operations similar to those available in array languages such as APL, NIAL, or J. As an example, consider the operations take and create as defined in Fig. 3. The function take expects two arguments v and a. It returns an array of shape v whose elements are copied from those in the corresponding positions of the argument array a. Note here, that the specification of 0*v as lower bound yields a vector of zeros of the same length as the vector v and, thus, ensures shape-invariance, i.e., it makes take applicable to arrays of arbitrary dimensionality.

```
take = λv,a.with ( 0*v <= iv < v): sel( iv, a)
           genarray( v, 0)
create = λs,x.with ( 0*s <= iv < s): x
             genarray( s, x)
```

Fig. 3. A definition of take and create in SAC$_\lambda$

The function create takes two arguments as well: a shape vector s and a value x. From these it computes an array of shape s with all elements identical to x. Again, shape-invariance is achieved by computing the bounds from the vector s that determines the shape of the result.

Both these functions are non-uniform, i.e., result shapes cannot be computed from the argument shapes only. Instead, argument values are required to determine the result shapes. Several application studies show that functions of this sort usually prove very useful when adopting a compositional programming style [Sch03, GS99]. A typical application of these operations is shown in Fig. 4. The

```
matmul = λdl,dm,v.let
                   maind = dm * v
               in let
                    lowerd = dl * take( shape( dl), v)
                 in let
                      zeros = create( shape( dm) - shape( dl), 0)
                   in maind + concat( zeros, lowerd)
```

Fig. 4. A definition of a sparse matrix vector multiply in SAC$_\lambda$

function matmul implements a special case for a matrix vector product where the matrix contains non-zero values on two diagonals only: the main diagonal (argument dm) and another diagonal dl located below the main one. A third argument v represents the vector the matrix is to be multiplied with and, thus, is expected to have as many elements as the main diagonal dm does. The difference in length between the two diagonals determines the exact location of the lower diagonal. Essentially, the matrix vector product consists of the sum of products dm * v and dl * v. However, the vector v needs to be shortened prior to the multiplication with dl to match its size, and the resulting vector (lowerd in Fig. 4) needs to be prepended by sufficient zeros in order to match the length of the main diagonal dm. The latter is achieved by concatenating a vector of zeros (zeros in Fig. 4) of appropriate length.

The most remarkable aspect of this function is that although it makes use of the two non-uniform operations take and create, matmul itself is uniform. This stems from the fact that the shape determining arguments of take and create are computed from the shape of the arguments dm and dl, a programming pattern that can be observed rather frequently.

A brute force approach to static inference based on specialisation to argument shapes only would only yield the dimensionalities for the results of the applications of take and create, not their shapes. This, in turn, would lead to the loss of static result shape knowledge for matmul itself. That knowledge can only be gained, if take and create both are specialised wrt. values in their first argument position, and if the subtraction in the first argument position of create is computed statically.

The overall goal of the analysis presented in this paper is to statically infer to what extent functions need to be specialised in order to achieve a certain level of information for their results. In the given example, the analysis should yield that take and create need to be specialised to values if the result shape is required, and that for matmul it suffices to specialise wrt. argument shapes. However, the analysis should also yield to which extent all subexpressions need to be calculated statically in order to achieve that goal.

4 Basic Approach

Traditionally, binding time analysis is based on a two element domain: all expressions are either attributed as *static* or as *dynamic*. In our approach, we distinguish four different levels of static array information[2]:

AUD (**A**rray of **U**nknown **D**imensionality):
  no shape information is available at all;
AKD (**A**rray of **K**nown **D**imensionality):
  dimensionality is known but not the exact shape;
AKS (**A**rray of **K**nown **S**hape):
  the exact shape is available at compile-time;
AKV (**A**rray of **K**nown **V**alue):
  not only the exact shape but also the value is statically known.

These four levels build the grounds for our analysis. We try to infer to which extent static knowledge of the arguments of a function is needed in order to achieve a certain level of static information about the result. Although we are primarily interested in the level of information that is required for statically computing the shape of the result only (AKS result), we need to infer the required levels for all possible result levels. This extended effort is required as we may find function applications in positions where other levels of shape information than just AKS are required. Consider, for example, the expression shape(dm) - shape(dl) of the matmul example. Here, it is essential for the inference to find out which level of information is required for dm and dl in order to compute the value of the expression statically.

As a consequence, we do not attribute each expression with one of these levels only, but we need to infer mappings from the set of levels {AUD, AKD, AKS,

---

[2] Readers familiar with SAC may notice that these levels directly correspond to the hierarchy of array types in SAC which is essential when it comes to implementing the specialisation phase.

AKV} into itself. Once we have inferred such mappings for all arguments of a function, we can use this information to find out which level of specialisation is required in order to achieve a certain level of result information.

Let us consider the built-in operation **shape** as an example. For its relation between result level and argument level, we find the following mapping in our four-element-domain:

$$\{ \; AUD \rightarrow AUD,$$
$$AKD \rightarrow AUD,$$
$$AKS \rightarrow AKD,$$
$$AKV \rightarrow AKS\}$$

As the result of the primitive function **shape** always is a vector, no array information at all is needed if we are interested in the dimensionality of the result. The shape of the result requires the dimensionality of the argument only, and the value of the result can be deduced from the shape of the argument.

In order to formalise this approach, we can identify the different levels of array information as coarsening steps in the value domain of SAC_λ. While AKV is identical to our original domain of values of the form

$$< [\; shp_1, \ldots, shp_n], [\; data_1, \ldots, data_m] >,$$

AKS can be described by values of the form

$$< [\; shp_1, \ldots, shp_n], - >.$$

Taking the use of the '−' symbol for irrelevant values further, we can use

$$< [\; \overbrace{-, \ldots, -}^{n}], - >$$

for AKD arrays and

$$< -, - >$$

for AUD arrays.

With these new domains, we can now deduce new semantic rules from those of Fig. 2. We successively weaken the preconditions to less precise domains and determine the effect of this information loss on the postconditions. Applying this approach to the SHAPE-rule, we obtain three new rules:

$$\text{AKSSHAPE} \; : \; \frac{e \Downarrow < [\; s_1, \ldots, s_n], - >}{\text{shape}(\; e) \Downarrow < [\; n], [\; s_1, \ldots, s_n] >}$$

$$\text{AKDSHAPE} \; : \; \frac{e \Downarrow < [\; \overbrace{-, \ldots, -}^{n}], - >}{\text{shape}(\; e) \Downarrow < [\; n], - >}$$

$$\text{AUDSHAPE} \; : \; \frac{e \Downarrow < -, - >}{\text{shape}(\; e) \Downarrow < [\; -], - >}$$

From these rules we observe that

- AKS arguments are mapped into AKV ones
- AKD arguments are mapped into AKS ones
- AUD arguments are mapped into AKD ones

As we are interested in predicting the required argument shape-levels for a desired return shape-level, we are actually looking for the inverse of the mapping deduced from the semantic rules. The inverse is well-defined as all functions are monotonic with respect to the array information hierarchy, i.e., providing more shape information can never lead to fewer shape information of the result. Furthermore, the finite domain/codomain guarantees an effective computability of the inverse.

In case of the **shape** operation, we obtain exactly the same mapping as the one we have derived earlier in an informal fashion.

Uniformity of a function can now easily be recognised from its associated mapping: whenever AKS is mapped into a shape-level less or equal to AKS, we know that the shape of the function's result does at most require the shape of the argument, not its value. The unpleasant non-uniform cases are those where AKS is mapped into AKV.

5 Towards an Inference Algorithm

Rather than just giving the coarsened semantic rules, in the sequel, we develop an algorithm for effectively inferring the shape-level mappings described in the previous section for arbitrary SAC_λ programs.

In order to achieve a more concise notation, we encode our four-element-domain by the numbers 0,1,2 and 3. This allows us to represent the mappings on that domain as four-element-vectors of these numbers. Applications of these mappings then boil down to selections into the vector. Using 0 for AUD, 1 for AKD, 2 for AKS, and 3 for AKV, we can encode the mapping for **shape** as $[0, 0, 1, 2]$. Similarly, we obtain the vector $[0, 0, 0, 1]$ for the primitive operation **dim**. It shows that only if we are interested in the result value itself we need to know something about the argument and all we need to know is its dimensionality.

We refer to these vectors as *propagation vectors* as they, for a given function application, propagate a given return value demand into a demand for the arguments. If we are, for example, interested in the value of an expression **shape(dm)**, i.e., we have a demand of 3 (AKV), this demand propagates into a demand on **dm** by selecting the third element of the propagation vector of **shape** yielding $[0,0,1,2][3] = 2$ (AKS) as demand for **dm**.

Functions with more than just one argument require as many propagation vectors as we have arguments. For example, the built-in selection operation **sel** has two propagation vectors: $\begin{bmatrix} [0, 2, 2, 3] \\ [0, 1, 2, 3] \end{bmatrix}$. If we are interested in the dimensionality of the result, we need to consult the second element in each propagation vector. It shows that the shape of the selection vector (first argument) is needed as well as the dimensionality of the array to be selected from (second argument).

Computing propagation vectors of entire functions essentially boils down to propagating all four possible demands through the body expression and collecting the resulting demands for the individual arguments as vectors. As an example, let us consider the expression λ a . sel([0] , shape(shape(a))). It computes the shape of the shape of an array a and selects the only component of the resulting vector which is identical to computing the array's dimensionality. Hence, we expect a propagation vector identical to that of the primitive operation dim to be computed for this function.

First, let us compute the demand for a assuming we need to statically compute the value of the overall expression, i.e., we have an initial demand of 3 (AKV). That demand propagates into the second argument of the selection by applying the second propagation vector of sel to it, i.e., we obtain $[0,1,2,3][3] = 3$ (AKV) as demand for the subexpression shape(shape(a)). Propagating that demand through the outer application of shape yields $[0,0,1,2][3] = 2$ (AKS) which subsequently is propagated through the inner application of shape resulting in $[0,0,1,2][2] = 1$ (AKD) as demand for a.

Similarly, the other three possible overall demands can be propagated through the function body. All these result in a demand of 0 (AUD) for a. Combining these results into a vector yields $[0,0,0,1]$ as propagation vector for the given function which corresponds to the propagation vector of the built-in operation dim.

As all four demands can be computed independently, the propagation in fact can be implemented as a data parallel operation that propagates entire demand vectors through the function bodies, starting out from the canonical demand vector $[0,1,2,3]$.

6   Inferring Propagation Vectors

So far, all our example functions were combinators, i.e., they did not contain any relatively free variables. Although that holds for all built-in operators and for all user-defined functions in SAC_λ, it does not hold for arbitrary expressions. These can be nested let-expressions or WITH-loops both of which introduce locally scoped variables. To address this situation, any inference scheme for propagation vectors needs to deal with environments that hold demands for relatively free variables.

We introduce a scheme $\mathcal{SD}(expr, dem, \mathcal{F})$ which computes an environment that contains demand vectors for all relatively free variables of an expression $expr$. It expects two additional parameters: an overall demand dem, and a function environment $\mathcal{F}$ that contains the propagation vectors of all functions. Fig. 5 shows a formal definition of that scheme. Constants meet any demand and do not raise any new demands, hence, an empty set is returned for constants. If a given demand dem is imposed on a variable Id then the singleton set is returned containing the pair of the identifier and the given demand.

For function applications, the demand is translated into argument demands by the appropriate propagation vectors first. These are either extracted from the function environment $\mathcal{F}$, or — in case of built-in operators — they are determined by an auxiliary scheme $\mathcal{PV}$. After the initial demand dem has been translated into demands dem_i for the individual arguments, the scheme is recursively applied to the argument expressions. The resulting sets of demands

$$SD(Const,\ dem,\ \mathcal{F}) = \{\}$$

$$SD(Id,\ dem,\ \mathcal{F}) = \{Id : dem\}$$

$$SD(FunId(e_1, ..., e_n),\ dem,\ \mathcal{F}) = \bigoplus_{i=1}^{n} SD(e_i,\ dem_i,\ \mathcal{F})$$
$$\text{where } dem_i = (\mathcal{F}(FunId)_i)[dem]$$

$$SD(Prf(e_1, ..., e_n),\ dem,\ \mathcal{F}) = \bigoplus_{i=1}^{n} SD(e_i,\ dem_i,\ \mathcal{F})$$
$$\text{where } dem_i = (\mathcal{PV}(Prf)_i)[dem]$$

$$SD(\texttt{let } Id = e_1 \texttt{ in } e_2,\ dem,\ \mathcal{F}) = \begin{pmatrix} (\ SD(e_2,\ dem,\ \mathcal{F}) \setminus \{Id\}\ ) \\ \oplus\ SD(e_1,\ dem',\ \mathcal{F}) \end{pmatrix}$$
$$\text{where } dem' = \mathcal{PV}(\lambda\, Id\,.\, e_2)[dem]$$

$$SD\begin{pmatrix} \texttt{with}(e_{lb}\texttt{<=}Id\texttt{<}e_{ub}) : e \\ \texttt{genarray}(e_{shp}, e_{def}) \end{pmatrix},\ dem,\ \mathcal{F}) = \begin{pmatrix} SD(e_{shp},\ dem_s,\ \mathcal{F}) \\ \oplus\ (\ SD(e,\ dem,\ \mathcal{F}) \setminus \{Id\}\ ) \\ \oplus\ SD(e_{def},\ dem,\ \mathcal{F}) \\ \oplus\ SD(e_{lb},\ dem_{Id},\ \mathcal{F}) \\ \oplus\ SD(e_{ub},\ dem_{Id},\ \mathcal{F}) \end{pmatrix}$$
$$\text{where } dem_s = [0,2,3,3][dem]$$
$$dem_{Id} = \mathcal{PV}(\lambda\, Id\,.\, e)[dem]$$

Fig. 5. Scheme for inferring specialisation demands

for relatively free variables are combined by an operation denoted as $\oplus$. It constitutes a union of sets for those variables that occur in one set only and an element-wise maximum on the demand vectors for all variables that occur in both sets.

Let-expressions essentially are a combination of the demands in the body and the demands in the defining expression. However, the external demand dem needs to be translated into the demand for the defining expression dem' by computing the propagation vector for the underlying λ-abstraction. Furthermore, we need to exclude the demand for the defined variable from the demands inferred from the body of the let-expression as relatively free occurrences in the body relate to this very definition.

The dominating rule for inferring specialisation demands of array operations is the rule for WITH-loops as these are the predominant language constructs for defining array operations in SAC. While the overall demand dem can be propagated without modification into the generator expression e and the default expression e_{def}, the most important effect is the increase in demand for the shape expression e_{shp}. Here, we have a propagation vector $[0,2,3,3]$ which indicates that we lose one level of shape information. As a consequence, we need to statically infer the exact value of this expression if we want to find out the shape of the result. The overall demand of the WITH-loop, again, is the combination of the demands of the individual components using the translated demands dem_s, dem_e, and dem_{Id} for the shape expression, defining expressions, and the boundary expressions, respectively.

All that remains to be defined is the auxiliary scheme for obtaining the propagation vectors $\mathcal{PV}$ as shown in Fig. 6. It takes a function and returns a vector

$$\mathcal{PV}(shape) = [[0, 0, 1, 2]]$$

$$\mathcal{PV}(dim) = [[0, 0, 0, 1]]$$

$$\mathcal{PV}(sel) = \begin{bmatrix} [0, 2, 2, 3] \\ [0, 1, 2, 3] \end{bmatrix}$$

$$\mathcal{PV}(*) = \begin{bmatrix} [0, 1, 2, 3] \\ [0, 1, 2, 3] \end{bmatrix}$$

$$\mathcal{PV}(\lambda\, Id_1, ..., Id_n\,.\, e) = \begin{bmatrix} \mathcal{SD}(e,\ [0, 1, 2, 3],\ \mathcal{F})(Id_1) \\ \vdots \\ \mathcal{SD}(e,\ [0, 1, 2, 3],\ \mathcal{F})(Id_n) \end{bmatrix}$$

Fig. 6. Computing propagation vectors

of propagation vectors. For built-in operations such as shape, dim, etc. these are constants defined as explained earlier. For user defined functions or abstract functions as introduced by the scheme $\mathcal{SD}$, the scheme $\mathcal{SD}$ itself can be utilised. It is applied to the body of the function, assuming demand for all four different levels ([0,1,2,3]). As this yields the demands for all relatively free variables it suffices to select those entries that relate to the binding λ. Variables that do not occur in these sets are not used within the body and, thus, obtain the propagation vector [0,0,0,0]. This is realised by the selection operation denoted as $\mathcal{SD}(...)(Id_i)$.

With these definitions, we can define the overall propagation vector environment for user-defined functions $\mathcal{F}$. Assuming a program of the form

$$f_1 = e_1$$
$$\vdots$$
$$f_n = e_n$$
$$\text{main} = e$$

we obtain:

$$\mathcal{F} = \bigoplus_{i=1}^{n} \{f_i : \mathcal{PV}(e_i)\} \qquad .$$

The interesting aspect of this definition, from an implementational point of view, is its recursive nature which arises from the reference to $\mathcal{F}$ in the definition of $\mathcal{PV}(e_i)$. However, due to the monotonicity of the maximum of the $\oplus$ operation and the finiteness of the domain, the computation of $\mathcal{F}$ can be implemented as a fixed-point iteration starting with propagation vectors [0,0,0,0].

7   Applying the Inference Algorithm

This section illustrates the formalism of the previous section by providing a formal derivation of the propagation for the functions `take` and `matmul` from Section 2. For `take`, we obtain:

$$\mathcal{PV}(\lambda \mathtt{v,a}.\, body_{take}) = \begin{bmatrix} \mathcal{SD}(body_{take},\ [0,1,2,3],\ \mathcal{F})(\mathtt{v}) \\ \mathcal{SD}(body_{take},\ [0,1,2,3],\ \mathcal{F})(\mathtt{a}) \end{bmatrix}$$

Propagating the canonical demand [0,1,2,3] into the body of `take`, we obtain demands for the subexpressions of the WITH-loop:

$\mathcal{SD}(body_{take},\ [0,1,2,3],\ \mathcal{F})$

$$= \mathcal{SD}\left(\begin{array}{l} \mathtt{with(0*v <= iv < v) : sel(iv,a)} \\ \mathtt{genarray(v,0)} \end{array},\ [0,1,2,3],\ \mathcal{F}\right)$$

$$= \left(\begin{array}{l} \mathcal{SD}(\mathtt{v},\ [0,1,2,3],\ \mathcal{F}) \\ \oplus\ (\ \mathcal{SD}(\mathtt{sel(iv,a)},\ [0,1,2,3],\ \mathcal{F}) \setminus \{\mathtt{iv}\}\ ) \\ \oplus\ \mathcal{SD}(0,\ [0,1,2,3],\ \mathcal{F}) \\ \oplus\ \mathcal{SD}(0*\mathtt{v},\ \mathcal{PV}(\lambda \mathtt{iv.sel(\ iv,\ a)})[0,1,2,3],\ \mathcal{F}) \\ \oplus\ \mathcal{SD}(\mathtt{v},\ \mathcal{PV}(\lambda \mathtt{iv.sel(\ iv,\ a)})[0,1,2,3],\ \mathcal{F}) \end{array} \right)$$

The demand for the lower and upper bound expressions of the generator of the WITH-loop is computed as demand for `iv` when propagating the actual demand through the body expression `sel( iv, a)`. This is done by first computing the propagation vector for the pseudo-function $\lambda \mathtt{iv.sel(\ iv,\ a)}$:

$\mathcal{PV}(\lambda \mathtt{iv.sel(\ iv,\ a)})$
$= [\mathcal{SD}(\mathtt{sel(iv,a)},\ [0,1,2,3],\ \mathcal{F})(\mathtt{iv})]$
$= [\{\mathtt{iv} : [0,2,2,3]\}(\mathtt{iv})]$
$= [[0,2,2,3]]$

With this propagation the demand for the bounds can be computed by mapping the actual demand [0,1,2,3] on a selection into [0,2,2,3] which yields [0,2,2,3]. With this demand we obtain

$\mathcal{SD}(\mathtt{v},\ \mathcal{PV}(\lambda \mathtt{iv.sel(\ iv,\ a)})[0,1,2,3],\ \mathcal{F})$
$= \mathcal{SD}(\mathtt{v},\ [[0,2,2,3]],\ \mathcal{F})$
$= \{\mathtt{v} : [0,2,2,3]\}$

and
$$SD(0 * v, \; \mathcal{PV}(\lambda\,iv.\,sel(\;iv,\;a))[0,1,2,3], \; \mathcal{F}) = \{v : [0,2,2,3]\}$$

For the result shape we have
$$SD(v, \; [0,2,3,3], \; \mathcal{F}) = \{v : [0,2,3,3]\}.$$

From the body expression a demand on a arises as
$$(\; SD(sel(iv,a), \; [0,1,2,3], \; \mathcal{F}) \setminus \{iv\} \;) = \{a : [0,1,2,3]\}.$$

As the default expression is constant we have
$$SD(0, \; [0,1,2,3], \; \mathcal{F}) = \{\}.$$

Taking these together, we eventually obtain
$$SD(body_{take}, \; [0,1,2,3], \; \mathcal{F}) = \{v : [0,2,3,3], a : [0,1,2,3]\}$$

which gives
$$\mathcal{PV}(\lambda\,v,a.\,body_{take}) = \begin{bmatrix} [0,2,3,3] \\ [0,1,2,3] \end{bmatrix}.$$

From this result, we can easily identify the non-uniformity in the first argument position of **take**. If the shape of the result is required, the demand of the individual arguments can be derived from the third position in the propagation vectors. They show that we do need to specialise the first argument wrt. to the argument value while it suffices to specialise the second argument wrt. its shape. Similarly, we obtain for **create**:
$$\mathcal{PV}(\lambda\,s,x.\,body_{take}) = \begin{bmatrix} [0,2,3,3] \\ [0,1,2,3] \end{bmatrix}.$$

Having these in place, we can now infer the propagation for **matmul**:
$$\mathcal{PV}(\lambda\,dl,dm,v.\,body_{mm}) = \begin{bmatrix} SD(body_{mm}, \; [0,1,2,3], \; \mathcal{F})(dl) \\ SD(body_{mm}, \; [0,1,2,3], \; \mathcal{F})(dm) \\ SD(body_{mm}, \; [0,1,2,3], \; \mathcal{F})(v) \end{bmatrix}$$

Propagating the canonical demand [0,1,2,3] into the body of **matmul** we obtain:
$$SD(body_{mm}, \; [0,1,2,3], \; \mathcal{F})$$

$$= SD\left(\begin{array}{l} \texttt{let} \\ \quad \texttt{maind} = dm * v, \; [0,1,2,3], \; \mathcal{F} \\ \texttt{in } letbody \end{array} \right)$$

$$= \left(\begin{array}{l} SD(letbody, \; [0,2,3,3], \; \mathcal{F}) \\ \oplus \, SD(dm * v, \; \mathcal{PV}(\lambda\,maind.\,letbody)[0,1,2,3], \; \mathcal{F}) \end{array} \right)$$

Since $\mathcal{PV}(\lambda\,maind.\,letbody) = [SD(letbody, \; [0,1,2,3], \; \mathcal{F})(maind)]$ we can see how the inference is driven bottom-up. Computing $SD(letbody, \; [0,1,2,3], \; \mathcal{F})$ recursively leads us into the innermost goal expression, i.e., **maind + concat(zeros, lowerd)**. As both, addition and concatenation are uniform, we have
$$SD(maind + concat(zeros,lowerd), \; [0,1,2,3], \; \mathcal{F})$$

$$= \{maind : [0,1,2,3], zeros : [0,1,2,3], lowerd : [0,1,2,3]\}$$

From this, we obtain that
$$\mathcal{PV}(\lambda\,\texttt{zeros.maind + concat(zeros, lowerd)})[0,1,2,3] = [0,1,2,3]$$

and thus
$$\mathcal{SD}\left(\begin{array}{l} \texttt{let} \\ \quad \texttt{zeros = create(shape(dm) - shape(dl), 0),}\ [0,1,2,3],\ \mathcal{F} \\ \quad \texttt{in maind + concat(zeros, lowerd)} \end{array}\right)$$
$$= \left(\begin{array}{l} \{\texttt{maind} : [0,1,2,3], \texttt{zeros} : [0,1,2,3], \texttt{lowerd} : [0,1,2,3]\} \\ \oplus \mathcal{SD}(\texttt{create(shape(dm)} - \texttt{shape(dl),0),}\ [0,1,2,3],\ \mathcal{F}) \end{array}\right).$$

Here, we have reached the most interesting aspect of the inference for $\texttt{matmul}$. Although $\texttt{create}$ is non-uniform, we expect this expression not to raise a demand higher than [0,1,2,3] for the variables $\texttt{dm}$ and $\texttt{dl}$. Following the inference algorithm rules, we obtain:
$$\mathcal{SD}(\texttt{create(shape(dm)} - \texttt{shape(dl),0),}\ [0,1,2,3],\ \mathcal{F})$$
$$= \mathcal{SD}(\texttt{shape(dm)} - \texttt{shape(dl),}\ [0,2,3,3],\ \mathcal{F})$$

as the constant 0 does not raise any demand. As subtraction is uniform the demand that was raised to [0,2,3,3] by $\texttt{create}$ is propagated into the individual subexpression, i.e., we have
$$\mathcal{SD}(\texttt{shape(dm)} - \texttt{shape(dl),}\ [0,2,3,3],\ \mathcal{F})$$
$$= \mathcal{SD}(\texttt{shape(dm),}\ [0,2,3,3],\ \mathcal{F}) \oplus \mathcal{SD}(\texttt{shape(dl),}\ [0,2,3,3],\ \mathcal{F})$$

According to the rule for primitive functions, we obtain as demand for $\texttt{dm}$ as well as $\texttt{dl}$: $[0,0,1,2][[0,2,3,3]] = [0,1,2,2]$. From this result, we can see that we obtain a demand of [0,1,2,2] which is even lower than the expected demand [0,1,2,3]. Having a closer look at the expression, we can observe that the value of the entire expression in fact does not depend on the values of $\texttt{dm}$ and $\texttt{dl}$ but their shapes only.

Using this result, we obtain
$$\mathcal{SD}\left(\begin{array}{l} \texttt{let} \\ \quad \texttt{zeros = create(shape(dm) - shape(dl), 0),}\ [0,1,2,3],\ \mathcal{F} \\ \quad \texttt{in maind + concat(zeros, lowerd)} \end{array}\right)$$
$$= \left(\begin{array}{l} \{\texttt{maind} : [0,1,2,3], \texttt{zeros} : [0,1,2,3], \texttt{lowerd} : [0,1,2,3]\} \\ \oplus \{\texttt{dm} : [0,1,2,2], \texttt{dl} : [0,1,2,2]\} \end{array}\right).$$

Propagating that information further up, we obtain
$$\mathcal{SD}(letbody,\ [0,1,2,3],\ \mathcal{F})$$
$$= \mathcal{SD}\left(\begin{array}{l} \texttt{let} \\ \quad \texttt{lowerd = dl * take(shape(dl), v),}\ [0,1,2,3],\ \mathcal{F} \\ \quad \texttt{in } letbody2 \end{array}\right)$$
$$= \left(\begin{array}{l} \{\texttt{maind} : [0,1,2,3], \texttt{dm} : [0,1,2,2], \texttt{dl} : [0,1,2,2]\} \\ \oplus\ \mathcal{SD}(\texttt{dl * take(shape(dl),v),}\ [0,1,2,3],\ \mathcal{F}) \end{array}\right).$$

As we have
$$\mathcal{SD}(\texttt{dl * take(shape(dl),v),}\ [0,1,2,3],\ \mathcal{F}) = \{\texttt{dl} : [0,1,2,3], \texttt{v} : [0,1,2,3]\}$$

we further obtain

$\mathcal{SD}(letbody,\ [0,1,2,3],\ \mathcal{F})$
$= \{\texttt{maind} : [0,1,2,3], \texttt{dm} : [0,1,2,2], \texttt{dl} : [0,1,2,3], \texttt{v} : [0,1,2,3]\}$

Note here how the multiplication with $\texttt{dl}$ increases the overall demand for that variable in the AKV case from AKS to AKV.

Eventually, we obtain for the entire body of $\texttt{matmul}$:

$\mathcal{SD}(body_{mm},\ [0,1,2,3],\ \mathcal{F})$
$= \{\texttt{dm} : [0,1,2,2], \texttt{dl} : [0,1,2,3], \texttt{v} : [0,1,2,3]\} \oplus \mathcal{SD}(\texttt{dm} * \texttt{v},\ [0,1,2,3],\ \mathcal{F})$
$= \{\texttt{dm} : [0,1,2,2], \texttt{dl} : [0,1,2,3], \texttt{v} : [0,1,2,3]\} \oplus \{\texttt{dm} : [0,1,2,3], \texttt{v} : [0,1,2,3]\}$
$= \{\texttt{dm} : [0,1,2,3], \texttt{dl} : [0,1,2,3], \texttt{v} : [0,1,2,3]\}$

Similar as with $\texttt{dl}$, the use of $\texttt{dm}$ as factor increases the demand for $\texttt{dm}$. This supports our intuitive result that $\texttt{matmul}$ is a uniform function with

$$\mathcal{PV}(\lambda\,\texttt{dl},\texttt{dm},\texttt{v}.\,body_{mm}) = \begin{bmatrix} [0,1,2,3] \\ [0,1,2,3] \\ [0,1,2,3] \end{bmatrix}.$$

8   Related Work

Generic programming on arrays can also be found in the programming language FISH [JMB98, JS98]. It is based on the idea to divide up all functions into two parts: one part that describes the actual computation of values and another part that describes the computation of result shapes from argument shapes. While the former is implemented at runtime, the latter is done statically by the compiler. This separation eases the specialisation as the static parts are identified by the programmer. In fact, it can be considered an offline approach to partially evaluating FISH programs. However, specialisation wrt. argument values in FISH cannot happen since all shape computations need to be defined in terms of argument shapes only. This vastly simplifies the specialisation process but comes at the price of lack in expressiveness. Only uniform array operations can be defined which immediately rules out the definition of operations such as $\texttt{take}$ or $\texttt{create}$.

A similar situation can be found in the C++ based approach to generic array programming called BLITZ [Vel98]. There, the rank information is made a template parameter which is resolved statically. Using the template mechanism as a tool for partial evaluation (for details see [Vel99]) results in rank specific C code that — at compile time — is derived from otherwise generic program specifications. This way, similar to the FISH approach, the rank computation is strictly separated from the value computation, as the template mechanism in C++ is strictly separated from the rest of the language.

Further work on specialising generic programs for data types rather than values can be found in the context of algebraic data types (ADT for short). Programs that are defined on generalisations of ADTs as they can be found in the generics of CLEAN [Ali05], the generic type classes of the Glasgow Haskell Compiler [HP00] or in GENERIC-HASKELL [CHJ$^+$01], when left unspecialised, lead to significant runtime overhead [AS04]. To ameliorate that problem, Alimarine and Smetsers in [AS04] propose specialisation to data types throughout generic programs. They show that for non-recursive data types this specialisation can be done always without risking non-termination which suggests a brute-force approach similar to online partial evaluation. Although this is similar to the specialisation approach in generic array programming there is a major difference to be observed: in CLEAN, the underlying type system precludes types to depend on argument values. As a consequence, generic array programming that would allow definitions of functions such as `take` or `create` can only be done, if array shapes are part of the data itself. In that case specialisation beyond the level of data types would be required which is outside the scope of the work described in [AS04].

9   Conclusions

This paper proposes an inference algorithm for analysing the relation between the shapes of arguments and the shapes of return values of function definitions in a first order functional array language. It determines for each function which level of argument shape knowledge is required in order to determine a certain level of return shape knowledge. This information can be used to steer function specialisation in a way that ensures that all shapes are computed statically, whenever possible. Once all functions are specialised to appropriate level, the provided shape information can be utilised for various optimisations that are essential for achieving highly efficient runtime behaviour.

With this apparatus at hand, abstractions can be chosen freely without preventing the compiler from applying sophisticated optimisations that are restricted to the intra-procedural case. As a consequence, non-uniform functions such as `take` can be used as building blocks for large applications without introducing considerable runtime degradation.

References

[Ali05]   A. Alimarine. *Generic Functional Programming*. PhD thesis, Radboud University of Nijmegen, Netherlands, 2005.

[AS04]   A. Alimarine and S. Smetsers. Optimizing Generic Functions. In D. Kozen, editor, *The 7th International Conference, Mathematics of Program Construction, Stirling, Scotland, UK*, volume 3125 of *LNCS*, pages 16–31. Springer, 2004.

[Can89]   D.C. Cann. Compilation Techniques for High Performance Applicative Computation. Technical Report CS-89-108, Lawrence Livermore National Laboratory, LLNL, Livermore California, 1989.

[CHJ+01]   D. Clarke, R. Hinze, J. Jeuring, A. Löh, and J. de Witt. *The Generic Haskell User's Guide*, 2001.

[GS99]   C. Grelck and S.B. Scholz. Accelerating APL Programs with SAC. *SIGAPL Quote Quad*, 29(2):50–58, 1999.

[GT04]   C. Grelck and K. Trojahner. Implicit Memory Management for SaC. In
          C. Grelck and F. Huch, editors, *Implementation and Application of Func-
          tional Languages, 16th International Workshop, IFL'04*, pages 335–348.
          University of Kiel, 2004.
[HP00]   R. Hinze and S. Peyton Jones. Derivable type classes. In G. Hutton, editor,
          Proceedings of the 4th Haskell Workshop, 2000.
[Hui95]   R. Hui. Rank and Uniformity. *APL Quote Quad*, 25(4):83–90, 1995.
[JGS93]   N.D. Jones, C.K. Gomard, and P. Sestoft. *Partial Evaluation and Auto-
          matic Program Generation*. Prentice-Hall, 1993.
[JMB98]   C.B. Jay, E. Moggi, and G. Bellè. Functors, Types and Shapes. In
          R. Backhouse and T. Sheard, editors, *Workshop on Generic Programming:
          Marstrand, Sweden, 18th June, 1998*, pages 21–4. Chalmers University of
          Technology, 1998.
[Jon96]   N.D. Jones. An Introduction to Partial Evaluation. *ACM Computing Sur-
          veys*, 28(3), 1996.
[JS98]   C.B. Jay and P.A. Steckler. The Functional Imperative: Shape! In Chris
          Hankin, editor, *Programming languages and systems: 7th European Sym-
          posium on Programming, ESOP'98 Held as part of the joint european con-
          ferences on theory and practice of software, ETAPS'98 Lisbon, Portugal,
          March/April 1998*, volume 1381 of *LNCS*, pages 139–53. Springer-Verlag,
          1998.
[Kre03]   D.J. Kreye. *A Compiler Backend for Generic Programming with Arrays*.
          PhD thesis, Institut für Informatik und Praktische Mathematik, Univer-
          sität Kiel, 2003.
[LLS98]   E.C. Lewis, C. Lin, and L. Snyder. The Implementation and Evaluation of
          Fusion and Contraction in Array Languages. In *Proceedings of the ACM
          SIGPLAN '98 Conference on Programming Language Design and Imple-
          mentation*. ACM, 1998.
[Pie02]   B.C. Pierce. *Types and Programming Languages*. MIT Press, 2002. ISBN
          0-262-16209-1.
[Sch03]   Sven-Bodo Scholz. Single Assignment C — efficient support for high-level
          array operations in a functional setting. *Journal of Functional Program-
          ming*, 13(6):1005–1059, 2003.
[Vel98]   T.L. Veldhuizen. Arrays in Blitz++. In *Proceedings of the 2nd Inter-
          national Scientific Computing in Object-Oriented Parallel Environments
          (ISCOPE'98)*, LNCS. Springer, 1998.
[Vel99]   T.L. Veldhuizen. C++ Templates as Partial Evaluation. In O. Danvy,
          editor, *Proceedings of PEPM'99, The ACM SIGPLAN Workshop on Par-
          tial Evaluation and Semantics-Based Program Manipulation*, pages 13–18.
          University of Aarhus, Dept. of Computer Science, 1999.

Author Index

Lecture Notes in Computer Science

For information about Vols. 1–4262

please contact your bookseller or Springer